Pasta and Rice Italian Style

Efrem Funghi Calingaert
Jacquelyn Days Serwer

Drawings by Paulette Dickerson

A PLUME BOOK

NEW AMERICAN LIBRARY

NEW YORK AND SCARBOROUGH, ONTARIO

Copyright © 1983 Efrem Funghi Calingaert and Jacquelyn Days Serwer

All rights reserved. No part of this book may be reproduced in any form
without the permission of Charles Scribner's Sons. For information address
Charles Scribner's Sons, 597 Fifth Avenue, New York, New York 10017.

This is an authorized reprint of a hardcover edition published by
Charles Scribner's Sons. Published simultaneously in Canada.

Library of Congress Cataloging in Publication Data

Calingaert, Efrem Funghi.
  Pasta and rice Italian style.

  Includes index.
  1. Cookery (Macaroni)   2. Cookery (Rice)   3. Cookery,
Italian.   I. Serwer, Jacquelyn Days.   II. Title.
TX809.M17C33   1984   641.8′22   84-4898
ISBN 0-452-25618-6

SIGNET, SIGNET CLASSIC, MENTOR, PLUME, MERIDIAN and
NAL BOOKS are published *in the United States* by New American Library,
1633 Broadway, New York, New York 10019, *in Canada* by
The New American Library of Canada Limited,
81 Mack Avenue, Scarborough, Ontario M1L 1M8

First Plume Printing, August, 1984

1 2 3 4 5 6 7 8 9

PRINTED IN THE UNITED STATES OF AMERICA

"HIGH MARKS FOR A FRESH, APPEALING BOOK!"
—*Library Journal*

Here is a small sampling of the sensuous eating you are about to dip into. Note that each recipe is timed for your convenience:

Quick Spring Menu
(about 60 minutes)

Stuffed Eggs, p. 53 (30 minutes)
Fusilli with Tuna and Butter, p. 176 (30 minutes)
Seasoned Tomato Halves, p. 255 (10 minutes)
Green apples with dried ricotta
Espresso
Wine: Valpolicella Bolla

Piedmontese Country Menu for Autumn
(about 60 minutes)

Rice with Four Cheeses, p. 117 (40 minutes)
White Beans with Tuna, p. 28 (15 minutes)
Orange Salad, p. 259 (15 minutes)
Dried figs and walnuts
Espresso
Wine: Chianti Colli Senesi

EFREM FUNGHI CALINGAERT and JACQUELYN DAYS SERWER met in Rome, where both their husbands were diplomats at the American Embassy. Their mutual interest in cooking, eating, and art history led to this cookbook. Efrem Calingaert, an art historian, was born in Turin and spent her childhood there and in Gorizia, near Trieste. Wherever she has lived, she has given demonstrations in Italian cooking. Jacquelyn Serwer, also an art historian, was born in New York. She has worked behind the scenes in an Italian restaurant and studied Italian cooking with professional chefs.

To our mothers,
Alma and Dorothea

Contents

Preface and Acknowledgments

*A*ppropriately enough, we first met in Rome over a delicious meal. Both our husbands were diplomats—the economic minister and the science counselor—at the American Embassy there. That first meal was one of many we ate together during a two-year period. Soon we shared many of the same friends and gradually discovered that we shared the same interests as well—cooking, eating, and art. These are, of course, the major preoccupations in Italy as well, so we found ourselves stimulated, inspired, and very much absorbed by the sensuousness of Italy. For Efrem this was nothing new, but rather the latest episode in her on and off life in Italy since her marriage to an American diplomat some fifteen years earlier. For Jackie, however, the experience of living in Italy greatly intensified her already considerable interest in food and cooking. Suddenly it was normal to begin every conversation with a discussion about who had had what for lunch; in what restaurant we planned to have dinner; where the best artichokes were to be found; which coffee bar had the best hot pastries in the morning, and so on—in short, heaven for those terminally obsessed with food.

As we became more and more involved in Italian food—eating in restaurants and in the homes of Italian friends as well as continually experimenting with new dishes ourselves—we began to consider the idea of collaborating on a cookbook. We envisioned one that would make available to Americans many wonderful dishes that were suited to American tastes yet, for the most part, were not well known in the United States.

By the time we actually decided to write the book, the Calingaerts had been transferred to Washington, D.C., while the Serwers were to remain in Rome for another year or so. For the better part of a year, the mail between Washington and Rome was full of suggestions for a proposal, chapter outlines, and drafts of recipes. Then, during July and August of 1981, we worked on the manuscript together in Rome. Each morning we emerged from the Serwers' apartment in a restored sixteenth-century palazzo to enjoy cappuccino and pastry before shopping in the magnificent open market nearby. Cooking together afterward was great fun, especially when Italian friends came to eat the results and offer helpful advice.

We both returned from Italy in late August of 1981, one to continue graduate work in art history, the other to await a new baby. During the next nine months, in spite of exams, papers, absent husbands, and pregnancy problems, we cooked mammoth meals—eight to ten recipes at a time—for the two families (and some adventurous friends) on the weekends. During the week we wrote, edited, and rewrote. The pace was often hectic, and our lives were very complicated at times, but the tasty results of our experiments and the enthusiastic response of our guinea-pig families encouraged us to finally complete the manuscript in the spring of 1982.

In the end, we realized we had written this cookbook for many reasons: logical and practical, personal and sentimental. Not least of all, we have assured ourselves of always having the recipes for our favorite dishes close by, in one convenient place, rather than on miscellaneous cards and scraps of paper. Moreover, the book represents a small capsule of Italy that we can always carry with us.

In the deepest sense, *Pasta and Rice Italian Style* is our homage to Italy, our acknowledgment of its ongoing influence on and enrichment of our lives. Since both of us are art historians, we hope one day to contribute to an understanding of an aspect of the fine arts of Italian culture. For the present, however, we are happy to share our experience that much of the originality, vitality, and pleasure of Italian life is communicated by the loving way in which food is prepared. In keeping with this attitude, our Italian friends could not have been more generous with us in sharing their delight in cooking, eating, and entertaining. Perhaps most of all, the book is an expression of the love, respect, and gratitude we feel toward all of them.

We want to thank our friends Marilu Bonanni, Ferdinando Cappabianca, Emma Caroleo, Milena Colombo, Bianca D'Antonio, Laura De Liguori, Michelangelo De Maria, Tina Boella Merzari, Maresa Pinto, Cecilia Sfligiotti, Giovanna Toti, Marcella Triolo, Giamberto Vanni, and Elio Sgambati, owner of the Trattoria Bella Napoli, for sharing some of their personal and most successful recipes with us. In addition, we are privileged to have had Arrigo Comar's illuminating comments on Italian coffee.

We are also grateful to Jo Crawford, who joined us in the kitchen on several occasions, lending her expertise in perfecting the crusts for our timballi. Jo, with Lois Roth, was helpful in proofreading portions of the manuscript.

In addition, we are very appreciative of all those friends on both sides of the ocean who so enthusiastically sampled our experiments, offering honest and valuable criticism as well as praise.

We are greatly indebted to our families, who, depending on the occasion, suffered at times from both overeating and near starvation but always maintained their good humor and unflagging confidence in our ultimate success. Daniel Serwer made it possible for us to work together by twice maintaining a separate household in another part of the world; Daniel Calingaert willingly typed the manuscript rather than play the piano during the most crucial times; and above all we are grateful to Michael Calingaert, without whose practical assistance, sleepless nights, and moral support the book could never have been finished.

Introduction

*T*here are many Italian cookbooks on the market today, but ours is different. While living in Italy, one of our most enjoyable eating events was the buffet dinner party, which was particularly popular in Rome. The highlight of the buffet for us was always the selection of antipasti, pasta, and rice dishes. After these so-called first courses, or *primi piatti*, had been savored, the meat course often seemed superfluous. As a result of going to these parties over a period of several years, we began to consider the idea of writing a cookbook for Americans that would concentrate on these very appealing foods. We felt that pasta- and rice-oriented meals could be satisfyingly full of carbohydrates without being heavy. Furthermore, they would eliminate the sometimes boring and often expensive meat focus, while presenting vegetables in a variety of unusual and attractive guises. Based on our experiences with cooking and eating in Italy and our familiarity with American food preferences and informal styles of entertaining, we have gathered a collection of favorite recipes featuring virtually meatless dishes that offer a new mealtime approach.

Most Italians still eat formal meals that include a meat course several times a week. The rest of the time, however, they eat more or less in the manner we propose. As a result, they consume less meat than Americans, and they tend to eat more grains in the form of pasta and rice as well as more fresh vegetables and fruits.

Though many people are convinced that high-carbohydrate diets are fattening, the Italian population does not have an obesity problem. Moreover, the level of heart disease is lower in Italy than in the United States. The high-carbohydrate diet is probably partly responsible.

In addition to the dietary benefits of pasta and rice meals, there are economic and practical advantages as well. In most cases these meals will make it possible both to feed the family and to entertain within a reasonable budget. You will find innumerable replacements for the commonplace lasagna or spaghetti and meatballs supper. Impressive yet convenient to prepare, many dishes lend themselves to quick last-minute meals, while others can be done, wholly or in part, in advance.

Perhaps the most novel aspect of *Pasta and Rice Italian Style*, besides the emphasis on non-meat dishes, is the selection of rice recipes. Pasta has been an American favorite for decades, but Italian rice dishes, especially risottos, are not so familiar. Our instructions on how to prepare many different risottos, along with an extensive offering of other rice dishes, should give you a new cooking repertoire.

With our sample menus as guides, we suggest you plan meals with pasta or rice as a main course, preceded by an antipasto, accompanied by a salad, and followed by fruit as dessert. However, most of our dishes are versatile enough to be incorporated into traditional meals as well. Many of our antipasti make perfect vegetable accompaniments for meat meals or can serve by themselves as light luncheon fare. Any of the rice preparations could replace other rice or potato dishes. Leftover risottos and many of the short pastas are especially appealing as side dishes the second time around. Most of the salads and soups can also stand by themselves as choices for a variety of mealtime occasions. And finally, we offer recipes in *Pasta and Rice Italian Style* that will gratify the accomplished cook as well as formulas for simple but delicious *piatti* that will assure culinary success for even the most apprehensive novice.

Pasta and Rice Italian Style

1 Equipment and Ingredients

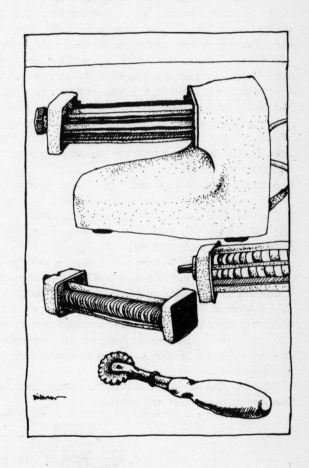

Equipment

The suggested list of cooking equipment below is relatively short, and most kitchens are likely to have almost all the items that are absolutely essential to prepare these recipes. Italian cooks are not terribly fussy about their equipment, relying on their imagination and resourcefulness, so no missing ideal pot or pan would prevent the undertaking of a wonderful meal. You should operate the same way. If you have these items already or feel inclined to add them to your kitchen, cooking may be easier and more enjoyable. If you don't have them, cook Italian style—improvise!

Stockpot: 6 to 8 quarts, tall, preferably made of stainless steel or aluminum, with handles; for pasta, soups, and broths.

Skillet: large, heavy, preferably aluminum or enameled cast iron, about 2½″ high and 10″ or 11″ in diameter (the French call it a *sautoir*); for dishes in which the pasta is added to the sauce and tossed on the stove.

Saucepan: heavy-bottomed 4-quart size, preferably aluminum, with a cover; for risotto and small quantities of soup.

Oven-to-table baking dish: rectangular, about 13″ x 9½″ and 2½″ to 3″ high, preferably earthenware or enameled cast iron; for baked antipasti and pasta dishes.

Colander: aluminum, with feet so that it can stand in the sink; for draining pasta and rice. In a pinch, use a large wire strainer.

Skimmer: extra-large, round metal slotted spoon or very shallow wire strainer with a long handle; for scooping up gnocchi, ravioli, and other filled pasta. A Chinese bamboo strainer will also work.

Large fork: long-handled, two-pronged, preferably and traditionally wood; for stirring spaghetti and other long pasta without breaking it.

Wooden spoons: long-handled for stirring short pasta; shorter ones for stirring sauces and risotto.

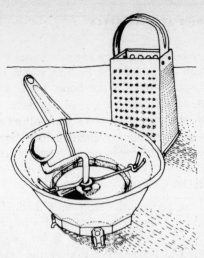

Also useful are a food mill, a four-sided standing cheese grater, and a fluted pastry wheel.

For making pasta at home you can use either an electric machine such as the Bialetti (our preference) or a hand machine for rolling out dough. The hand machine is much less expensive. There are also machines that will mix, knead, and cut the dough.

A food processor is not an essential piece of equipment, but it is a great convenience.

Ingredients

As in any kind of ethnic cuisine, some ingredients are essential to achieve a result that tastes genuinely Italian. The following ingredients are for the most part readily available in either a well-stocked supermarket or in specialty stores. In addition, a list of mail order suppliers appears at the end of the book.

ANCHOVIES

There are two kinds of preserved anchovies—fillets packed in oil and whole fish packed in salt. In Italy anchovies in oil are generally served raw as part of an antipasto platter and are used only rarely in cooking. Anchovies packed in salt have a more concentrated flavor and are the common cooking ingredient.

Salted anchovies are sold in specialty stores rather than supermarkets, where you'll find those packed in oil. They store well in the refrigerator so you may purchase them in advance. Before using them, rinse the salt off under cold running water, then split the anchovies and carefully remove the bone, head, and tail. Each half counts as one fillet.

If neither type of anchovy is available, anchovy paste can be substituted in recipes that call for chopped anchovies. Use ¼ teaspoon paste in place of one fillet.

BOUILLON CUBES

Bouillon cubes are perhaps the most basic method of seasoning in the Italian home kitchen. Italian cooks use them to give broth, soup, sauces—almost anything—added flavor, much the way Americans use salt and pepper. We achieve the best results with Knorr brand, the one most widely used in Italy, which comes in three flavors—beef, chicken, and fish. Keep a large supply on hand since their uses are infinite, and they can be stored on the shelf indefinitely.

BREAD CRUMBS

It's easy to make your own bread crumbs, and they will give more life to your recipes. Use leftover stale bread to make dry crumbs. It can be ground in a blender or processor or grated by hand. Fresh crumbs are made from fresh bread with the crusts trimmed off.

CAPERS

Italian cooks favor large capers, not the smaller French variety. Although most Italian cooks prefer to use capers packed in salt, any imported variety packed in vinegar and salt will work well. Always drain capers before using them. After opening a jar, refrigerate the remaining capers in their liquid.

CHEESES

Fontina: A popular Italian cheese from the Val d'Aosta in northern Italy that has a nutty taste and firm texture. Use the imported kind (you can be sure by checking the Italian markings on the rind); the domestic versions are bland and rubbery. Danish Fontina is a reasonable substitute, however.

Gorgonzola: A blue-veined cheese that comes either mild or sharp. For cooking we recommend mild Gorgonzola. Although we discourage using substitutes, Danish soft blue cheese gives a different but tasty result.

Mozzarella: The best mozzarella, which in Italy is made from the milk of water buffaloes, is not widely available outside Italy, although it is carried by some specialty and cheese stores. Domestic varieties bear little resemblance to Italian mozzarella, but for cooking they are satisfactory. Among the supermarket packaged mozzarelle, we prefer the cheese made from whole milk. If you live in a city with a sizable Italian population, you may find shops that make their own mozzarella. Fresh mozzarella is usually significantly better in both texture and flavor.

Parmesan: The imported Parmesan, known as Parmigiano Reggiano, is the finest available, and it really has no equivalent. Parmigiano Reggiano is made according to a centuries-old formula and is aged for at least two years. Its taste is so prized by Italians that they eat it as a delicacy with wine in addition to cherishing it as a cooking ingredient. To be certain that you are getting genuine Parmigiano Reggiano, check the rind, which will show at least parts of these two words etched in what looks like pinpricks. Other imported Parmesan or Parmesan-type grating cheeses, including plain Parmesan and Grana, are not of the same high caliber but are certainly satisfactory. Parmesan should be straw colored and crumbly rather than dry. Try to avoid buying it if it is hard, dry, and colorless. Parmesan will keep for several weeks in the refrigerator if it is wrapped first in a layer of waxed paper and then in aluminum foil. Domestic grating cheese is characterless compared with any of the imported brands, but if you absolutely cannot find real Parmesan, use the ungrated domestic kind. Never use the bottled grated cheese, which is invariably tasteless, stale, and full of additives.

Pecorino: Although pecorino—sheep's cheese—comes in many varieties in Italy, only those that are aged and suitable for grating are exported. The two common grating types found in the United States are pecorino Sardo and pecorino Romano. Pecorino Sardo, called simply Sardo, is slightly sharp and tangy, with a dry, somewhat crumbly consistency that is close to Parmesan. Pecorino Romano, often referred to as Romano, is considerably sharper and more pungent than Sardo. Imported pecorino Sardo and Romano are usually available in any cheese shop or Italian specialty store. The Romano found in supermarkets, usually in a triangular wedge in the dairy case, can be substituted if the real thing is not available. Like Parmesan, pecorino will keep for several weeks in the refrigerator if it is well wrapped.

Ricotta: In Italy ricotta is usually made from the whey of other cheeses, such as mozzarella or pecorino. Domestic ricotta, however, is made from whole or partially skimmed milk. Somewhat similar in appearance to cottage cheese, ricotta is really unique in its smooth texture and flavor. It varies in consistency from rather dry to very creamy. The amount of liquid in any recipe calling for ricotta will vary a bit depending upon its consistency. Although the domestic varieties are not as tasty and are often somewhat creamier than the Italian ricotta, they are satisfactory for cooking. You can usually find ricotta in the supermarket dairy case. It will keep for several days in the refrigerator.

Ricotta salata: Usually labeled dry ricotta, this is an aged ricotta, imported from Italy. It is very white in color with a dry somewhat crumbly consistency. Ricotta salata is mainly an eating cheese, but it is also used in cooking in Sardinia and southern Italy.

DRIED MUSHROOMS

The porcini mushroom is the most common dried Italian mushroom exported to the United States. These mushrooms are beige to dark brown in color and come in tiny, seemingly inordinately expensive-for-their-size, packages of about one-half ounce (15 to 18 grams). Nevertheless, when they are reconstituted in warm water, these mushrooms impart a special woodsy, robust flavor to sauces that is worth the expense. Fresh mushrooms are never an appropriate substitute. Most gourmet shops and Italian specialty stores carry this precious item. They also carry a more ordinary variety of dried mushrooms, labeled simply "dried imported mushrooms," that give a satisfactory result. Dried mushrooms will keep in a tightly sealed tin box or glass jar for months.

HERBS

Basil: Fresh basil leaves are a must in many recipes and highly desirable in most recipes that call for basil. In the spring, summer,

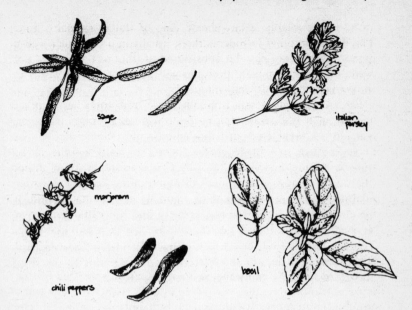

sage

italian parsley

marjoram

basil

chili peppers

and early fall, it is available at most good produce markets. Basil is also easy to grow at home in a garden or window box. Hearty plants may even last the winter indoors if placed in a sunny spot. Avoid those recipes that require fresh basil when none is to be found. Some recipes indicate when dried basil can be substituted— but always with a loss of flavor. Some experts recommend preserving fresh basil leaves in coarse salt or olive oil for out-of-season use. If you have a good warm-weather supply and the time, put some aside, for either form of preserved basil is preferable to the dried variety. Basil packed in salt should be wiped gently—not rinsed—before it is used. Basil preserved in oil would be best used in pesto or other sauces that include oil. The leaves should be drained before they're used.

Oregano: Oregano is commonly used in southern Italian cuisine. It is usually used dried even in Italy.

Marjoram: Related to oregano, marjoram is a mild herb with tiny leaves. Look for the plants in herb stores or supermarkets. Substitute dried marjoram if fresh isn't available.

Parsley: Italian parsley differs from the more common American type in having larger, flatter leaves and a more definite taste. When you can find the Italian variety, use it.

Red chili pepper: The red chili pepper (peperoncino) is small and thin and, either fresh or dried, is an essential ingredient in many spicy pasta sauces. Red pepper flakes are an acceptable substitute, but whole red chili peppers are better. If you find a supply in the summer or fall, dry them yourself for later use by hanging them up, away from moisture. They look decorative and will last you through the winter. If you don't find whole dried peppers in your supermarket, try Italian specialty stores.

Sage: Fresh sage, like fresh basil, is far removed from the dried version. Sage will grow readily in a garden or window box during the warmer months. You may even be able to preserve a modest plant all year round in a sunny spot indoors. If you cannot cultivate an indoor plant during the winter, dried sage is an alternative. You may also dry your own sage leaves for out-of-season use. Some people preserve fresh sage under coarse salt, just as they do basil. The flavor and texture of preserved sage is superior to the dried leaves. Again, wipe the leaves before using them.

OLIVE OIL

The best olive oil—the purest and most richly flavorful—is known as *extra vergine,* or extra virgin. The term refers to oil produced in the first of three pressings. Extra virgin also means oil low in acidity, with no additives. Although fine Italian and French olive oils are currently very much in fashion, their high cost and limited availability put them outside the budgets of most people. Among the affordable imported olive oils, Progresso, Bertolli, and Goya are good-tasting products.

OLIVES

Italian olives—both green and black—have a much stronger taste than American olives. If possible, look for Italian varieties (large green Sicilian, black Gaeta) or other seasoned Italian olives sold from barrels or in jars at Italian specialty stores and supermarkets. Greek olives are a good substitute. Italian olives are never pitted, but a cherry pitter, available at kitchen stores, can make the pitting fast and simple.

PASTA (DRY)

There is a detailed discussion of various types of dry pasta in the chapter on pasta, p. 147. In general buy the highest-quality durum wheat (semolina) pasta, either imported or domestic. The purists consider the best available imported pasta to be De Cecco. American brands made from durum wheat or semolina are practically indistinguishable and are less expensive.

RICE

There is a detailed discussion of various types of rice in the chapter on rice, p. 81. Most of the recipes here call for Italian arborio, Carolina long grain, and Uncle Ben's converted long grain rice.

PANCETTA

Pancetta comes from the same part of the hog as bacon, but the curing is entirely different. Pancetta is cured with salt and with spices and is shaped like a large salami. Look for pancetta in Italian specialty stores, and buy it in slices about one-half-inch thick. Kept in the freezer, pancetta will last indefinitely; it is also easier to cut when frozen. There is no need to thaw it beforehand. Pancetta will thaw almost instantly.

PROSCIUTTO

In Italy prosciutto means any kind of ham—what Americans call prosciutto is cured, uncooked ham (prosciutto crudo in Italy), as well as ordinary varieties of baked or boiled ham. Here we use prosciutto in the American way—to mean cured, uncooked ham with a deep pink color and a rather salty taste. Authentic prosciutto from Italy is not available in America because of import restrictions on cured meats. However, Italian meat-processing companies such as Citterio now produce prosciutto in the United States using the Italian method, and the result is very satisfactory. You will find this kind of prosciutto in Italian specialty stores, delicatessens, and some supermarkets. Sliced prosciutto dries out quickly, so don't buy it more than one or two days in advance, and keep it in the refrigerator in its wrapper inside a plastic bag. After being in the refrigerator, the slices will be easier to separate if you let them come to room temperature before removing them from their covering. Thinly sliced, packaged, Smithfield-type cured country ham, found in good supermarkets, makes a fine substitute.

TOMATOES (CANNED) AND TOMATO PASTE

Canned tomatoes: Although canned tomatoes exist in many varieties in America, you should use plum tomatoes in preparing Italian dishes. The best canned kind is San Marzano, imported from the Naples area, but Progresso Italian-Style Tomatoes (rather than their Imported Italian Tomatoes) are very satisfactory. Though the finest imported Italian tomatoes are found primarily in Italian specialty stores, Rosa imported Italian tomatoes and Progresso Italian-Style Tomatoes are readily available in good supermarkets. Once you find a brand you like, purchase cans in quantity since they will keep for months.

Tomato paste: Finding a good tomato paste should not be a problem. Any of the well-known brands are acceptable, although imported paste is richer tasting. If you use part of a can, you can freeze the leftovers. A very convenient way to buy tomato paste, if you can find it, is in tubes of about five ounces. Some stores now carry tubes of tomato paste imported from Italy (Cirio is one good brand). With a tube you can use a little at a time without wasting what remains. The reclosed tube lasts for a couple of months in the refrigerator.

2 Basic Stocks and Sauces
Brodi e Salse

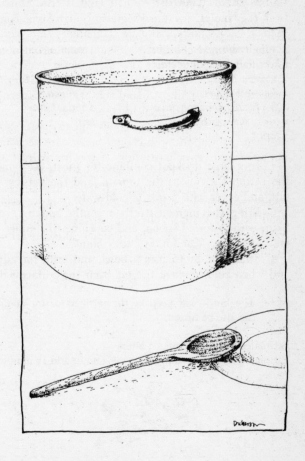

*T*here are always shortcuts to avoid the inconvenience of making stocks and sauces, but there are times when only the real thing will do. Here is a basic selection of essential stocks and sauces. They impart a classic, freshly made taste to the dishes you use them in yet are simple and straightforward to prepare.

∾ BRODO DI CARNE ∾
Meat Broth

Makes 1½ quarts

1½ lbs. beef shank or brisket
2 beef soup bones, preferably
    marrow bones
2 veal soup bones
1 lb. chicken bones or carcass
1 celery stalk with leaves
1 carrot

1 medium onion stuck with a
    clove
1 ripe peeled tomato, fresh or
    canned
2 sprigs parsley
salt

1. In a large stockpot combine the meat, the bones, the celery, the carrot, the onion, the tomato, and the parsley. Add 1½ tsp. salt, and cover with 3 quarts cold water.

2. Bring the ingredients to a gentle boil over medium heat. Skim with a slotted spoon, and continue to simmer, partially covered, over low heat for 2½ to 3 hours.

3. Strain the broth into a bowl, and taste for salt. Refrigerate, and when cold, remove the fat from the surface with a spoon.

Note: The broth will keep in the refrigerator for about five days. It can also be frozen.

Estimated Cooking Time: 3 hours
Estimated Total Preparation Time: 3 hours and 15 minutes

∾ BRODO DI POLLO ∾
Chicken Broth
Makes 1½ quarts

1 lb. chicken gizzards
2 lbs. chicken bones, necks, or
   other scraps
2 lbs. chicken wings or other parts
1 celery stalk with leaves

1 carrot
1 medium onion
1 leek
2 sprigs parsley
salt

1. In a large stockpot combine the chicken gizzards, bones, and wings, the celery, the carrot, the onion, the leek, and the parsley. Add 1½ tsp. salt, and cover with 3 quarts cold water.
2. Bring the ingredients to a gentle boil over medium heat. Skim with a slotted spoon, and continue to simmer, partially covered, over low heat for 2½ to 3 hours.
3. Strain the broth into a bowl, and taste for salt. Refrigerate, and when cold, remove the fat from the surface with a spoon.

Note: The broth will keep in the refrigerator for about five days. It can also be frozen.

Estimated Cooking Time: 3 hours
Estimated Total Preparation Time: 3 hours and 15 minutes

∾ BRODO DI PESCE ∾
Fish Stock
Makes 1½ quarts

3 lbs. fish bones, trimmings, and
   heads (with gills removed)
   from white lean fish such as
   flounder or whiting
1 small carrot, sliced
1 medium onion, sliced

1 celery stalk without leaves,
   sliced
3 sprigs parsley
1 cup dry white wine
salt

1. In a large stockpot combine the fish bones, trimmings, and heads with the carrot, the onion, the celery, the parsley, the wine, and 1 tsp. salt. Cover them with 2½ quarts cold water.
2. Bring the ingredients to a gentle boil over medium heat. Skim

with a slotted spoon, and continue to simmer, partially covered, for about 40 minutes.

3. Strain the stock into a bowl, and taste for salt.

Note: The stock will keep in the refrigerator for three to four days. It can also be frozen.

Estimated Cooking Time: 40 minutes
Estimated Total Preparation Time: 1 hour

∽ SALSA DI POMODORO I ∽

Basic Tomato Sauce I
Makes 2 cups

This is the purest and simplest tomato sauce to prepare. It is also the lowest in calories since it contains no fats. It keeps in the refrigerator for several days and in the freezer for several months.

*2 lbs. ripe plum tomatoes,
    washed and quartered
        or
1 28-oz. can Italian-style plum
    tomatoes
1 medium onion, quartered*

*1 sprig parsley
6 to 8 fresh basil leaves, whole,
        or
½ tsp. dried sweet basil
pinch of sugar
¾ tsp. salt*

1. Place all the ingredients in a saucepan. Cover and cook over medium heat, stirring from time to time, for 15 minutes. Remove the cover, and continue cooking, uncovered, until thickened (about 30 minutes).

2. Puree the sauce through a food mill. Taste for salt.

Note: If you prefer to puree the sauce in a blender or food processor, be sure to peel the tomatoes before cooking them and remove the parsley stems.

Estimated Cooking Time: 45 minutes
Estimated Total Preparation Time: 1 hour

∾ SALSA DI POMODORO II ∾
Basic Tomato Sauce II

Makes 2 cups

2 tbs. olive oil
2 tbs. butter
1 small onion, minced
2 lbs. ripe plum tomatoes,
   peeled and chopped
         or
1 28-oz. can Italian-style plum
   tomatoes, chopped

5 to 6 fresh basil leaves, torn into
   pieces
         or
½ tsp. dried sweet basil
pinch of sugar
salt

1. Heat the oil and the butter in a saucepan, and sauté the onion over medium heat until soft and translucent.

2. Add the tomatoes, the basil, the sugar, and 1 tsp. salt. Cook, uncovered, over medium-high heat until thickened, stirring from time to time. This should take about 30 minutes. Taste for salt.

Note: If you prefer a smoother sauce, puree it through a food mill or in a food processor or blender.

Estimated Cooking Time: 30 minutes
Estimated Total Preparation Time: 1 hour (fresh tomatoes); 45 minutes (canned tomatoes)

∽ SALSA DI POMODORO III ∽
Basic Tomato Sauce III

Makes 2 cups

2 tbs. olive oil
1 small onion, minced
⅓ cup dry white wine
2 lbs. ripe tomatoes, peeled
  and chopped
          or
1 28-oz. can Italian-style plum
  tomatoes, chopped

¼ cup fresh basil leaves, torn
  into pieces
          or
½ tsp. dried sweet basil
salt

1. Heat the oil in a saucepan, and sauté the onion over medium heat until soft and translucent.

2. Add the wine, and cook over high heat until the wine is almost completely evaporated.

3. Add the tomatoes, the basil, and 1 tsp. salt, and cook over medium heat for about 45 minutes, or until thickened. Taste for salt.

Note: Use the sauce as is, or if you prefer a smoother sauce, puree through a food mill before using. The sauce will keep for several days in the refrigerator or for several months in the freezer.

Estimated Cooking Time: 45 minutes
Estimated Total Preparation Time: 1 hour and 15 minutes (fresh tomatoes); 1 hour (canned tomatoes)

∽ SALSA BESCIAMELLA ∽
Bechamel Sauce

Makes 2 scant cups

This versatile easy-to-make white sauce is an essential element of many of the recipes here. Depending on the requirements of any given recipe, the sauce will be thin, medium, or thick. The basic method of preparation is the same; it is the proportion of the ingredients, more specifically the flour-liquid ratio, that varies. Note the changes in these proportions called for in the recipes throughout the book.

Medium bechamel sauce:

2 cups milk	4 tbs. butter
or	3 tbs. all-purpose flour
2 cups meat, chicken, or fish stock	salt (not necessary when using
(as required)	salted stock)

1. Bring the milk or stock almost to a boil (when small bubbles begin to appear on the surface) in a small saucepan over medium heat.
2. Meanwhile melt the butter in a small heavy saucepan over low heat. Add the flour, and cook, stirring constantly, with a wire whisk, for 1 to 2 minutes. Be sure not to let the flour brown. Remove from the heat. Add the milk all at once, stirring vigorously with the whisk to prevent lumps from forming. Add salt, and stir.
3. Return the pan to the burner, and cook the sauce a few minutes longer, stirring constantly, until it is thick, smooth, and creamy.

Note: For a thick sauce, use 2 cups milk or stock, 5 tbs. butter, and 4 tbs. flour.
   For a very thick sauce, use 1½ cups milk.
   For a thin sauce, use 2 cups milk or stock, 3 tbs. butter, and 2 tbs. flour.

Estimated Cooking Time: 10 minutes
Estimated Total Preparation Time: 10 minutes

∽ MAIONESE ∽

Mayonnaise

Makes about 1½ cups

2 egg yolks	2 tsp. wine vinegar
salt	¾ cup light vegetable oil
1½ tbs. lemon juice	combined with ½ cup olive oil

1. Place the egg yolks, ¼ tsp. salt, 1 tbs. lemon juice, and the vinegar in a 4 to 5 cup bowl. Beat the ingredients with an electric beater at medium speed for about 30 seconds.
2. Start adding the oil, dribbling it between the blades of the beater so that it combines with the egg mixture immediately. Beat continuously, but stop the flow of oil every 15 or 20 seconds to

make sure that the oil is being fully absorbed by the eggs. When you have used about a ½ cup of oil, turn the beater to high, and add the remaining oil in a heavier flow. Add the remaining lemon juice, and beat the mayonnaise a few more seconds. Taste for salt, lemon, and/or vinegar.

Note: Both the ingredients and the utensils must be at room temperature. Mayonnaise will keep for a week refrigerated in a closed jar.

Estimated Total Preparation Time: 5 minutes

3 Antipasti

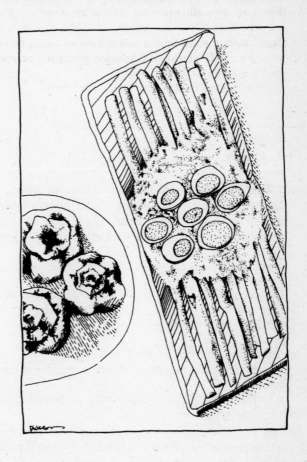

*I*n Italy no culinary display is more impressive than the typical antipasto table laden with a variety of seasonal vegetable dishes. Even the most modest restaurants feature an attractive selection. These dishes are not only excellent appetizers. Most can play many different mealtime roles—first courses or side dishes in traditional meals; light lunches when served alone, with a salad; and cocktail, picnic, or snack food. You may also enjoy preparing several, to be served together, in the Italian manner.

∽ BAGNA CAUDA ∽

Hot Dip for Raw Vegetables For 6

This is a popular Piedmontese winter antipasto. The vegetable-dipping often concludes with a couple of eggs being scrambled in the leftover sauce. Bagna Cauda also makes an elegant choice for cocktails accompanied by a more elaborate selection of vegetables.

1 *small cauliflower*	6 *anchovy fillets, minced*
2 *green peppers*	*or*
½ *bunch celery*	2 *tbs. anchovy paste*
½ *cup olive oil*	4 *tbs. butter*
6 *garlic cloves, minced*	

1. Wash and dry all the vegetables.
2. Remove the hard core from the cauliflower, and separate the florets.
3. Halve the peppers, remove the seeds and filaments, and cut into wide strips.
4. Peel the tough outer layer from the celery stalks, and cut each crosswise into two pieces. One piece will have the celery leaves and a short stem, and the other will be all stem. Cut the stem pieces in half lengthwise.
5. Arrange the vegetables on a platter in a decorative manner, and put it on the table.
6. In a 2 to 3 cup flameproof earthenware pot, place ¼ cup olive oil and the garlic over very low heat. Add the anchovies, and con-

tinue cooking, stirring, and mashing, for about 15 minutes. Add the butter, and cook over a very low heat for another 10 minutes while the ingredients melt and thicken. If the heat is too high, the anchovies will taste fried. Add the rest of the oil gradually, stirring constantly, and cook for 2 to 3 minutes more. Set aside.

7. Bring the sauce to the table, and place it on a small food warmer, heated with a candle. Diners can dip the vegetables into the hot sauce.

Note: The sauce is even more flavorful when made a few hours in advance or the day before and reheated just before serving.

Estimated Cooking Time: 30 minutes
Estimated Total Preparation Time: 45 minutes

❧ CARCIOFI ALLA MOZZARELLA ❧
Artichokes with Mozzarella   For 4

4 large artichokes	salt
1 lemon, halved	freshly ground black pepper
2 tbs. olive oil	½ lb. mozzarella, diced
1 cup homemade chicken broth	2 tbs. freshly grated pecorino
or	Romano cheese
1 chicken bouillon cube,	1 tbs. plain dry bread crumbs
dissolved in 1 cup water	2 tbs. fresh parsley, minced
1 egg	4 rolled anchovy fillets

1. Preheat the oven to 350°F.
2. Cut off the artichoke stems. Break off the small leaves at the base of each, and cut off about 1″ from the top. Snap off the hard

upper part of the leaves. With a small sharp knife or a grapefruit spoon remove the fuzzy choke and the small prickly leaves around it, being careful not to remove the heart. Rub the artichokes with the lemon to prevent discoloration.

3. Put the artichokes—standing up—in an earthenware or Pyrex dish just large enough to hold them. Drizzle with the oil, pour the broth into the dish, and bake, covered, for about 40 minutes.

4. In a bowl beat the egg with ½ tsp. salt and the pepper. Add the mozzarella, the pecorino cheese, the bread crumbs, and the parsley, and mix well.

5. Remove the artichokes from the oven, and fill the cavities with the mozzarella mixture. Return the artichokes to the oven, covered, for 15 minutes more, or until the mozzarella is completely melted.

6. Remove the artichokes to a serving dish, and decorate each top with a rolled anchovy fillet. Serve hot.

Estimated Cooking Time: 55 minutes
Estimated Total Preparation Time: 1 hour and 25 minutes

∽ CARCIOFI ALLA PIZZAIOLA ∽
Baked Artichokes with Tomatoes For 4

4 artichokes	salt
1 lemon, halved	freshly ground black pepper
2 tbs. olive oil	¼ tsp. dried oregano
1 1-lb. can Italian-style plum	1 cup mozzarella, diced
tomatoes, chopped (discard	5 to 6 fresh basil leaves, torn into
the juice)	small pieces

1. Preheat the oven to 350°F.

2. Cut off the artichoke stems. Break off the small leaves at the base of each, and cut off about 1″ from the top. Snap off the hard upper part of the leaves. With a small sharp knife or a grapefruit spoon remove the fuzzy choke and the small prickly leaves around it, being careful not to remove the heart. Rub the artichokes with the lemon to prevent discoloration.

3. In the bottom of an earthenware or Pyrex dish just large

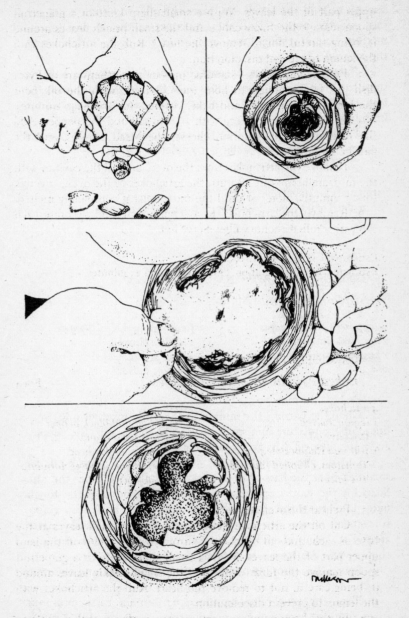

enough to hold the artichokes, place the oil, the tomatoes, ¼ tsp. salt, and the pepper. Roll the artichokes in the oil and tomato mixture before setting them upright in the dish. Sprinkle with the oregano.

4. Bake the artichokes, covered, for about 40 minutes. Remove from the oven, and fill the cavities with the mozzarella. Spoon the tomato sauce over the tops of the artichokes, and sprinkle with the fresh basil leaves.

5. Return the artichokes to the oven, covered, for 15 minutes more, or until the mozzarella is completely melted.

6. Serve the artichokes hot.

Estimated Cooking Time: 55 minutes
Estimated Total Preparation Time: 1 hour and 20 minutes

∽ CARCIOFI ALLA ROMANA ∽
Artichokes Roman Style   For 4

¼ cup fresh parsley leaves
2 tbs. fresh mint leaves
1 large garlic clove, peeled
salt

freshly ground black pepper
1¼ cups olive oil
4 large artichokes
1 lemon, halved

1. Preheat the oven to 350°F.

2. Chop the parsley, the mint, and the garlic together until very fine. Put the mixture in a small bowl. Add ½ tsp. salt, the pepper, and 4 tbs. olive oil. Mix the ingredients well.

3. Cut off the artichoke stems, leaving about 1". Break off the small leaves at the base of each, and cut off about 1" from the top. Snap off the hard upper part of the leaves, and peel the tough outer layer from the stems. With a small sharp knife or a grapefruit spoon remove the fuzzy choke and the small prickly leaves around it, being careful not to remove the heart. Rub the artichokes with the lemon to prevent discoloration.

4. Spoon the seasoning mixture into the artichokes, and close the leaves.

5. Place the artichokes—upside down—in an earthenware or Pyrex dish just large enough to hold them. Sprinkle with a pinch

of salt, pour the remaining oil and ¾ cup water over them, and bake, covered, for about 1 hour.

6. Remove the liquid to a small saucepan, and boil it down, over medium-high heat, to about 1 cup. Pour over the cooked artichokes.

7. Serve the artichokes at room temperature.

Note: These artichokes must be prepared a few hours ahead of time. They can also be prepared the day before and do not need to be refrigerated. If any oil is left over, it can be used for salad dressing.

Estimated Cooking Time: 1 hour
Estimated Total Preparation Time: 1 hour and 30 minutes

∾ ANTIPASTO LUIGI ∾
Raw Artichoke Salad   For 4

juice of 2 lemons
4 artichokes
¼ cup olive oil
salt
½ cup Parmesan cheese,
  shredded

freshly ground black pepper
parsley sprigs
1 lemon, cut in half lengthwise
  and thinly sliced

1. Put the lemon juice into a medium bowl.

2. Cut off the artichoke stems. Break off the small leaves at the base of each, and cut off about 1" from the top. Snap off the hard upper part of the leaves. Cut the artichokes in half lengthwise, and remove the fuzzy choke and the prickly leaves around it, being careful not to remove the heart. Slice each half lengthwise

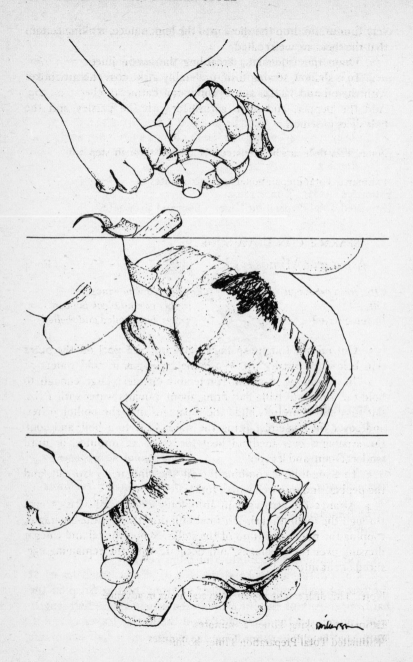

very thinly, and drop the slices into the lemon juice, making certain that the slices are well coated.

3. Drain the artichokes, discarding the lemon juice.

4. In a shallow serving dish, preferably glass, toss the artichokes with the oil and ¼ tsp. salt. Sprinkle the Parmesan cheese on top. Add the pepper, and serve garnished with the parsley and the half slices of lemon.

Note: This dish can be prepared beforehand through step 2.

Estimated Total Preparation Time: 30 minutes

∽ ASPARAGI CON UOVA SODE ∽

Asparagus Mimosa   For 4

2 lbs. fresh asparagus	3 tbs. red wine vinegar
salt	freshly ground black pepper
½ cup olive oil	3 eggs, hard-boiled and shelled

1. Cut off the tough asparagus bottoms, and peel off the outer skin below the tender tip. Wash the asparagus in cold water.

2. In an oblong casserole (preferably enamel) large enough to hold the asparagus lying flat, bring about 3 quarts water with 1 tbs. salt to a boil. Carefully slide the asparagus into the boiling water, and cover the casserole. Bring the water back to a boil, and cook the asparagus over medium heat for 10 to 12 minutes, or until tender. Drain, and let cool.

3. In a small bowl combine the oil, the vinegar, ½ tsp. salt, and the pepper, and mix well with a fork.

4. Arrange the asparagus in an oblong serving dish. Pass 2 eggs through the medium disk of a food mill directly over the asparagus, topping the upper one third of the stalks. Spoon the oil and vinegar dressing over the asparagus, and decorate with the remaining egg, sliced or cut into wedges.

Note: This dish can be prepared several hours in advance.

Estimated Cooking Time: 20 minutes
Estimated Total Preparation Time: 40 minutes

∽ FAGIOLI CON TONNO ∽
White Beans with Tuna   For 4

1 cup dry navy beans or white
   kidney beans
1 small onion stuck with a clove
1 small celery stalk
1 sprig fresh sage or ½ tsp.
   dried sage
         or
1½ 1-lb. cans Italian cannellini
   beans

1 small red onion, sliced thinly,
   rinsed under cold water, and
   dried
½ cup olive oil
1 tbs. lemon juice
salt
1 6½-oz. can chunk light tuna
   packed in oil, drained and
   broken into large flakes

1. If using the dry beans, soak them overnight in 4 cups cold water. Drain the beans, and place them in a medium saucepan with enough water to cover and go 2 to 3 inches above the beans. Add the whole onion, the celery, and the sage, and cook for about 1 hour over medium heat, or until the beans are tender but not soft. Drain the beans, and place in a serving bowl to cool slightly.

If you are using canned beans, drain in a colander, and rinse under cold water to remove any sediment. Drain again, and place in a serving bowl.

2. In a shallow serving dish combine the beans with the sliced onion, the oil, the lemon juice, and ½ tsp. salt. Mix. Add the tuna, and toss gently. Serve at room temperature.

Note: This recipe can be prepared hours in advance but should be kept at room temperature rather than refrigerated. It is equally good after one or two days. In that case it should be refrigerated but brought back to room temperature before serving.

Estimated Cooking Time: 1 hour (dried beans)
Estimated Total Preparation Time: 1 hour and 15 minutes (dried beans); 15 minutes (canned beans)

∾ FAGIOLINI AL FORMAGGIO ∾
Cooked Green Beans with Fontina Cheese   For 4

1 lb. green beans
salt
4 oz. Fontina cheese, diced
1 tbs. capers, drained

2 tbs. lemon juice
¼ cup olive oil
freshly ground black pepper

1. Snap off the ends of the beans, and remove any strings. Rinse in cold water.
2. Bring 1½ to 2 quarts water with 2 tsp. salt to a boil. Add the green beans, and cook, uncovered, over medium-high heat for 10 to 12 minutes, or until barely tender.
3. Drain the beans in a colander. Refresh quickly under cold water, and remove to a bowl.
4. Add the cheese, the capers, the lemon juice, the oil, ¼ tsp. salt, and the pepper. Toss well. Arrange the beans in a shallow dish, and serve.

Estimated Cooking Time: 25 minutes
Estimated Total Preparation Time: 25 minutes

∾ INSALATA DI RINFORZO ∾
Seasoned Broccoli Antipasto   For 4

1 lb. broccoli
4 anchovy fillets, chopped
1 tsp. capers, drained
1 egg, hard-boiled, shelled,
   and chopped

1 tbs. red wine vinegar
¼ cup olive oil
freshly ground black pepper

1. Wash and dry the broccoli. Cut off and discard the tough stem bottoms. Peel the remaining stems, and cut them into matchsticks. Separate the tops into florets.
2. Steam the broccoli in a vegetable steamer over medium-high heat for about 2 minutes, or just until it turns bright green. Remove the broccoli from the steamer, and let cool.

3. In a serving bowl combine the broccoli with the anchovies, the capers, and the egg. Drizzle the broccoli mixture with the vinegar and the oil. Add the pepper, toss well, and serve.

Note: The salad can be prepared several hours in advance.

Estimated Cooking Time: 7 minutes
Estimated Total Preparation Time: 20 minutes

∾ CAVOLFIORE CON OLIVE ∾
Cauliflower with Black Olives   For 4 to 5

1 lb. cauliflower
4 anchovy fillets, chopped
1/4 cup Italian or Greek black
  olives, slivered

2 tbs. white wine vinegar
1/4 cup olive oil

1. Wash and dry the cauliflower. Cut the cauliflower florets into thin slices, and discard the core.
2. In a serving bowl combine the cauliflower with the anchovies and the olives. Drizzle with the vinegar and the oil. Toss well, and serve.

Note: Do not season the cauliflower until just before serving it. The white vinegar is recommended to avoid discoloring the cauliflower.

Estimated Total Preparation Time: 20 minutes

∾ INDIVIA ALLA ROMANA ∾
Curly Chicory with Braised Tomatoes   For 4

Although American curly chicory differs somewhat from the Italian version, it adapts beautifully to this Roman appetizer. The textures and colors complement each other well. You don't need to be hesitant about the anchovies. No one will ever guess what ingredient provides the tangy flavor.

3 heads curly chicory
salt
⅓ cup olive oil
3 garlic cloves, peeled

6 anchovy fillets, chopped
¾ lb. ripe plum tomatoes,
    peeled, seeded, and coarsely
    chopped
freshly ground black pepper

1. Remove and discard any dark green or bruised outer leaves, and wash the chicory thoroughly in 2 or 3 changes of water. Drain, and cut the leaves in half.

2. Bring 3 to 4 quarts water to a boil with 1 tbs. salt. Add the chicory, and cook over medium heat for 10 to 15 minutes, or until tender. Drain the chicory.

3. In a large skillet heat the oil. Add the garlic cloves, and sauté over medium heat until golden. Discard the garlic, and add the anchovies. Cook over low heat, stirring and mashing with a wooden spoon. Add the tomatoes, raise the heat to medium, and cook for about 10 minutes longer.

4. Squeeze the chicory to remove any excess liquid. Add it to the skillet along with ½ tsp. salt and pepper to taste. Simmer for about 10 minutes. Serve hot or at room temperature.

Estimated Cooking Time: 45 minutes
Estimated Total Preparation Time: 1 hour

✧ CAPONATA ✧
Eggplant Appetizer   For 4

2 lbs. eggplants, preferably the
    small Italian type
salt
4 tbs. olive oil
2 medium onions, sliced thin
1½ lbs. ripe tomatoes, peeled,
    seeded, and cut into strips

1 celery heart, sliced
2 tbs. capers, drained
½ cup Italian green olives, pitted
    and quartered
⅔ cup vegetable oil
½ cup red wine vinegar
1 tbs. sugar

1. Wash and dry the eggplants, and cut into ¼″ cubes. Place in a colander, sprinkle with 2 tsp. salt, and let drain for 30 to 40 minutes.

2. Heat the olive oil in a medium saucepan over medium heat. Add the onions, and sauté until slightly golden. Add the tomatoes and the celery heart, and cook for 10 to 15 minutes, until the tomatoes are soft. Add the capers and the olives, and stir.

3. Heat the vegetable oil in a large skillet over medium-high heat until quite hot. Dry the eggplant, and fry until tender and lightly browned, stirring from time to time. Add to the tomato mixture.

4. In a small saucepan heat the vinegar and the sugar over medium heat. Stir until the sugar is dissolved. Add it to the eggplant-tomato mixture, stir, and cook a few minutes longer, until the vinegar has evaporated.

5. Serve the caponata cold or at room temperature.

Note: This dish can be prepared several days in advance and refrigerated.

Estimated Cooking Time: 50 minutes
Estimated Total Preparation Time: 1 hour and 30 minutes

∽ MELANZANE AL FUNGHETTO ∽
Sautéed Seasoned Eggplants For 4

*1½ lbs. eggplants, preferably the
    small Italian type
salt
2 tbs. vegetable oil*

*2 tbs. olive oil
1 garlic clove, mashed
3 tbs. fresh parsley, minced*

1. Wash and dry the eggplants, and cut into ¼" cubes. Place the cubes in a colander, sprinkle with 1 tsp. salt, and let drain for 30 to 40 minutes.

2. Heat the oils in a wide, heavy-bottomed casserole. Dry the eggplant, and sauté over high heat, stirring frequently, until slightly browned. Add the garlic and the parsley, stir well, and cook the eggplant, partially covered, over medium-low heat for another 10 to 15 minutes, or until tender. Taste for salt.

Note: This dish can be prepared the day before. It should be kept in a
cool place but not necessarily in a refrigerator. An Italian cook
would store it in a cold oven. The eggplant is equally delicious
warm or cold.

Estimated Cooking Time: 25 minutes
Estimated Total Preparation Time: 1 hour and 15 minutes

∽ MELANZANE ALLA CALABRESE ∽

Eggplant Calabrese For 4

The olives add a delightful spiciness to the always delicious
eggplant-mozzarella combination.

1 large eggplant	8 oz. mozzarella, cut into thin
or	slices
4 small Italian eggplants	1/3 cup Italian or Greek black
salt	olives, pitted and sliced
1 cup vegetable oil	1 tbs. olive oil
1 recipe Basic Tomato Sauce II,	
p. 15	

1. Wash and dry the eggplant, and cut into 1/4" slices. Place
the slices in a colander, sprinkle with 1 tsp. salt, and let drain for
30 to 40 minutes.
2. Heat the oil in a large skillet over medium-high heat. Dry
the eggplant slices, and fry until they are golden on both sides.
Drain the slices on brown paper.
3. Preheat the oven to 400° F.
4. Cover the bottom of an oven-to-table baking dish with 1/3 of
the eggplant. Top it with 1/3 of the tomato sauce, half the mozzarella, and half the olives. Repeat the process twice, ending with
the tomato sauce. Drizzle with the olive oil.
5. Bake the dish for about 15 minutes. Allow it to settle for at
least 5 minutes before serving.

Note: This dish can be prepared in advance through step 4.

Estimated Cooking Time: 40 minutes
Estimated Total Preparation Time: 1 hour and 20 minutes

∽ MELANZANE MARINATE ∽
Marinated Eggplant For 4

1 eggplant (1¼ to 1½ lbs.)
salt
1 cup vegetable oil
1 large garlic clove, mashed

¼ cup fresh parsley, chopped
8 to 10 fresh sage leaves, chopped,
or
½ tsp. dried sage
⅓ cup red wine vinegar

1. Wash and dry the eggplant, and cut crosswise into ⅛" slices. Place the slices in a colander, sprinkle with 1 tsp. salt, and let drain for 30 to 40 minutes.
2. Heat the oil in a large skillet over medium-high heat. Dry the eggplant thoroughly with paper towels. When the oil is very hot, slide in the eggplant slices in a single layer. Fry quickly over high heat until tender and slightly browned. Drain on brown paper. Continue this process with the rest of the eggplant.
3. Place a layer of eggplant on the bottom of a shallow serving dish. Sprinkle with some of the garlic, some of the parsley, and a little sage. Repeat the process with one or two more layers.
4. In a small saucepan bring the vinegar to a boil over high heat. Pour the vinegar over the eggplant.
5. Cover the eggplant, and let marinate for at least 12 hours.

Note: For best results this dish should be prepared a day in advance. It does not have to be refrigerated.

Estimated Cooking Time: 30 minutes
Estimated Total Preparation Time: 1 hour and 30 minutes

∽ MELANZANE SOTT'OLIO ∽
Marinated Eggplant Dressed in Oil For 4

Unlike most recipes for eggplant, this one doesn't require you to salt and drain the eggplant beforehand because it is seared rather than fried.

4 to 6 small Italian eggplants
⅓ cup olive oil
¼ cup red wine vinegar

2 garlic cloves, thinly sliced
1 red chili pepper, crushed
salt

1. Wash and dry the eggplants, and cut lengthwise into ⅛" slices.

2. Heat a heavy griddle, and sprinkle with a few drops of olive oil.

3. Add the eggplant slices in one layer, searing quickly over high heat on both sides until dark brown and almost crisp. Continue in this manner with the remaining slices.

4. Arrange the slices on a platter in two layers, sprinkling each layer with vinegar, the garlic, the chili pepper, and salt to taste. Drizzle the remaining oil on top. Let the eggplant marinate for at least 2 hours before serving.

Note: This dish can be prepared two days in advance and stored in the refrigerator. Let it sit two or three hours at room temperature before serving.

Estimated Cooking Time: 30 minutes
Estimated Total Preparation Time: 45 minutes

∽ MELANZANE PICCANTI ∽
Piquant Eggplant For 4

salt	1 red chili pepper
1½ lbs. small Italian eggplants	or
¼ cup fresh parsley	¼ tsp. red pepper flakes
4 anchovy fillets	½ tsp. dried oregano
1 large garlic clove, peeled	⅓ cup red wine vinegar

1. Bring 4 quarts of water to a boil in a large saucepan. Add 2 tbs. salt, and stir.

2. Meanwhile cut the eggplants lengthwise into ¼" slices, and drop into the boiling water. Cook for 5 to 7 minutes, or until just tender. Drain the slices, and dry with paper towels.

3. In a food processor combine the parsley, the anchovies, the garlic, the chili pepper, the oregano, and the vinegar, and chop for about 20 seconds, or by hand chop all the ingredients except the vinegar together until fine, and then add the vinegar.

4. Place half the eggplant in a shallow serving dish, and cover with half the sauce. Make a second layer of eggplant, and top with sauce.

5. Cover the dish, and let the eggplant marinate for at least 8 hours.

Note: For best results this dish should be prepared one day in advance. It does not have to be refrigerated.

Estimated Cooking Time: 30 minutes
Estimated Total Preparation Time: 40 minutes

∽ MELANZANE ALLA SICILIANA ∽
Deep-Fried Eggplant with Mozzarella   For 4

In this dish the eggplant slices and the mozzarella are made into elegant "sandwiches." Each diner garnishes the "sandwiches" with a fresh tomato sauce that is served separately.

1 large eggplant (about 2½ lbs.)
salt
½ cup flour
1 cup vegetable oil
1 tsp. dried oregano

½ lb. mozzarella, thinly sliced
1 tbs. olive oil
1 recipe Basic Tomato Sauce II,
p. 15

1. Wash and dry the eggplant, and cut into ¼" slices. Place the slices in a colander, sprinkle with 1 tsp. salt, and let drain for 30 to 40 minutes.
2. Preheat the oven to 350° F.
3. Place the flour on a plate or a sheet of waxed paper. Heat the oil in a skillet over medium-high heat. Quickly dry the eggplant slices, dip into the flour, and fry in one layer until browned on both sides. Drain the slices on brown paper.
4. In an oven-to-table baking dish arrange half the eggplant slices in one layer. Sprinkle with the oregano. Top each slice with mozzarella and a second slice of the eggplant. Drizzle with the olive oil.
5. Bake the eggplant for 10 to 15 minutes, or until the cheese is melted.
6. While the eggplant is in the oven, warm the tomato sauce in a small saucepan over low heat.
7. Serve the eggplant with the tomato sauce on the side.

Estimated Cooking Time: 30 minutes
Estimated Total Preparation Time: 1 hour and 10 minutes

∽ MELANZANE RIPIENE ∽
Stuffed Eggplants   For 4

6 small Italian eggplants (about
   2 lbs.)
salt
1 cup fresh bread crumbs made
   from Italian bread
¼ cup Italian or Greek black
   olives, pitted and quartered
2 tbs. capers, drained

5 anchovy fillets, coarsely
   chopped
⅓ cup fresh parsley, minced
1 large garlic clove, mashed
¼ tsp. dried oregano
½ cup olive oil
4 canned Italian-style plum
   tomatoes, seeded and cut into
   strips

1. Wash and dry the eggplants. Remove the stems, and halve eggplants lengthwise. Cut deep slashes into the pulp, being careful not to rupture the skin. Sprinkle with 1 tsp. salt, and place the eggplants, upside down, in a colander to drain for 30 to 40 minutes.

2. Meanwhile combine the bread crumbs, the olives, the capers, the anchovies, the parsley, the garlic, and the oregano in a bowl. Blend well.

3. Preheat the oven to 350°F.

4. Dry the eggplants thoroughly with paper towels, and place in an oiled oven-to-table baking dish. Top each eggplant with the olive mixture, pushing it down into the slashes.

5. Distribute the tomatoes on top, drizzle with the oil, and sprinkle with a pinch of salt. Bake for 1 hour. Serve at room temperature.

Note: These eggplants must be made several hours in advance. They can be prepared one or two days ahead of time and refrigerated. In that case, remove them from the refrigerator several hours before serving to bring them to room temperature.

Estimated Cooking Time: 1 hour
Estimated Total Preparation Time: 2 hours

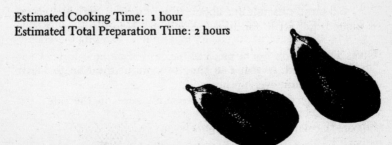

∽ MELANZANE E ZUCCHINE ALLA PARMIGIANA ∽
Baked Eggplant and Zucchini   For 4

This variation on the typical eggplant Parmesan casserole was perfected by a Calabrese friend. The combined eggplant and zucchini flavors, along with the addition of the potato, makes for a very satisfying dish.

1 lb. eggplants, preferably the small Italian type	1 cup vegetable oil
salt	1 cup Basic Tomato Sauce I, p. 14
1 lb. thin zucchini	½ lb. mozzarella, thinly sliced
1 large new potato	½ cup freshly grated Parmesan cheese

1. Wash and dry the eggplants, and cut into ¼" slices. Place the slices in a colander, sprinkle with ½ tsp. salt, and let drain for 30 to 40 minutes. Follow the same procedure with the zucchini.

2. Scrub and dry the potato but do not peel. Cut into thin slices.

3. Preheat the oven to 350° F.

4. Heat the oil in a large skillet over medium-high heat. Fry the potato slices in one layer until slightly browned on both sides. Drain on brown paper. Dry the eggplant and the zucchini, and fry the same way.

5. Coat the bottom of an oven-to-table baking dish with a little tomato sauce. Spread the eggplant slices in one layer. Cover with half the mozzarella and ⅓ cup tomato sauce, and sprinkle with ¼ cup Parmesan cheese. Follow with a layer of the potatoes, a layer of the zucchini, and the remaining mozzarella. Top with the rest of the tomato sauce, and finish with the remaining Parmesan cheese.

6. Bake the casserole for about 15 minutes, or until the cheese is melted. Let settle for about 20 minutes before serving.

Note: This casserole can be prepared the day before through step 5 and refrigerated. In that case bring to room temperature, and bake for 30 minutes.

Estimated Cooking Time: 45 minutes
Estimated Total Preparation Time: 2 hours

∾ INSALATA SICILIANA ∾

Marinated Eggplants, Peppers, and Tomatoes

For 4 to 6

3 small Italian eggplants	4 ripe medium tomatoes
salt	4 tbs. olive oil
3 red or green sweet peppers	1 garlic clove, crushed

1. Wash and dry the eggplants, and cut lengthwise into ½" slices. Place the slices in a colander, sprinkle with ¼ tsp. salt, and let drain for 30 to 40 minutes.

2. While the eggplants are draining, wash and dry the peppers. Place them on a rack as close as possible to the broiler, and sear on all sides. When the skins of the peppers have loosened and are slightly charred (5 to 10 minutes), remove the peppers from the broiler, and peel them. Halve the peppers, remove the seeds, and cut into ¼" strips.

3. Dip the tomatoes into boiling water. Peel, seed, and mash into a coarse puree.

4. Dry the eggplants, place them on a cookie sheet, and brush with 1 tbs. oil. Broil for about 15 minutes on each side. Remove from the broiler, and cut into ¼" strips.

5. In a shallow serving bowl combine the peppers, the eggplants, the tomatoes, the garlic, the remaining olive oil, and ¼ tsp. salt. Toss gently. Serve the dish cold or at room temperature.

Note: This dish can be prepared a day in advance. Store in the refrigerator.

Estimated Cooking Time: 25 minutes
Estimated Total Preparation Time: 1 hour

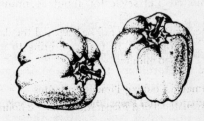

∽ FUNGHI CRUDI CONDITI ∽
Fresh Mushroom Salad   For 4

1 lb. fresh mushrooms   salt
2 tbs. lemon juice   freshly ground black pepper
4 tbs. olive oil

1. Remove the mushroom stems. If the caps are relatively clean, wipe them thoroughly with a damp paper towel. If there is a lot of soil and dirt clinging to them, rinse thoroughly but quickly in cold water, rubbing the mushrooms against each other to dislodge the dirt. Dry with paper towels. Slice the mushrooms thinly, lengthwise.

2. Place the mushrooms in a round shallow bowl. Pour the lemon juice and the oil over them, and sprinkle with the salt and pepper. Toss gently.

Note: This dish should be prepared within one hour of serving time. The mushroom stems may be used for risottos, in the filling for cannelloni, and in the sauces for the Pasta Roll with Cooked Ham and Fontina (p. 215) and the Green Raviolini Baked in a Crust (p. 233).

Estimated Total Preparation Time: 30 minutes

∽ FUNGHI ALLA LANGAROLA ∽
Raw Mushrooms in Piquant Sauce   For 4

1 lb. fresh mushrooms   2 tbs. fresh parsley, minced
½ cup olive oil   6 anchovy fillets, chopped
2 tbs. lemon juice   1 garlic clove, slightly crushed
2 egg yolks

1. Remove the mushroom stems. If the caps are relatively clean, wipe them thoroughly with a damp paper towel. If there is a lot of soil and dirt clinging to them, rinse thoroughly but quickly in cold water, rubbing the mushrooms against each other to dislodge the dirt. Dry with paper towels. Slice the mushrooms thinly, lengthwise, and place in a shallow serving dish.

2. In a small bowl combine the oil, the lemon juice, the egg

yolks, the parsley, and the anchovies. Spear the garlic clove with a fork, and use it to stir the ingredients until they form a thick, smooth sauce.

3. Pour the sauce over the mushrooms, and toss gently.

Note: This dish should be prepared within an hour of serving time. The mushroom stems may be used for risottos, in the filling for cannelloni, and in the sauces for Pasta Roll with Cooked Ham and Fontina (p. 215) and the Green Raviolini Baked in a Crust (p. 233).

Estimated Total Preparation Time: 40 minutes

◇ FUNGHI ALL'OLIO D'OLIVA ◇
Mushrooms in Olive Oil   For 4

1½ lbs. fresh mushrooms   ½ large beef bouillon cube
1 cup olive oil   1 tbs. fresh parsley, chopped

1. Trim off the ends of the mushroom stems. If the mushrooms are relatively clean, wipe them thoroughly with a damp paper towel. If there is a lot of soil and dirt clinging to the caps, rinse thoroughly but quickly in cold water, rubbing them against each other to dislodge the dirt. Dry with paper towels. Leave the small mushrooms whole. Halve or quarter the larger ones.

2. Put the oil and the bouillon cube into a heavy-bottomed saucepan. Add the mushrooms, and cook over medium-low heat until the mushrooms have given off their liquid. Simmer over low heat for about 15 minutes more, or until the mushrooms are tender but still firm.

3. Let the mushrooms cool in their liquid, then refrigerate them in the liquid for several hours or overnight.

4. Just before serving drain the mushrooms, reserving the liquid, and toss them with the parsley.

Note: If there are leftover mushrooms, refrigerate them in the reserved liquid. You can also use liquid to season cooked vegetables.

Estimated Cooking Time: 35 minutes
Estimated Total Preparation Time: 1 hour

∾ FUNGHI SAPORITI ∾
Savory Mushrooms
For 4

1½ lbs. fresh mushrooms
2 tbs. olive oil
2 tbs. butter
1 garlic clove, peeled
1 lb. ripe tomatoes (preferably
   plum), peeled, seeded, and
   coarsely chopped

8 to 10 fresh mint leaves, chopped
salt
¼ tsp. ground white pepper

1. Trim off the ends of the mushroom stems. If the mushrooms are relatively clean, wipe them thoroughly with a damp paper towel. If there is a lot of soil and dirt clinging to them, rinse thoroughly but quickly in cold water, rubbing the mushrooms against each other to dislodge the dirt. Dry with paper towels. Cut the mushrooms in half vertically.

2. In a medium saucepan, preferably enamel or earthenware, heat the oil and the butter over medium-low heat. Add the garlic, and sauté until golden. Remove the garlic.

3. Add the mushrooms, the tomatoes, the mint, ¼ tsp. salt, and the pepper, and cook over medium-high heat for about 15 minutes, or until fairly dry. Serve the mushrooms at room temperature.

Note: These mushrooms can be prepared in advance. If they are refrigerated, bring them to room temperature before serving.

Estimated Cooking Time: 25 minutes
Estimated Total Preparation Time: 45 minutes

∽ INSALATA DI PEPERONI ∽
Salad of Sweet Red Peppers   For 4

6 sweet red peppers
4 tbs. olive oil
2 garlic cloves, peeled
8 Italian or Greek black olives,
    pitted and slivered

2 anchovy fillets, minced
½ cup red wine vinegar
salt

1. Wash and dry the peppers. Place them on a rack as close as possible to the broiler, and sear on all sides. When the skins of the peppers have loosened and are slightly charred (5 to 10 minutes), remove the peppers from the broiler, and peel them. Halve the peppers, remove the seeds, and cut into ¼" strips.

2. Heat the oil in a skillet with the garlic over medium-high heat. When the garlic is golden, remove it, and add the olives, the anchovies, and the vinegar. Cook for 2 to 3 minutes. Lower the heat to medium, add the peppers, and cook until the liquid is reduced to about 1 tbs. Taste for salt.

3. Remove the peppers with their sauce to a shallow serving dish, and let cool. Serve at room temperature.

Note: This dish can be prepared one or two days in advance.

Estimated Cooking Time: 20 minutes
Estimated Total Preparation Time: 40 minutes

∽ PEPERONATA ∽
Stewed Peppers with Tomatoes   For 4

4 to 5 green or red sweet peppers
2 tbs. vegetable oil
2 tbs. olive oil
1 large onion, thinly sliced

5 ripe plum tomatoes
or
3 ripe medium tomatoes
salt

1. Wash and dry the peppers. Halve them, remove the seeds, and cut into ¼" slices.

2. Heat the oils in a heavy saucepan. Add the onion, and sauté over medium heat until slightly golden. Add the peppers, and sauté for 8 to 10 minutes.

3. While the peppers are cooking, dip the tomatoes into boiling water, and peel them. Cut into strips, and add to the saucepan. Add ½ tsp. salt, stir, and cook the mixture, covered, over medium-low heat for about 15 minutes. Remove the cover, and cook for 10 minutes longer, or until the vegetables are tender and the stew is thick but still moist.

4. Remove the stew from the heat, and cool before serving.

Note: This dish can be prepared a day or two in advance and kept in the refrigerator.

Estimated Cooking Time: 45 minutes
Estimated Total Preparation Time: 1 hour

∽ PEPERONI ARROSTO ∽
Roasted Peppers   For 4

6 large yellow or green peppers   3 tbs. fresh parsley, minced
salt   ⅓ cup olive oil
1 garlic clove, mashed

1. Wash and dry the peppers. Place them on a rack as close as possible to the broiler, and sear on all sides. When the skins of the peppers have loosened and are slightly charred (5 to 10 minutes), remove the peppers from the broiler, and peel them. Halve them, remove the seeds, and cut into ¼" strips.

2. Arrange the peppers in a shallow serving dish. Sprinkle with ¼ tsp. salt, the garlic, the parsley, and the oil.

3. Let peppers marinate for at least 30 minutes.

Note: This dish can be prepared the day before. It does not have to be refrigerated.

Estimated Cooking Time: 10 minutes
Estimated Total Preparation Time: 25 minutes

ᔔ PEPERONI IMBOTTITI ᔔ
Stuffed Red Peppers

For 4

4 *large sweet red peppers, washed
   and dried*
1 *cup fresh bread crumbs*
¼ *cup plain dry bread crumbs*
½ *lb. ripe tomatoes, peeled,
   seeded, and chopped*
4 *anchovy fillets, chopped*
2 *tbs. capers, drained and
   chopped*
12 to 15 *Italian or Greek black
   olives, pitted and chopped*
3 *tbs. fresh parsley, minced*
⅓ *cup freshly grated pecorino
   Romano cheese*
6 *tbs. olive oil*
freshly ground black pepper
salt

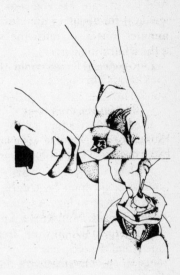

1. Preheat the oven to 350° F.
2. Cut the tops off the peppers in such a way that they can be put back in place. Remove all the seeds and filaments. Set peppers aside.
3. Soak the fresh bread crumbs in a little cold water, and squeeze to remove excess moisture.
4. In a medium bowl combine the fresh bread crumbs, the dry bread crumbs, the tomatoes, the anchovies, the capers, the olives, the parsley, the cheese, 2 tbs. oil, and the pepper. Mix thoroughly, and taste for salt.
5. Stuff the peppers with the mixture, put their tops back on, and place in a shallow baking dish just large enough to hold the standing peppers. Drizzle with the remaining oil.
6. Bake the peppers for 1 hour, basting from time to time with the oil. Serve warm or at room temperature.

Note: This recipe can be prepared the day before and does not need
      to be refrigerated.

Estimated Cooking Time: 1 hour
Estimated Total Preparation Time: 1 hour and 30 minutes

∽ POMODORI GRATINATI ∽
Savory Grilled Tomatoes   For 4

4 medium tomatoes
salt
4 tbs. olive oil
3½ tbs. plain dry bread crumbs
3 anchovy fillets, chopped

1 garlic clove, minced
2 tbs. fresh parsley, minced
1 tbs. capers, drained and
    chopped
½ tsp. dried oregano

1. Preheat the oven to 450° F.
2. Slice off the tops of the tomatoes. Seed them, and remove the hard core. Sprinkle with ¼ tsp. salt, and turn upside down to drain for about 30 minutes.
3. Heat 3 tbs. oil in a small skillet. Add 2 tbs. bread crumbs, and sauté over medium heat until lightly browned (2 to 3 minutes). Turn the heat to low. Add the anchovies and the garlic, and cook, stirring and mashing with a wooden spoon for 2 to 3 minutes.
4. Remove the mixture from the heat. Add the parsley, the capers, and the oregano.
5. Fill the tomatoes with the mixture. Sprinkle with the rest of the bread crumbs, and drizzle with the remaining oil. Bake for about 15 minutes. Let cool.
6. Serve the tomatoes at room temperature.

Estimated Cooking Time: 25 minutes
Estimated Total Preparation Time: 1 hour

∽ POMODORI RIPIENI ALLA PIEMONTESE ∽
Stuffed Tomatoes with Green Sauce   For 4

4 medium tomatoes
salt
½ cup fresh bread crumbs
3 tbs. red wine vinegar
4 anchovy fillets

1 garlic clove, peeled
1 tbs. capers, drained
1 hard-boiled egg yolk
½ cup fresh parsley, minced
⅓ cup olive oil

1. Slice the tops off the tomatoes. Scoop out the pulp, reserving it for another use. Sprinkle the inside of the tomatoes with salt, and turn the tomatoes upside down to drain for about 30 minutes.

2. In a bowl soak the bread crumbs in the vinegar.

3. Chop the anchovies, the garlic, the capers, and the egg yolk together until fine.

4. Add the anchovy mixture and the parsley to the bread crumbs, and blend thoroughly with a wooden spoon. Add the olive oil, a little at a time, stirring well until the sauce is smooth and creamy.

5. Fill the tomatoes with the stuffing, and let cool in the refrigerator for about 30 minutes.

Note: This recipe can be prepared hours ahead of time. In that case remove the tomatoes from the refrigerator 20 minutes before serving so that they are cool but not chilled.

Estimated Total Preparation Time: 45 minutes

∾ POMODORI RIPIENI AL TONNO ∾
Fresh Tomatoes Stuffed with Tuna   For 4

4 firm medium tomatoes	*1½ tbs. fresh parsley, minced*
salt	*freshly ground black pepper*
1 6½-oz. can chunk light tuna,	*⅓ cup mayonnaise (see*
drained and flaked	*Mayonnaise, p. 17)*

1. Slice the tops off the tomatoes. Scoop out the pulp, reserving it for another use.

2. In a bowl combine the tuna with the parsley, ¼ tsp. salt, and the pepper.

3. Fill the tomatoes with the tuna mixture, and top each tomato with 1½ tbs. mayonnaise.

Note: These tomatoes can be prepared several hours in advance and chilled. In that case remove them from the refrigerator about 30 minutes before serving. Add the mayonnaise topping at the last minute.

Estimated Total Preparation Time: 20 minutes

~ ZUCCHINE MARINATE ~
Marinated Zucchini   For 4

1 lb. zucchini
salt
1 cup vegetable oil
1 large garlic clove, minced

¼ cup fresh parsley, minced
⅓ cup red wine vinegar
½ red chili pepper
or
¼ tsp. red pepper flakes

1. Wash and dry the zucchini, and cut into ¼″ slices. Place in a colander, sprinkle with ½ tsp. salt, and drain for 30 to 40 minutes.

2. Heat the oil in a large skillet over high heat. Dry the zucchini, and slide the pieces into the oil in a single layer. Fry quickly until tender and slightly browned. Drain slices on brown paper. Continue this process with the rest of the zucchini.

3. Place one layer of the zucchini on the bottom of a shallow serving dish. Sprinkle with some of the garlic and some of the parsley. Repeat the procedure with one or two more layers.

4. Put the vinegar and the chili pepper in a small saucepan and bring to a boil. Remove the chili pepper, and pour the vinegar over the zucchini. If you use pepper flakes, strain the vinegar.

5. Cover the zucchini with foil, and let marinate for at least 12 hours.

Note: For best results this dish should be prepared one day in advance.

Estimated Cooking Time: 30 minutes
Estimated Total Preparation Time: 1 hour and 30 minutes

∽ ZUCCHINE RIPIENE ∽
Stuffed Zucchini   For 4

4 large ripe tomatoes
    or
8 canned Italian-style plum
    tomatoes
salt
7 tbs. olive oil
5 medium zucchini (about 1½
    lbs.)

8 to 10 fresh basil leaves, torn
    into small pieces
    or
½ tsp. dried sweet basil
¼ cup fresh bread crumbs from
    Italian bread
1 egg, slightly beaten
⅓ cup freshly grated pecorino
    Sardo cheese
freshly ground black pepper

1. Preheat the oven to 425° F.
2. Cut two tomatoes into thin slices, and spread them over the bottom of an oven-to-table baking dish. Sprinkle with ¼ tsp. salt and 2 tbs. oil.
3. Wash four zucchini, scraping off any dirt, and dry thoroughly. Halve the zucchini lengthwise, and remove the pulp from the center, leaving a shell about ¼" thick.
4. Place the zucchini shells in the baking dish, sprinkle with a pinch of salt, drizzle with 2 tbs. oil, and bake for 15 minutes. Remove from the oven.
5. Meanwhile peel the remaining zucchini, and with the pulp from the other zucchini, chop it fine.
6. Heat 1 tbs. oil in a medium saucepan over medium heat. Add the zucchini pulp, and sauté for about 10 minutes. Chop the remaining tomatoes, and add to the zucchini, with the basil and ½ tsp. salt. Cook for about 10 minutes.
7. In a bowl combine the zucchini mixture, the bread crumbs, the egg, the cheese, and the pepper. Blend well.
8. Lower the oven temperature to 350° F.
9. Divide the mixture among the zucchini shells, making oblong mounds. Drizzle the remaining oil on top.
10. Bake the zucchini for about 25 minutes. Remove from the oven, and let sit for 20 to 30 minutes before serving.

Note: These zucchini are as good at room temperature as they are warm. They can be prepared up to two days in advance. If you do prepare the zucchini in advance, be sure to remove them from the refrigerator several hours ahead of time to bring them to room temperature.

Pecorino Sardo is less sharp than Romano; it is often labeled Sardo-Romano.

Estimated Cooking Time: 1 hour and 20 minutes
Estimated Total Preparation Time: 2 hours

❖ CROSTINI ALLA NAPOLETANA ❖

Bread Pizzas   For 4

Crostini make an ideal light meal for children. If they object to the anchovies, leave them out, but try to get them to taste crostini with the anchovies. Our children have learned to love the salty, tangy taste they add.

8 slices Italian bread
3 tbs. butter, softened
½ lb. mozzarella, thinly sliced
8 anchovy fillets

2 large tomatoes, peeled and
  thinly sliced
½ tsp. dried oregano
2 tbs. olive oil

1. Preheat the oven to 400° F.
2. Butter the slices of bread.
3. On each slice of bread place a layer of mozzarella, an anchovy fillet cut into 2 pieces, and a layer of tomato. Sprinkle oregano over the tomatoes, and drizzle with oil.
4. Bake the bread pizzas for about 15 minutes, or until the mozzarella is melted. Serve immediately.

Estimated Cooking Time: 15 minutes
Estimated Total Preparation Time: 30 minutes

∽ CROSTINI AL SALMONE ∽
Smoked Salmon Toasts For 4

This is a great antipasto to have with drinks before sitting down at the table.

5 slices thin white bread
1½ tbs. butter, softened
½ lb. mozzarella, thinly sliced

4 to 5 oz. smoked salmon,
*   shredded*
1 lemon, cut into wedges
freshly ground black pepper

1. Preheat the oven to 400° F.
2. Remove the crusts from the bread, and butter the slices. Cut each slice into quarters.
3. Top each quarter with a slice of mozzarella and some of the salmon.
4. Place the crostini on a cookie sheet, and bake for about 7 minutes, or until the mozzarella is melted. Serve immediately with lemon wedges and a grinding of black pepper.

Estimated Cooking Time: 10 minutes
Estimated Total Preparation Time: 25 minutes

∽ INSALATA CAPRESE ∽
Tomato and Mozzarella Salad with Fresh Basil For 4

1 lb. mozzarella, preferably fresh,
*   cut into bite-sized cubes*
12 firm plum tomatoes, cubed
*   or*
4 to 5 firm medium tomatoes,
*   cubed*

salt
¼ cup olive oil
8 to 12 fresh basil leaves, torn
*   into pieces*

1. Combine the mozzarella and the tomatoes in a shallow serving dish. Sprinkle with ⅛ tsp. salt, drizzle with the oil, and toss gently.
2. Add the basil leaves, toss again, and taste for salt. Serve immediately.

Estimated Total Preparation Time: 15 minutes

∽ MOZZARELLA IN CARROZZA ∽
Deep-Fried Mozzarella Sandwiches   For 4

8 slices white sandwich bread
½ lb. mozzarella, thinly sliced
2 tbs. flour

2 eggs, slightly beaten with
    ¼ tsp. salt
2 cups vegetable oil or shortening

1. Remove the crusts from the bread.
2. Place the mozzarella on four slices of the bread, making sure that the mozzarella remains within ⅛" of the edges. Cover with the remaining four slices, pressing them together around the edges.
3. Pour the flour into a flat dish, and coat the edges of the sandwiches with it. Put ½ cup water in a shallow bowl, and dip the floured edges in carefully so that they are well sealed.
4. Place the sandwiches in a large shallow dish, making sure that they don't touch each other. Pour the eggs over them. Let the sandwiches rest for about 15 minutes to absorb the eggs, then carefully lift the sandwiches up to allow the egg to slide under the bottoms and soak them. Let the sandwiches rest another 15 minutes.
5. Heat the oil in a heavy skillet, and deep fry the sandwiches until golden on both sides. Drain on brown paper, and serve immediately on a heated platter.

Estimated Cooking Time: 10 minutes
Estimated Total Preparation Time: 50 minutes

∽ FRICO ∽
Potato and Cheese Pancake   For 4

Frico comes from Friuli, in the northeastern area of the Veneto region. Latteria, the cheese used there, is locally produced and unavailable elsewhere. Appenzeller, the firm, slightly tangy Swiss cheese, is the best substitute. This is one of the Funghi family specialties, prepared by Lido, Efrem's father. Although his repertoire consists of only three dishes, these pancakes, like his other two specialties, are always very successful.

1 *lb. potatoes*   1 *lb. Appenzeller cheese,*
2 *tbs. vegetable oil*   *shredded*

1. Peel and shred the potatoes, using the largest holes on a
standing grater.

2. Heat the oil in a heavy 9″ skillet over high heat. Add the
potatoes, and sauté for about 5 minutes, stirring constantly with a
wooden spoon. Lower the heat to medium, and continue cooking,
stirring the potatoes, for 10 to 15 minutes longer, or until they
are tender and browned.

3. Add ⅓ of the cheese, stirring until melted and thoroughly
mixed into the potatoes. Repeat the process with the remaining
cheese. When all the cheese is melted, push it down with the
spoon to release the fat. Pour off the fat, and put the pan back
on the burner, pressing the mixture down until a crust forms on
the bottom. Turn the frico over with a large spatula, and cook
until a crust forms on the second side.

4. Turn the frico onto a round dish, and serve cut into wedges.

Note: Do not shred the potatoes until just before cooking, or they will
turn brown.

Estimated Cooking Time: 30 minutes
Estimated Total Preparation Time: 40 minutes

∽ UOVA RIPIENE ∽
Stuffed Eggs   For 4

4 *eggs, hard-boiled and shelled*   3 *anchovy fillets, mashed*
4 *tbs. mayonnaise (see*   1 *tbs. fresh parsley, minced*
  Mayonnaise, p. 17)   8 *capers, drained*

1. Cut the hard-boiled eggs in half crosswise. Cut about ⅛″ off
each end so that the eggs can stand.

2. Remove the yolks, and place them in a bowl. Add the
mayonnaise, the anchovies, and the parsley, and mix with a wooden
spoon, blending the ingredients thoroughly.

3. Put the mixture in a pastry bag fitted with a big star or a

petal tip. Pipe the mixture into the egg whites in a flower petal pattern. Decorate each half egg with a caper.

Estimated Cooking Time: 15 minutes
Estimated Total Preparation Time: 30 minutes

Although the Italian frittata is not as well known as the French omelet, it is one of the most versatile dishes in Italian cuisine. Warm, it is eaten as a light meal, while cold frittatas are often included in a mixed antipasto or a summer picnic basket. The frittata is also an excellent accompaniment for cocktails.

∽ FRITTATA DI ASPARAGI ∽

Asparagus Frittata   For 4

1 lb. asparagus
6 tbs. butter
½ chicken bouillon cube
 dissolved in ½ cup water

6 eggs
½ cup grated Gruyère cheese
1 tbs. fresh parsley, minced
freshly ground black pepper

1. Cut off the tough asparagus bottoms, and peel off the outer skin below the tender tip. Rinse, and cut the stalks into ½" pieces, reserving the tips.

2. Heat 2 tbs. butter in a medium saucepan over medium-low heat. Add the asparagus pieces and the bouillon, and cook, covered, for 5 minutes. Add the tips, and continue cooking, partially covered, for 10 more minutes, or until just tender. The liquid should dry out; if not drain it.

3. In a large bowl beat the eggs slightly with a fork. Add the asparagus, the cheese, the parsley, and the pepper, and mix the ingredients thoroughly.

4. Heat 3 tbs. butter in a 10" skillet over medium heat. Pour the egg mixture into the skillet, turn the heat to low, and cook for about 10 minutes, or until the frittata has set (the top will still be somewhat runny). Turn the frittata upside down onto a dish.

5. Add the remaining butter to the skillet. When melted, slide the frittata, soft side down, back into the skillet, and cook for 3 minutes, or until well set. Press on the top to make sure there is no liquid egg in the center.

6. Turn the frittata onto a platter, and let sit for 5 to 10 minutes before serving.

Note: Frittatas are eaten both warm and at room temperature.

Estimated Cooking Time: 35 minutes
Estimated Total Preparation Time: 50 minutes

Frittatas, like omelets, can be prepared with any number of vegetables or other ingredients using the same basic techniques, as the recipes that follow demonstrate.

∽ FRITTATA DI CARCIOFI ∽
Artichoke Frittata For 4

3 artichokes
1 lemon, halved
1 tbs. vegetable oil
5 tbs. butter
¼ large chicken bouillon cube
  dissolved in ¼ cup water

6 eggs
salt
freshly ground black pepper
2 tbs. fresh parsley, minced

1. Cut off the artichoke stems, leaving about 1". Break off the small leaves at the base, and cut off about 1" from the top. Snap off the hard upper part from the leaves, and peel the tough outer layer from the stem. Cut the artichokes in half lengthwise and remove the fuzzy choke and the prickly leaves around it, being careful not to remove the heart. Rub the halves with the lemon to prevent discoloration. Slice each half lengthwise very thinly.

2. Heat the oil and 1 tbs. butter in a medium saucepan, preferably enamel or stainless steel. Add the artichokes, and sauté for about 5 minutes over low heat. Add the bouillon, and cook the artichokes, covered, for about 20 minutes, or until tender.

3. In a large bowl beat the eggs, ¼ tsp. salt, and the pepper slightly with a fork. Add the artichokes and the parsley, and mix the ingredients thoroughly. Follow steps 4 to 6 of Asparagus Frittata (p. 54).

Estimated Cooking Time: 45 minutes
Estimated Total Preparation Time: 1 hour

∼ FRITTATA DI CIPOLLE ∼
Onion Frittata   For 4

6 tbs. butter
2 large white onions (about
 1 lb.), thinly sliced

salt
6 eggs
freshly ground black pepper

1. Heat 2 tbs. butter in a medium skillet over medium-low heat. Add the onions, sprinkle with ¼ tsp. salt, and cook until soft and slightly golden, 15 to 20 minutes. Remove from the heat.

2. In a large bowl beat the eggs, ¼ tsp. salt, and the pepper slightly with a fork. Add the onions, and mix well. Follow steps 4 to 6 of Asparagus Frittata (p. 54).

Estimated Cooking Time: 35 minutes
Estimated Total Preparation Time: 45 minutes

∼ FRITTATA DI CRESCIONE ∼
Watercress Frittata   For 4

1 bunch watercress
6 large eggs

salt
4 tbs. butter

1. Wash the watercress, and pluck off the leaves, discarding the stems, to make about 1½ cups. Chop coarsely.

2. In a medium bowl, beat the eggs and ¼ tsp. salt slightly with a fork. Add the watercress, and mix well. Follow steps 4 to 6 of Asparagus Frittata (p. 54).

Estimated Cooking Time: 15 minutes
Estimated Total Preparation Time: 30 minutes

∽ FRITTATA DI ERBE ∾

Frittata with Fresh Herbs For 4

5 tbs. butter
¼ cup scallions, chopped
2 tbs. fennel greens (wispy green
    leaves), chopped
1 tbs. chives, chopped

2 tbs. arugola, chopped
    or
2 tbs. watercress, chopped
¼ cup fresh parsley, minced
6 eggs
salt
freshly ground black pepper

1. Heat 1 tbs. butter in a small skillet over low heat. Add the scallions, and cook for about 10 minutes, or until soft. Add the fennel greens, and cook 1 minute longer. Add the chives, the arugola, and the parsley, stir and remove from the heat.

2. In a medium bowl beat the eggs, ¼ tsp. salt, and the pepper slightly with a fork. Add the herb mixture, and combine thoroughly. Follow steps 4 to 6 of Asparagus Frittata (p. 54).

Estimated Cooking Time: 25 minutes
Estimated Total Preparation Time: 35 minutes

∽ FRITTATA DI PEPERONI ∾

Green Pepper Frittata For 4

2 medium green sweet peppers
1½ tbs. vegetable oil
1 small onion, thinly sliced
salt

6 eggs
1 tbs. fresh parsley, minced
4 tbs. butter

1. Wash and dry the peppers. Halve them, remove the seeds, and cut into ¼" strips.

2. Heat the oil in a 10" skillet. Sauté the onion over medium heat for about 1 minute. Add the peppers and ¼ tsp. salt, and sauté for 10 to 12 minutes, or until the peppers are tender but still firm.

3. In a large bowl beat the eggs and ¼ tsp. salt slightly with a

fork. Add the peppers and the parsley, and mix well. Follow steps 4 to 6 of Asparagus Frittata (p. 54).

Estimated Cooking Time: 30 minutes
Estimated Total Preparation Time: 40 minutes

∽ FRITTATA DI ZUCCHINE ∽

Zucchini Frittata

For 4

2 tbs. vegetable oil
2 cups zucchini, thinly sliced
salt
2 tbs. fresh parsley, minced

6 large eggs
2 tbs. Emmenthal (Swiss) cheese, shredded
4 tbs. butter

1. Heat the oil in a skillet. Sauté the zucchini over medium heat for about 15 minutes, or until tender, stirring from time to time. Add ¼ tsp. salt and the parsley.

2. In a large bowl beat the eggs and ¼ tsp. salt slightly with a fork. Add the zucchini and the cheese, and mix well. Follow steps 4 to 6 for Asparagus Frittata (p. 54).

Estimated Cooking Time: 30 minutes
Estimated Total Preparation Time: 45 minutes

∽ ANTIPASTO DI CALAMARI ∽

Squid Salad

For 4

3 lbs. squid
1 carrot
½ celery stalk with leaves, plus
   1 celery stalk, chopped
½ small onion
2 sprigs parsley
1 small bay leaf
4 juniper berries

1 cup dry white wine
salt
2 anchovy fillets
2 garlic cloves, peeled
⅓ cup olive oil
1 tbs. lemon juice
3 tsp. capers, drained
freshly ground black pepper

1. To clean the squid, gently remove the tentacles from the sacs, cut them above the eyes, and discard the rest. Rinse the

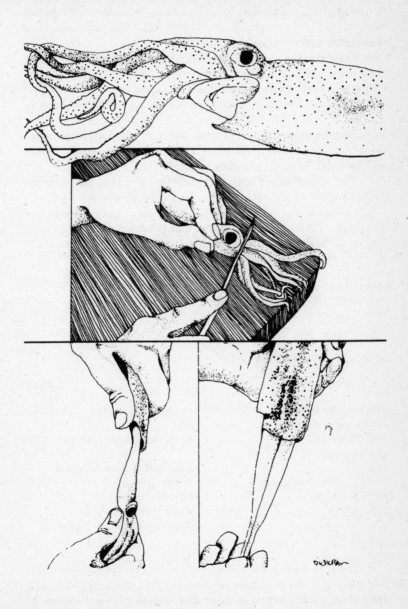

tentacles under cold running water, and set aside. Peel the sacs by pulling the skin off with your fingers. Remove the cartilage-like bone as well as any gelatinous matter from the sacs, and rinse thoroughly under cold running water.

2. Combine the carrot, the celery stalk with leaves, the onion, the parsley, the bay leaf, the juniper berries, the white wine, ¼ tsp. salt, and 1 quart water in a medium saucepan, and bring to a boil over high heat. Lower the heat, and simmer, covered, for about 10 minutes.

3. Add the squid to the saucepan, and cook for about 10 minutes, or until tender. Drain, and let cool. Slice the sacs into ¼" rings and the tentacles into ½" pieces. Set aside.

4. Mash together the anchovies and the garlic. Add the anchovy-garlic mixture to the oil. Add the lemon juice, and stir well.

5. Distribute the pieces of squid in a shallow serving bowl. Add the chopped celery and the capers, and pour the oil mixture over the squid. Sprinkle with the freshly ground pepper, and taste for salt. Serve at room temperature.

Estimated Cooking Time: 30 minutes
Estimated Total Preparation Time: 1 hour

∽ INSALATA DI MARE ∽
Seafood Salad

For 4

6 fresh littleneck clams
1½ lbs. fresh mussels
3 tbs. cornmeal
1½ lbs. squid
1 carrot
½ celery stalk with leaves
½ small onion
2 sprigs parsley
1 small bay leaf
4 juniper berries

1 cup dry white wine
salt
½ lb. small fresh shrimp
    or
6 oz. cooked shrimp, peeled
⅓ cup olive oil
3 tbs. lemon juice
1 garlic clove, mashed
freshly ground black pepper

1. Wash and scrub the clams and the mussels thoroughly under cold running water to remove all sand and dirt, discarding any open ones. With a knife scrape off any hair protruding from the mussels.

Soak the clams and mussels in cold water with 1 tbs. cornmeal for 1 hour, changing the water twice and adding 1 tbs. of fresh cornmeal each time.

2. While the clams and the mussels are soaking, clean the squid. Gently remove the tentacles from the sacs, cut them above the eyes, and discard the rest. Rinse the tentacles under cold running water, and set aside. Peel the sacs by pulling the skin off with your fingers. Remove the cartilage-like bone as well as any gelatinous matter from the sacs, and rinse thoroughly under cold running water.

3. Combine the carrot, the celery, the onion, the parsley, the bay leaf, the juniper berries, the white wine, ¼ tsp. salt, and 1 quart water in a medium saucepan, and bring to a boil over high heat. Lower the heat, and simmer, covered, for about 10 minutes.

4. Add the shrimp to the simmering liquid, and cook for 4 to 5 minutes over medium heat. Remove with a slotted spoon, and cool. Shell and devein the shrimp, and set aside. If you use cooked shrimp, do not cook them again. Combine them with the other seafood in step 7.

5. Add the squid to the saucepan, and cook for about 10 minutes or until tender. Drain, and let cool. Slice the sacs into ¼″ rings, and the tentacles into ½″ pieces, and set aside.

6. Drain the clams and mussels, rinse in cold water, and place in a large heavy saucepan, over medium-high heat. Cover the saucepan, and shake every few minutes so that the mussels and clams will open evenly. When they have all opened, remove from the shells. Discard any that do not open. Strain the liquid through a sieve lined with a cloth or paper towel, and set aside.

7. In a shallow serving dish combine the squid, the shrimp, the clams, and the mussels. Drizzle with oil, and sprinkle with the lemon juice, the mashed garlic, ½ tsp. salt, and the pepper. Toss gently but thoroughly.

8. Let the salad marinate for at least 1 hour before serving.

Note: This salad can be prepared several hours ahead of time but should be kept at room temperature. Mussels must be used the day they are bought.

Estimated Cooking Time: 25 minutes
Estimated Total Preparation Time: 1 hour and 45 minutes

∾ PROSCIUTTO E MELONE ∾
Italian Cured Ham and Cantaloupe   For 4

1 large cantaloupe   12 oz. thinly sliced prosciutto
                                      (about 12 thin slices)

1. Seed and peel the cantaloupe. Cut into 12 wedges.
2. Arrange the wedges on four individual dishes and drape the prosciutto slices over them.

Estimated Total Preparation Time: 15 minutes

4 Soups
Minestre

*A*lthough northern Italy has perhaps contributed the greatest number and variety of soups for Italian menus, all regions of the country offer some specialties that combine locally popular ingredients. These selections include samples from all over. Some are rich and can serve as a meal, accompanied by antipasto and salad, others are delicate openers for a full-course dinner.

∽ MINESTRONE ALLA MILANESE ∽
Minestrone Milanese Style with Rice   For 4 to 6

With Pasta e Fagioli, Minestrone alla Milanese is the classic fare of northern cuisine. Not as hearty as Pasta e Fagioli (p. 72), this tasty, healthful, and colorful soup is eaten all year around, hot or cold, depending on the season.

2 oz. salt pork
1 small onion
1 leek
1 garlic clove, peeled
2 tbs. fresh parsley leaves
2 tbs. butter
2 oz. lean pancetta, cut into
    small strips
        or
2 oz. bacon, cut into small strips
2 small celery stalks, washed and
    diced
2 carrots, peeled and diced
2 zucchini, washed and diced
2 ripe medium tomatoes, peeled,
    seeded, and diced
        or
3 canned tomatoes, seeded and
    diced

1 lb. fresh cranberry beans (also
    called October beans), shelled
        or
½ cup dry cranberry beans,
    soaked overnight in 3 cups
    water and drained
3 baking potatoes, peeled
salt
1 lb. fresh peas, shelled
        or
½ 10-oz. package frozen peas
⅓ small green cabbage, coarsely
    shredded
⅔ cup Carolina long grain rice
4 to 5 fresh sage leaves
        or
6 to 8 fresh basil leaves
        or
½ tsp. dried sage leaves
½ cup freshly grated Parmesan
    cheese

1. Make a *battuto* by chopping together the salt pork, the onion, the leek, the garlic, and the parsley.
2. Place the *battuto*, the butter, and the pancetta or bacon in a stockpot, and sauté over medium heat for 2 to 3 minutes. Add the

celery, the carrots, the zucchini, the tomatoes, the beans, the potatoes, 2 quarts water, and 1 tsp. salt. Bring to a boil, and simmer over medium-low heat for about 1 hour. Add the peas and the cabbage, and cook 30 minutes longer. Remove the potatoes to a dish, roughly mash them with a fork, and return them to the pot. If dried beans are used, partially cook them in 3 to 4 cups water, over medium-low heat, for about 1 hour. Drain them.

3. Add the rice and the sage or basil, and continue cooking for 12 to 14 minutes, or until the rice is al dente—tender but still "firm to the bite." (If you are cooking the minestrone a day or two before you are serving it, see note.) Taste for salt.

4. Serve the minestrone in individual soup bowls, with a bowl of Parmesan cheese at the table.

Note: This soup can be prepared two or three days in advance and refrigerated and served hot or cold. If it is eaten cold, remove it from the refrigerator several hours before the meal to bring it to room temperature. If you are going to serve it hot, do not cook the rice with the soup. Cook it separately, and add it just before serving.

Estimated Cooking Time: 1 hour and 50 minutes (fresh beans); 2 hours and 50 minutes (dried beans)
Estimated Total Preparation Time: 3 hours (fresh beans and peas); 3 hours and 30 minutes (dried beans and frozen peas)

∽ RISI E BISI ∾
Pea and Rice Soup Venetian Style For 4

3 tbs. bacon, chopped (about 2 strips)
1 small onion, minced
2 tbs. butter
4 cups homemade meat broth
2 lbs. fresh peas, shelled
or
1 10-oz. package frozen peas

pinch of sugar
1 cup Carolina long grain rice
2 tbs. fresh parsley, minced
salt
1/3 cup freshly grated Parmesan cheese

1. Combine the bacon, the onion, and the butter in a heavy saucepan, and sauté over medium heat until the onion is soft and translucent.

2. Meanwhile bring the broth to a simmer. If you are using fresh peas, add them, the sugar, and 1 cup broth to the bacon, and cook, uncovered, over low heat for about 10 minutes. Add the remaining broth, and bring to a boil. Go on to step 4.

3. If you are using frozen peas, add the broth to the bacon, bring to a boil, and add the peas. Bring to a boil again.

4. Add the rice. Cook, covered, for about 15 minutes, or until al dente, stirring from time to time. Add the parsley, and taste for salt. Add the Parmesan cheese. Stir well, and let the soup rest for 1 minute before serving.

Estimated Cooking Time: 35 minutes (fresh peas); 25 minutes (frozen peas)

Estimated Total Preparation Time: 1 hour (fresh peas); 45 minutes (frozen peas)

∽ MINESTRA DI RISO E CECI ∽
Rice and Chickpea Soup   For 4

1 cup dried chickpeas
2 slices bacon (2 oz.)
1 medium onion
1 garlic clove, peeled
3 tbs. olive oil
1 celery stalk, chopped
3 to 4 escarole leaves, chopped

4 to 5 ripe plum tomatoes, chopped

or

4 to 5 canned Italian-style plum tomatoes, chopped
salt
½ cup Carolina long grain rice
2 tbs. fresh parsley, minced
¼ cup freshly grated pecorino Romano cheese

1. Soak the chickpeas, covered with 2 to 3 inches of cold water for about 24 hours.

2. Chop the bacon, the onion, and the garlic together until fine, or place in a food processor and chop until fine (about 15 seconds) to make a *battuto*.

3. Combine the oil and the *battuto* in a stockpot, and sauté over medium heat for 4 to 5 minutes. Add the chickpeas, the celery, the escarole, the tomatoes, and 1½ to 2 quarts water. Bring the soup to a boil and simmer over low heat, covered, for 3 to 4 hours. Add ½ tsp. salt, keeping in mind that the pecorino will be very salty.

4. Add the rice, cook 12 to 14 minutes longer, or until tender stirring from time to time. Add the parsley, and stir. Serve the soup with the pecorino on the side.

Note: The soup can be prepared two to three days in advance through step 3 and then refrigerated. Cook the rice just before serving, and add to the soup.

Although we don't recommend using canned chickpeas, they can be substituted if dried ones aren't available. To adjust the recipe, in step 3 combine oil and *battuto*, and add the celery, the tomatoes, the escarole, and 1½ quarts of water. Bring the soup to a boil, and simmer over low heat, covered, for about 1 hour. Add the chickpeas and ½ tsp. salt, and simmer 30 minutes more.

Estimated Cooking Time: 4 to 4 hours and 30 minutes (dried chickpeas); 1 hour and 45 minutes (canned chickpeas)

Estimated Total Preparation Time: 5 hours, not including the soaking (dried chickpeas); 2 hours (canned chickpeas)

∽ MINESTRA DI RISO E FAGIOLI ∽
Rice and Bean Soup   For 4

1 *lb. white navy beans*
or
1 *1-lb. can white kidney beans*
2 *oz. prosciutto, with the fat*
or
2 *oz. cured ham*
1 *medium onion*
1 *large garlic clove, peeled*
1 *small celery stalk*
2 *sprigs parsley*
1 *small red chili pepper*
or
¼ *tsp. red pepper flakes*

4 *tbs. olive oil*
1 *lb. ripe plum tomatoes, peeled, seeded, and chopped*
or
1 *1-lb. can Italian-style plum tomatoes, chopped*
6 to 7 *fresh basil leaves, torn into pieces*
salt
¾ *cup Carolina long grain rice*

1. Soak the beans overnight covered with 2 to 3 inches of cold water. Drain.
2. Cook the beans with 2 quarts water, covered, in a large

stockpot over medium heat for about 1 hour and 15 minutes, or until the beans are tender.

3. While the beans are cooking, prepare the *battuto* by chopping the prosciutto, the onion, the garlic, the celery, the parsley, and the chili pepper together until very fine; if you use a food processor this will take about 15 seconds.

4. Combine 2 tbs. oil and the *battuto* in a medium saucepan, and sauté over low heat for 5 to 10 minutes. Add the tomatoes, the basil, and ½ tsp. salt, and cook, covered, for about 20 minutes.

5. Add the tomato sauce to the beans and cook, covered, for 10 more minutes. If you are using canned beans add 3 cups water to the sauce, and cook for 10 minutes longer. Add the beans and stir.

6. Add the rice, and cook for 12 to 14 minutes, or until al dente, stirring from time to time.

7. Pour the soup into a tureen, and serve immediately. Drizzle each serving with about ½ tbs. olive oil.

Estimated Cooking Time: 1 hour and 45 minutes (dried beans); 1 hour (canned beans)
Estimated Total Preparation Time: 2 hours, not including soaking time (dried beans); 1 hour and 15 minutes (canned beans)

⌁ MINESTRA DI RISO E LENTICCHIE ⌁
Rice and Lentil Soup For 4

½ 1-lb. package small lentils, washed and drained
2 slices bacon (2 oz.)
1 garlic clove, peeled
2 sprigs parsley
2 tbs. olive oil

5 to 6 ripe plum tomatoes, peeled, seeded, and chopped
or
5 to 6 canned Italian-style plum tomatoes, seeded and chopped
salt
½ large beef bouillon cube
½ cup Carolina long grain rice
¼ cup freshly grated pecorino Romano cheese

1. Combine the lentils and 2 quarts water in a large saucepan, and bring to a boil, covered, over medium-high heat. Turn the

heat to medium-low, and simmer for about 25 minutes, or until the lentils are tender but still hold their shape. Drain.

2. Meanwhile prepare the *battuto* by chopping the bacon, the garlic, and the parsley together until fine; in a food processor this takes about 15 seconds.

3. Combine the *battuto* and the oil in a large saucepan, and sauté over medium heat for 5 minutes. Add the tomatoes, ¼ tsp. salt, and the bouillon, and cook for 10 minutes more. Add 5 cups water, and continue cooking, covered, for another 10 minutes.

4. Add the lentils, stir the soup, and add the rice. Stir again, and cook for 10 to 12 minutes, or until the rice is al dente. (If you are preparing the soup in advance, see note.)

5. Pour the soup into a tureen, and serve sprinkled with the cheese.

Note: This soup can be prepared several days in advance. In that case, do not cook the rice with the soup. Cook it separately, and add it just before serving.

Estimated Cooking Time: 1 hour and 10 minutes
Estimated Total Preparation Time: 1 hour and 20 minutes

ᴖ MINESTRA DI RISO E ZUCCA ᴖ
Acorn Squash Soup with Rice   For 4

6 tbs. butter	1 large beef bouillon cube
1 lb. acorn squash, peeled,	dissolved in 5 cups boiling
seeded, and cubed (about 2	water
cups)	½ cup freshly grated Parmesan
1 large onion, minced	cheese
1 cup Carolina long grain rice	salt
	freshly ground black pepper

1. Heat 2 tbs. butter in a medium saucepan. Add the squash, and sauté over low heat for 5 minutes. Add ½ cup water, and cook, covered, for about 20 minutes. Mash the squash with a wooden spoon, and if necessary, continue cooking for another 5 minutes, or until soft.

2. While the squash is cooking, heat 2 tbs. butter in a large

saucepan over medium-low heat. Add the onion, and sauté until soft and translucent. Add the rice, and sauté for 1 to 2 minutes, stirring well. Add the squash, and stir the mixture again. Raise the heat to medium-high. Pour in the bouillon, one-third at a time, stirring well after each addition. Cook the soup for 10 more minutes, or until the rice is al dente. Turn the heat off.

3. Add the remaining butter and the Parmesan cheese and taste for salt.

4. Pour the soup into a tureen, sprinkle with pepper, and serve immediately.

Estimated Cooking Time: 40 minutes
Estimated Total Preparation Time: 55 minutes

∽ TIELLA PUGLIESE ∽

Soup with Rice, Potatoes, and Mussels   For 4

An unusual creation from the coast along the heel of Italy, this intriguing combination of fresh vegetables and mussels is both decorative and delicious.

3 lbs. fresh mussels
3 tbs. cornmeal
4 tbs. olive oil
1 large onion, minced
1 large garlic clove, mashed
6 small ripe tomatoes, peeled and
  coarsely chopped

3 medium potatoes (about ¾ lb.),
  peeled and thinly sliced
¾ cup Carolina long grain rice
salt
2 tbs. fresh parsley, minced
freshly ground black pepper

1. Wash and scrub the mussels thoroughly under cold running water to remove all sand and dirt, discarding any open ones. With a knife scrape off any protruding hair. Soak the mussels in cold water with 1 tbs. cornmeal for 1 hour, changing the water twice, and adding 1 tbs. of fresh cornmeal each time. Drain the mussels, and rinse under cold water.

2. Place the mussels and 2 tbs. oil in a heavy-bottomed saucepan over medium-high heat. Cover the saucepan, and shake every few minutes so the mussels will open evenly. When they are open, remove them from the shells, and set aside. Do not use any mussels that do not open. Strain the liquid through a sieve lined with a cloth, and reserve.

3. Heat the remaining oil in a large saucepan over medium heat. Add the onion, and sauté until soft and translucent. Add the garlic and the tomatoes, and sauté 5 minutes longer.

4. Add the potatoes, stir, and sauté for 5 to 8 minutes. Add 4 to 5 cups water and the liquid from the mussels, raise the heat to high, and bring the soup to a boil. Add the rice and ¾ tbs. salt. Stir, turn the heat to low, and cook, covered, for 12 to 15 minutes, or until the rice is almost done.

5. Add the mussels, the parsley, and abundant pepper, and cook 2 to 3 minutes longer. Taste for salt, and serve immediately.

Note: Mussels must be used the same day they are bought.

Estimated Cooking Time: 50 minutes
Estimated Total Preparation Time: 2 hours

⬤ MINESTRA DI PASTA E CECI ⬤
Chickpea and Pasta Soup   For 4

1 cup dried chickpeas
    or
2 1-lb. cans chickpeas
2 sprigs fresh rosemary
    or
¾ tsp. dried rosemary leaves
2 garlic cloves, peeled
2 tbs. olive oil
1 tbs. tomato paste, diluted
    with ½ cup water

salt
1 cup tubetti
    or
7 oz. maltagliati (fresh egg pasta
    rolled thin and cut into
    random small pieces; ½ Basic
    Fresh Egg Pasta, p. 200)
freshly ground black pepper
4 tbs. olive oil (optional)

1. If you are using dried chickpeas, soak them covered with 2 to 3 inches of cold water for about 24 hours.

2. Drain the chickpeas, and put them in a stockpot, preferably terracotta. Add 2 quarts water and a sprig of rosemary (or ½ tsp. dried rosemary leaves), and cook, covered, over low heat for 3 to 4 hours, or until the chickpeas are tender.

3. Prepare a *battuto* by chopping the remaining rosemary leaves and the garlic together until fine.

4. Heat 2 tbs. oil in a large saucepan. Add the garlic-rosemary *battuto*, and sauté over medium heat for 2 minutes. Add the diluted tomato paste, and cook over low heat for 10 to 15 minutes longer.

Add the chickpeas, their cooking liquid, and the salt. Bring the soup to a boil. If you are using canned chickpeas, add them to the *battuto*–tomato paste mixture with their liquid, 4 cups of water, and ½ tsp. salt. Bring the soup to a boil, and simmer 15–20 minutes.

5. Add the pasta, and cook until done. If tubetti are used, it will take about 15 minutes. If fresh maltagliati are used, they will cook in 3 to 4 minutes. Sprinkle with the pepper, and stir. (If you are cooking the soup ahead, see note.)

6. Serve in individual soup bowls, drizzling each serving with 1 tbs. olive oil.

Note: This soup is also very good at room temperature. It can be prepared two to three days in advance. In that case, don't cook the pasta with the soup. Cook it separately on the day you are using the soup, and add it just before serving.

Estimated Cooking Time: 4 hours to 4 hours and 30 minutes (dried chickpeas); 45 minutes (canned chickpeas)

Estimated Preparation Time: 4 hours and 45 minutes, not including the soaking (dried chickpeas); 1 hour (canned chickpeas)

∽ PASTA E FAGIOLI ∽
Bean Soup with Pasta   For 6

1 lb. package dry cranberry beans
  (also called October beans)
1 large onion
2 celery stalks
2 small carrots
6 slices bacon (about 5 oz.)
2 tbs. vegetable oil
3 medium potatoes, peeled

1 large beef bouillon cube,
  dissolved in 1 cup of water
¾ cup tubetti or ditali pasta
salt
3 to 4 tbs. olive oil (optional)
  or
6 tbs. freshly grated Parmesan
  cheese (optional)

1. Soak the beans overnight covered with 2 to 3 inches of cold water. Drain them.

2. Prepare the *battuto* by chopping the onion, the celery, the carrots, and the bacon together until fine; in a food processor this takes about 15 seconds.

3. Heat the oil in a large heavy pot. Add the *battuto*, and sauté

over medium heat for about 5 minutes. Add the beans and the potatoes, and stir. Add the bouillon cube, dissolved in 1 cup water, plus 8 to 9 additional cups of water. Cover the soup, bring to a boil, and simmer over low heat for about 2 hours, or until the beans are tender. Remove the potatoes, mash them roughly with a fork, and return to the soup.

4. Add the pasta, raise the heat to medium, and cook for about 15 minutes, or until the pasta is tender. Stir the soup from time to time to prevent the pasta from sticking. Taste for salt.

5. Serve the soup in individual bowls, drizzling each serving with about 2 tsp. olive oil or sprinkling with 1 tbs. freshly grated Parmesan cheese. Do not serve with both.

Estimated Cooking Time: 2 hours and 30 minutes
Estimated Total Preparation Time: 3 hours, not including the soaking

∽ MINESTRA DI PASTA E FAGIOLI ESTIVA ∽
Cold Bean and Pasta Soup   For 4 to 6

1 lb. great northern beans
2 celery stalks
1 medium onion
1 carrot
1 1-lb. can Italian-style plum
   tomatoes, coarsely chopped
5 to 6 fresh basil leaves
   or
¼ tsp. dried sweet basil
salt

3 slices (about 4 oz.) bacon, finely
   chopped
1 small red chili pepper, chopped
   or
¼ tsp. red pepper flakes
7 oz. maltagliati (fresh egg pasta
   rolled thin and cut into
   random small pieces; ½ Basic
   Fresh Egg Pasta, p. 200)
2 tbs. olive oil

1. Soak the beans overnight covered with 2 to 3 inches of cold water. Drain.

2. In a large stockpot combine the beans, the celery, the onion, and the carrot. Cover with 2½ quarts water, and bring to a boil over medium-high heat. Lower the heat to medium, and continue cooking for 1 hour and 15 minutes, or until tender. Drain the beans, reserving the liquid.

3. While the beans are cooking, cook the tomatoes, the basil, and ½ tsp. salt in a small saucepan, over medium heat, for about 20 minutes. Remove the basil leaves.

4. Puree the onion, the carrot, the celery, and half the beans through a food mill or in a food processor.

5. In the stockpot sauté the bacon and the red chili pepper over medium heat for 4 to 5 minutes. Add the vegetable puree, the tomato sauce, the beans and their cooking water, and ½ tsp. salt, and cook for 10 minutes longer. Taste for salt. Remove the soup from the fire, and let cool.

6. Drop the maltagliati into 2 to 3 quarts boiling salted water, and cook for 2 minutes if fresh or 5 minutes if frozen. Drain, and toss with the oil in a bowl. Cool. (If you are cooking the soup ahead, see note.)

7. Add the maltagliati to the soup, and stir. Serve at room temperature.

Note: This soup can be made two to three days in advance. In that case, cook the pasta, let it cool, and add just before serving.

Estimated Cooking Time: 1 hour and 40 minutes
Estimated Total Preparation Time: 2 hours, not including the soaking

∽ ZUPPA DI LENTICCHIE ALLA SICILIANA ∽
Lentil Soup Sicilian Style   For 4

1½ heads escarole lettuce
½ 1-lb. package small lentils,
   washed and drained
1 medium onion, minced
½ large beef bouillon cube
salt
4 tbs. olive oil

1 garlic clove, mashed
½ red chili pepper, seeded and
   chopped (optional)
       or
¼ tsp. red pepper flakes
   (optional)
½ cup bucatini broken into
   ½" pieces

1. Remove and discard any dark green or bruised outer leaves from the escarole, and wash in 2 or 3 changes of water. Drain.

2. Place the lentils, the onion, the bouillon cube, ½ tsp. salt, and about 1½ quarts water into a large pot, and bring to a boil, covered, on medium-high heat. Turn the heat to medium-low, and simmer for about 40 minutes to 1 hour (depending on the type of lentils), until the lentils are tender but still hold their shape. Turn the heat off.

3. In another large saucepan bring 2 quarts water to a boil. Add the escarole and ½ tsp. salt, and cook, covered, over medium-low heat for about 35 minutes, or until tender. Drain the lettuce, and chop it coarsely.

4. Heat the oil in a skillet. Add the lettuce, the garlic, and the chili pepper, and sauté over medium heat for about 5 minutes.

5. Add the lettuce to the lentils and stir well. Taste for salt.

6. Drop the bucatini into 1 quart boiling salted water, and cook briefly, until very al dente.

7. Bring the soup to a boil, add the pasta, and stir. Cook until the pasta is done (1 to 2 minutes).

Note: This soup tastes better when made a day in advance through step 5.

Estimated Cooking Time: 1 hour and 15 minutes
Estimated Total Preparation Time: 1 hour and 30 minutes

∽ MINESTRA DI PASTA E PATATE ∽
Potato and Pasta Soup For 4

2 slices bacon (about 2 oz.)
1 large onion
2 tbs. butter
4 medium potatoes, peeled and
   sliced thin

5 cups homemade meat broth
salt
1 cup tubetti or other very small
   pasta
1 tbs. fresh parsley, minced

1. Chop the bacon and the onion together to make a *battuto*.

2. Heat the butter in a large saucepan over medium heat. Add the *battuto*, and sauté for about 5 minutes.

3. Add the potatoes, stir, and sauté for 1 to 2 minutes. Add the broth, and bring it to a boil over high heat. Taste for salt. Add the tubetti, lower the heat to medium, and cook for 10 to 15 minutes, or until the pasta is done, stirring from time to time.

4. Stir in the parsley, and serve in a soup tureen.

Estimated Cooking Time: 30 minutes
Estimated Total Preparation Time: 45 minutes

∾ MINESTRA DI PASTA E ZUCCA ∾
Squash and Pasta Soup   For 4

3 tbs. olive oil
2 garlic cloves, peeled
1½ lbs. butternut squash, peeled,
    seeded, and sliced thin (about
    3 cups)
salt

1 red chili pepper (optional)
1 large beef bouillon cube,
    dissolved in 5 cups water
1 cup tubetti or ditali pasta
⅓ cup fresh parsley, minced
½ cup freshly grated Parmesan
    cheese

1. Heat the oil in a large saucepan over medium heat. Add the garlic cloves, and sauté until slightly colored. Add the squash, ½ tsp. salt, and the chili pepper, and sauté for a few minutes. Remove the garlic.

2. Add the bouillon, cover the pot, and bring the soup to a boil over medium-high heat. Turn the heat down to low, and simmer, covered, for about 40 minutes, or until the squash is very soft. Remove the chili pepper.

3. Drop the tubetti into 2 quarts boiling salted water, and cook for 5 minutes. Drain the pasta.

4. Add the pasta to the soup, and cook for another 5 to 10 minutes, or until done. Add the parsley, and stir. Taste for salt. This soup must be thin. If it is too thick, add more bouillon.

5. Pour the soup into a tureen, sprinkle with Parmesan cheese, and serve.

Estimated Cooking Time: 1 hour and 10 minutes
Estimated Total Preparation Time: 1 hour and 25 minutes

∾ MILLECOSEDDE ALLA CALABRESE ∾
Vegetable Soup Calabrian Style   For 4

6 oz. fresh mushrooms (about
    1¼ cups)
4 tbs. olive oil
1 medium onion, minced
1 celery stalk, chopped
½ small savoy (or green) cabbage,
    blanched and thinly sliced
1 cup canned white kidney beans

1 cup canned fava beans
1 cup canned chickpeas
1 cup canned lentils
salt
freshly ground black pepper
1 cup small elbow macaroni
½ cup freshly grated pecorino
    Romano cheese

1. Trim off the ends of the mushroom stems. If the mushrooms are relatively clean, wipe them thoroughly with a damp paper towel. If there is a lot of soil and dirt clinging to the caps, rinse them thoroughly but quickly in cold water, rubbing them against each other to dislodge the dirt. Dry with paper towels. Slice the mushrooms thinly.

2. Heat the oil in a large saucepan, preferably earthenware or enamel, over medium-low heat. Add the onion and the celery, and sauté until the onion is soft and translucent. Add the cabbage and the mushrooms, and continue cooking for 10 to 15 minutes. Add the kidney and fava beans, the chickpeas, the lentils, 1 tsp. salt, the pepper, and 5 cups water. Bring to a boil, and simmer, covered, for about 20 minutes.

3. Drop the pasta into 2 to 3 quarts boiling salted water, and cook for 5 minutes. Drain.

4. Add the pasta to the soup. Stir well, and cook for 5 to 7 minutes longer, or until done.

5. Serve the soup sprinkled with the cheese.

Note: We recommend removing the skins from the fava beans since they are very thick.

Estimated Cooking Time: 1 hour and 10 minutes
Estimated Total Preparation Time: 1 hour and 35 minutes

∽ MINESTRA ALLA MAGGIORANA ∽
Vegetable Soup with Marjoram   For 4 to 6

2 tbs. olive oil
1 garlic clove, peeled
2 large potatoes, peeled and diced
½ lb. fresh green beans, cut into
    ¼" pieces
1 cup frozen peas
salt

1 tbs. fresh marjoram leaves,
    chopped
1 cup canned Roman or pinto
    beans
¾ cup ditali or small elbow
    macaroni
½ cup freshly grated Parmesan
    cheese

1. Put the oil and the garlic in a large saucepan, and sauté over medium heat until the garlic is golden. Discard the garlic.

2. Add the potatoes and the green beans to the saucepan, stir, and cover them with 5 cups water. Bring the soup to a boil, covered, and cook it over medium-low heat for about 15 minutes.

3. Add the peas, ¾ tsp. salt, and the marjoram, and cook 5 minutes longer.

4. Add the beans and the pasta, and continue cooking the soup for 10 to 15 minutes more, or until the pasta is done, stirring from time to time. If the soup is too thick, add some stock or bouillon. Taste for salt.

5. Serve the soup hot with the Parmesan cheese on the side.

Estimated Cooking Time: 40 minutes
Estimated Total Preparation Time: 1 hour

∽ GNOCCHETTI DI SEMOLINO IN BRODO ∽
Broth with Semolina Dumplings For 4

7 cups homemade meat or
  chicken broth
2 tbs. butter, softened
2 eggs, separated
½ cup semolina flour

salt
⅛ tsp. freshly ground nutmeg
½ cup freshly grated Parmesan
  cheese

1. Bring the broth to a simmer.

2. In a large bowl, cream the butter with a wooden spoon until light and fluffy. Add the egg yolks, one at a time, beating well after each addition. Add the semolina, ¼ tsp. salt, and the nutmeg, blending the ingredients thoroughly.

3. Beat the egg whites until stiff, and gently fold into the semolina mixture.

4. Bring the broth to a boil.

5. With a teaspoon make little oblong balls about the size of a hazelnut, and drop them into the broth. Cook the gnocchetti for about 5 minutes over medium heat.

6. Pour the broth and the gnocchetti into a soup tureen, and serve with the Parmesan cheese on the side.

Estimated Cooking Time: 15 minutes
Estimated Total Preparation Time: 40 minutes

◇ PASSATELLI IN BRODO ◇
Broth with Cheese and Bread Crumb Dumplings
For 4

Although most of our soups are hearty and substantial, this creation from Emilia-Romagna, like the previous recipe, is light and elegant. It is equally appropriate for a children's supper and a formal dinner.

7 cups homemade meat broth
3 eggs
salt
¼ tsp. freshly grated nutmeg
½ lemon rind, grated

1 cup freshly grated Parmesan
    cheese
¾ cup plain dry bread crumbs
2 tbs. beef marrow chopped
    (optional)

1. Bring the broth to a simmer.
2. To make the passatelli, beat the eggs slightly with ½ tsp. salt, the nutmeg, and the lemon rind. Add the Parmesan cheese, the bread crumbs, and the marrow, and stir until the ingredients are thoroughly blended and the mixture is smooth. It should be soft but dry at the same time. If it is too moist, add more bread crumbs.
3. Bring the broth to a boil. Drop the passatelli into the broth by passing the mixture through the largest holes of a food mill.
4. When the passatelli come to the surface, remove the soup from the heat, pour into a tureen, and serve.

Estimated Cooking Time: 15 minutes
Estimated Total Preparation Time: 20 minutes

5 Rice
Riso

*R*ice, like pasta, is a staple in Italy. Known to the wealthy even in medieval times, it became a common food in the late sixteenth and early seventeenth centuries. By the eighteenth century, Italian rice dishes, especially those from northern Italy—Piedmont, Lombardy, and the Veneto—had achieved national renown. There continue to be some generally recognized northern classics like Risotto alla Parmigiana, but today every region of Italy has its own favorite typical rice dishes.

Rice is a popular Italian food for many reasons. Versatile and relatively inexpensive, rice is also healthy—it's easily digested and full of minerals (phosphorus and potassium) and has almost no sodium or fat. Although people may occasionally resist the temptation to eat rice because of its high carbohydrate and caloric content, these recipes, intended as main courses for four to six or as side dishes for twice that number, should pose no serious problems for most people's diet.

Risotto is perhaps the most common way that Italians cook rice. The rice is browned in oil or butter and then cooked slowly by adding small amounts of simmering broth. Different cooking techniques, described in the individual recipes, are used for other rice dishes such as stuffed vegetables, molds and rings, and salads.

Several varieties of rice are used in Italy. For risotto, vialone and arborio are the preferred varieties of Italian short grain rice. A cheaper rice, known as *riso comune* (ordinary rice), is used for stuffing vegetables. For soups and rice salads Italians generally choose a longer grain called ribe or R.B.

Of the several kinds of rice widely available in North America that we tested, we recommend Carolina or Uncle Ben's long grain, depending on the recipe. Although American short and medium grain rice are closer in appearance to Italian rice, neither holds the proper cooked texture (*cottura*) required for Italian dishes. Carolina is perhaps closer to Italian rice because it absorbs water more readily than Uncle Ben's, although not as quickly as arborio. However, we find that Uncle Ben's works more successfully in some recipes. Interestingly, all the Italians living in the United States whom we surveyed said they had adapted to using American long grain rice of one sort or another. Although the results achieved with American rice are a little different from those achieved with Italian-grown rice, they are delicious.

Risotto

Risotto is a typically Italian style of cooking rice. Traditionally it is served as a first course, not as a side dish, but accompanied by a simple antipasto and a salad, a risotto is a very satisfying main dish.

Preparing a risotto involves cooking the rice over medium-high heat and adding the liquid—usually a simmering broth—gradually, by cupfuls, constantly stirring the mixture until the rice has absorbed enough liquid to be tender but firm. A finished risotto always has a creamy consistency.

A perfect risotto becomes easier with practice since exact measurements of time and liquid cannot be given; some rice cooks faster, some absorbs more liquid than others. However, the master risotto recipe and the others that follow provide the necessary guidelines to ensure good results.

Type of Rice

Italian short grain rice (arborio) is the best choice for risotto if it is available. Most Italian groceries and specialty stores carry it. Italian rice takes from 18 to 25 minutes to cook. Today, however, even Italians use long grain rice for such dishes as Risotto with Champagne, considering it more elegant. This rice takes less time to cook—17 to 20 minutes.

As we mentioned before, among domestic brands we recommend Carolina long grain for most of these recipes; however, in some cases Uncle Ben's converted long grain rice works well. These recipes have been adapted to get good results with domestic rice. In each case the preference for the type of rice is indicated.

Procedure for Basic Risotto

1. In a heavy-bottomed saucepan sauté the chopped onion in butter or butter and oil over medium heat until soft and translucent.
2. Add the rice, stir well with a wooden spoon, and sauté for 1 to 2 minutes over medium-high heat so that the rice keeps its texture.

3. Lower the heat to medium, and add 1 cup simmering broth, stirring well around the sides and bottom until the liquid is absorbed but the rice is not completely dry. Keep adding broth, 1 cup at a time, stirring constantly to prevent sticking. Wait until the liquid is absorbed each time before adding more liquid. Rice does not always absorb the same amount of liquid, so adjust the recommended amount as needed. *The consistency should always be creamy.* Depending on the rice, it will take from 18 to 25 minutes to cook. Near the end, it is advisable to add the liquid cautiously, in smaller quantities, since the rice will absorb the liquid more readily when close to being done. If you run out of broth, simply add hot water. Uncle Ben's converted long grain rice absorbs considerably less liquid than other rices. Therefore keep the risotto fairly dry near the end when using this rice, especially if cream is added to the dish at the end.

4. The risotto is done when the rice is tender but still firm (al dente—"firm to the bite") and is incorporated into a creamy but not too liquidy sauce.

5. Taste for seasoning, keeping in mind that less salt should be added if the risotto is to be served with grated cheese.

6. Serve at once.

A risotto should be very creamy though not runny and, above all, not sticky. Until you feel confident, it is better to err on the creamy side, since the rice will continue to absorb liquid even after it is removed from the stove.

Many risottos need to rest a minute or two with the cover on and the heat off before serving. This helps combine the flavors and ingredients perfectly.

Risotto must be served immediately following this short rest period. When you're making up your cooking schedule, plan to prepare the risotto last.

❧ RISOTTO ALLA MILANESE ❧
Risotto with Saffron   For 4

5 to 6 cups homemade meat
  broth
              or
2 large beef bouillon cubes plus
  1 large chicken cube, dissolved
  in 5 to 6 cups water
½ tsp. whole saffron, chopped
              or
⅓ tsp. powdered saffron
6 tbs. butter

4 tbs. beef marrow, chopped
1 small onion, minced
2 cups Carolina long grain rice
              or
Italian arborio
⅔ cup dry white wine
salt
freshly ground black pepper
½ cup freshly grated Parmesan
  cheese

1. Bring the broth to a simmer.

2. Dissolve the saffron in a small bowl with 1 cup broth, and set aside.

3. Heat 4 tbs. butter in a heavy-bottomed saucepan over medium heat. Add the beef marrow and the onion, and sauté until the onion is soft and translucent.

4. Add the rice, turn the heat to medium-high, and sauté for 1 to 2 minutes, stirring well. Add the wine, and cook until it is evaporated. Add the broth, 1 cup at a time, and continue cooking, over medium heat, adjusting the recommended amount of liquid as needed, and following the directions for Basic Risotto (p. 83).

5. When the rice is done, remove the pan from the heat. Taste for salt. Add the pepper, the remaining butter, and the cheese. Stir well, and serve at once.

Note: Ask the butcher to crack the bones for easy removal of the marrow. If you cannot buy a cracked marrow bone, scoop the marrow out with a small spoon. Otherwise, boil the bone for a few minutes; the marrow will soften, and slide out easily.

Estimated Cooking Time: 25 minutes
Estimated Total Preparation Time: 40 minutes

∽ RISOTTO ALLA PARMIGIANA ∽
Risotto with Parmesan Cheese For 4

This recipe, which is the most basic of all the risottos, is used by Italians as a separate course and also as a component of more complex preparations such as anelli and timballi di riso.

5 to 6 cups homemade meat broth

or

2 large chicken bouillon cubes plus 1 large beef cube, dissolved in 5 to 6 cups water
2 tbs. vegetable oil
4 tbs. butter

1 small onion, minced
2 cups Carolina long grain rice

or

Italian arborio
¾ cups freshly grated Parmesan cheese
salt

1. Bring the broth to a simmer.
2. Heat the oil and 1 tbs. butter in a heavy-bottomed saucepan, and sauté the onion over medium heat until soft and translucent.
3. Add the rice, turn the heat to medium-high, and sauté for 1 to 2 minutes, stirring well. Add the broth 1 cup at a time, and continue cooking, over medium heat, adjusting the recommended amount of liquid as needed, and following the directions for Basic Risotto (p. 83).
4. After 12 minutes, or 7 to 8 minutes before the rice is done, add 2 tbs. butter and half the Parmesan cheese. Stir well, and continue to cook, adding the liquid.
5. When the rice is still very al dente (1 to 2 minutes before it is done), add the remaining cheese and butter, stir well, and taste for salt. Serve immediately in a heated dish.

Estimated Cooking Time: 25 minutes
Estimated Total Preparation Time: 35 minutes

✧ RISOTTO ALLA GORGONZOLA ✧
Risotto with Gorgonzola Cheese   For 4

*5 to 6 cups homemade meat
  broth*
            or
*2 large chicken bouillon cubes,
  dissolved in 5 to 6 cups water*
2 tbs. vegetable oil
4 tbs. butter
1 small onion, minced

2 cups Carolina long grain rice
            or
Italian arborio
*½ cup mild Gorgonzola cheese
  cut into small pieces*
*¼ cup freshly grated Parmesan
  cheese*
salt

1. Follow steps 1 to 3 of Risotto with Parmesan Cheese (p. 86).
2. After 15 minutes add the Gorgonzola cheese, the Parmesan cheese, and the remaining butter. Stir well until the cheese is melted. Taste for salt. Turn the heat off. Cover, and let rest 2 to 3 minutes, or until the rice is done. Then serve immediately on a heated dish.

Note: For this recipe mild Gorgonzola works well.

Estimated Cooking Time: 25 minutes
Estimated Total Preparation Time: 35 minutes

✧ RISOTTO ALLO CHAMPAGNE ✧
Risotto with Champagne   For 4

A recent addition to Italian cuisine, Risotto with Champagne is usually reserved for special evenings. Both elegant and simple, it is perfect for impressing the unexpected yet important guest.

4 cups homemade chicken broth
            or
*1½ large chicken bouillon cubes,
  dissolved in 4 cups water*
5 tbs. butter
1 small onion, minced (optional)
2 cups Uncle Ben's long grain rice

2 cups dry champagne
            or
*2 cups other good dry sparkling
  white wine*
1 cup heavy cream
*¾ cup Emmenthal (Swiss)
  cheese, shredded*
salt

1. Bring the broth to a simmer.
2. Heat 5 tbs. butter in a heavy-bottomed saucepan, and sauté the onion over medium heat until soft and translucent.

3. Add the rice, turn the heat to medium-high, and sauté for 1 to 2 minutes, stirring well. Add 1 cup broth, and continue cooking, over medium heat. Add 1 cup champagne and another cup broth, followed by ¾ cup champagne and the last 1 to 2 cups of broth. Adjust the recommended amount of liquid as needed, and follow the directions for Basic Risotto (p. 83). Since Uncle Ben's does not need much liquid, keep the rice fairly dry near the end.

4. When the rice is still very al dente (1 to 2 minutes before the rice is done), add the cream, the cheese, and the remaining champagne, stirring well until the cheese is completely melted. Taste for salt.

5. Turn the heat off, cover, and let rest for 1 to 2 minutes. Then serve the risotto immediately in a heated dish.

Estimated Cooking Time: 25 minutes
Estimated Total Preparation Time: 40 minutes

∽ RISOTTO AL BAROLO SEMPLICE ∽
Risotto with Barolo (Simplified Version)

For 4

Barolo is a rich red wine from Piedmont comparable to a good Bordeaux or to a California Zinfandel.

5 to 6 cups homemade meat broth	2 cups Carolina long grain rice
or	or
2 large beef bouillon cubes, dissolved in 5 to 6 cups water	Italian arborio
5 tbs. butter	1 cup Barolo or Zinfandel
1 small onion, minced	1 cup freshly grated Parmesan cheese
	salt

1. Bring the broth to a simmer.

2. Heat 3 tbs. butter in a heavy-bottomed saucepan, and sauté the onion over medium heat until soft and translucent.

3. Add the rice, turn the heat to medium-high, and sauté for 1 to 2 minutes, stirring well. Add the wine, stir well, and let it evaporate. Add the broth, 1 cup at a time, and continue cooking over medium heat, adjusting the recommended amount of liquid as needed, and following the directions for Basic Risotto (p. 83).

4. When the rice is done, add the Parmesan cheese and the remaining butter, and stir well. Taste for salt. Serve immediately on a heated dish.

Estimated Cooking Time: 25 minutes
Estimated Total Preparation Time: 40 minutes

∽ RISOTTO AL BAROLO ∽

Risotto with Barolo   For 4 to 5

This rich and substantial dish that comes from the wine, mushroom, and truffle area of northern Italy is saturated with the flavors and aromas of the hunt and the countryside in the fall.

1 oz. Italian or French dried
  mushrooms
1 small onion
½ medium carrot
4 slices bacon
2 sprigs parsley
¼ tsp. dry thyme
¾ lb. fresh mushrooms
3 to 3½ cups homemade meat
  broth
        or
1½ large beef bouillon cubes,
  dissolved in 3½ cups water

4 tbs. butter
2 cups Carolina long grain rice
        or
Italian arborio
2 cups Barolo or Zinfandel
½ cup heavy cream
¾ cup freshly grated Parmesan
  cheese
salt

1. Soak the dried mushrooms in 1 cup hot water at least 30 minutes. Drain, reserving the liquid, and chop coarsely. Strain the liquid through a sieve lined with a cloth or paper towel, and set aside.

2. Chop the onion, the carrot, the bacon, and the parsley all together into a *battuto*, and mix with the thyme.

3. Trim off the ends of the mushroom stems. If the mushrooms are relatively clean, wipe them thoroughly with a damp paper towel. If there is a lot of soil and dirt clinging to them, rinse thoroughly but quickly in cold water, rubbing them against each other to dislodge the dirt. Dry with paper towels. Remove and chop the stems. Cut the caps into thin slices.

4. Bring the broth to a simmer.

5. Heat 2 tbs. butter in a heavy-bottomed saucepan, and sauté the *battuto* over medium heat for about 5 minutes.

6. Add the chopped mushroom stems and the dried mushrooms to the saucepan. Cook for 3 to 5 minutes.

7. Add the rice, turn the heat to medium-high, and sauté for 1 to 2 minutes, stirring well. Add the wine, one cup at a time. Add the mushroom liquid and the broth, and continue cooking, over medium heat, adjusting the recommended amount of liquid as needed, and following the directions for Basic Risotto (p. 83).

8. After about 15 minutes, add the sliced mushroom caps, the cream, the Parmesan cheese, and the remaining butter. Stir well, and taste for salt. Turn the heat off, cover, and let rest 2 to 3 minutes, or until the rice is done. Then serve immediately on a heated platter.

Estimated Cooking Time: 30 minutes
Estimated Total Preparation Time: 1 hour and 20 minutes

∽ RISOTTO AL PEPE VERDE ∽

Green Peppercorn Risotto   For 4

We first sampled this unusual risotto at a restaurant outside of Padua frequented by the Italian racehorse crowd. The taste of the peppercorns is strong but not at all overwhelming.

5 to 6 cups homemade chicken
   broth
           or
2 large chicken bouillon cubes,
   dissolved in 5 to 6 cups water
5 tbs. butter
1 medium onion, minced
2 cups Carolina long grain rice
           or
Italian arborio

½ cup green peppercorns with
   brine
⅓ cup plus 2 tbs. dry white
   vermouth
1 cup heavy cream
½ cup Emmenthal (Swiss)
   cheese, shredded
salt

1. Bring the broth to a simmer.

2. Heat 3 tbs. butter in a heavy-bottomed saucepan, and sauté the onion over medium heat until soft and translucent.

3. Add the rice, turn the heat to medium-high, and sauté for 1 to 2 minutes, stirring well. Pour in the peppercorns with their liquid, stir again, and sauté for 2 to 3 minutes. Add ⅓ cup vermouth, stir, and let it evaporate. Add the broth 1 cup at a time, stirring well, and continue cooking, over medium heat, adjusting the recommended amount of liquid as needed, and following the directions for Basic Risotto (p. 83).

4. When the rice is still very al dente (1 to 2 minutes before it is done), add the cream, the cheese, the remaining butter, and 2 tbs. vermouth. Stir well, and taste for salt. Turn the heat off, cover, and let rest 1 to 2 minutes. Then serve immediately in a heated bowl.

Estimated Cooking Time: 25 minutes
Estimated Total Preparation Time: 35 minutes

⟳ RISOTTO PRIMAVERA ALLA VENETA ⟳
Risotto with Spring Vegetables   For 6

Literally "spring risotto," this is a beautiful dish full of color and delicate flavors that truly celebrates the season. It was always the centerpiece of the spring buffets of a gifted Roman hostess.

1 artichoke
½ lemon
4 asparagus
1 medium zucchini
8 to 10 small green beans
½ cup fresh spinach leaves
5 tbs. butter
3 tbs. vegetable oil
5 cups homemade chicken broth
    or
2 large chicken bouillon cubes, dissolved in 5 cups water
1 carrot, peeled and diced

¼ cup fresh peas, shelled
salt
1 small onion, minced
1 celery stalk, chopped
2 small tomatoes, seeded and cubed
2 cups Uncle Ben's long grain rice
    or
Italian arborio
1 cup cream
¾ cup freshly grated Parmesan cheese

1. Cut off the artichoke stem, leaving about 1". Break off the small leaves at the base, and cut off about 1" from the top. Snap

off the hard upper part of the leaves, and peel the tough outer layer from the stem. Cut the artichoke in half lengthwise, and remove the fuzzy choke and prickly leaves around it, being careful not to remove the heart. Rub the halves with a lemon half to prevent discoloration. Slice each half crosswise, very thinly.

2. Cut off the tough asparagus bottoms, and peel off the outer skin below the tender tip. Rinse. Cut into ¼" pieces.

3. Wash the zucchini, scraping off any dirt, and cut into ¼" cubes.

4. Snap off the ends of the green beans, and remove any strings. Wash in cold water, and cut into ½" pieces.

5. Wash the spinach well, and chop the leaves coarsely.

6. Heat 1 tbs. butter and 2 tbs. oil in a casserole over medium heat. Add the artichoke and ¼ cup broth. Cook over low heat for 10 minutes. Add the asparagus, the zucchini, the beans, the carrot, and the peas. Add ½ tsp. salt. Sauté over low heat for a few minutes, add 2 to 3 tbs. broth to keep the vegetables moist, and cook for about 10 minutes.

7. Bring the broth to a simmer.

8. Heat 2 tbs. butter and the remaining oil in a heavy-bottomed saucepan. Add the onion and the celery, and sauté over medium heat until the onion is soft and translucent. Add the tomatoes, and sauté for 4 to 5 minutes. Add the spinach, and stir.

9. Add the rice, turn the heat to medium-high, and sauté for 2 minutes, stirring well. Add the broth, 1 cup at a time, over medium heat, adjusting the recommended amount of liquid as needed, and following the directions for Basic Risotto (p. 83).

10. After 13 to 14 minutes, add the remaining cooked vegetables, stirring well. Cook for 2 to 3 minutes, and add the cream, the Parmesan cheese, and the remaining butter. Stir well, and taste for salt. Turn the heat off, cover, and let rest 1 to 2 minutes. Then serve immediately on a heated platter.

Note: The leftovers make a delicious accompaniment for cold sliced meat or cold chicken.

Estimated Cooking Time: 45 minutes
Estimated Total Preparation Time: 1 hour and 30 minutes

∾ RISOTTO PRIMAVERA ∾

Risotto with Spring Vegetables (Simplified Version)

For 6

This risotto makes a particularly fine side dish with lamb.

2 carrots
salt
½ 10-oz. package frozen
  asparagus
¼ 10-oz. package frozen chopped
  spinach
5 cups homemade chicken broth
                or
2 large chicken bouillon cubes,
  dissolved in 5 cups water

4 tbs. butter
4 tbs. vegetable oil
1 small onion, minced
½ 10-oz. package frozen tiny peas
2 cups Carolina long grain rice
                or
Italian arborio
1 cup heavy cream
½ cup freshly grated Parmesan
  cheese

1. Peel the carrots. Bring 1 quart water to a boil with a pinch of salt. Add the carrots, and cook at a moderate boil for about 10 minutes, or until tender. Drain, and set aside to cool. Cut into ¼" cubes.

2. Cut the asparagus tips into ¼" cubes.

3. Cut the spinach into 3 to 4 pieces without defrosting it.

4. Bring the broth to a simmer.

5. Heat 2 tbs. butter and the oil in a heavy-bottomed saucepan. Sauté the onion over medium heat until soft and translucent. Add the frozen asparagus, the spinach, the peas, and ½ tsp. salt. Stir, and cook over low heat for 5 minutes.

6. Add the rice, turn the heat to medium-high, and sauté for 1 to 2 minutes, stirring well. Add the broth, 1 cup at a time, and continue cooking over medium heat, adjusting recommended amount of liquid as needed, and following the directions for Basic Risotto (p. 83).

7. After 15 minutes, add the carrots and stir.

8. When the rice is still very al dente (1 to 2 minutes before it is done), add the cream, the Parmesan cheese, and the remaining butter. Taste for salt. Turn the heat off, cover, and let rest 1 to 2 minutes. Then serve immediately on a heated platter.

Estimated Cooking Time: 45 minutes
Estimated Total Preparation Time: 1 hour

∽ RISOTTO CON CARCIOFI ∽
Risotto with Artichokes   For 4

4 artichokes
1 lemon, halved
6 tbs. butter
5 to 6 cups homemade meat
   broth
        or
2 large chicken bouillon cubes,
   dissolved in 5 to 6 cups water
2 cups Carolina long grain rice
        or
Italian arborio

2 oz. prosciutto, cut into very thin
   strips
        or
2 oz. cured country ham, cut into
   very thin strips
¼ cup fresh parsley, minced
freshly ground black pepper
salt
½ cup freshly grated Parmesan
   cheese

1. Cut off the artichoke stems leaving about 1". Break off the small leaves at the base and cut off about 1" from the top. Snap off the hard upper part of the leaves, and peel the tough outer layer from the stems. Cut the artichokes in half lengthwise, and remove the fuzzy choke and prickly leaves around it, being careful not to remove the heart. Rub the halves with a piece of lemon to prevent discoloration. Slice each half lengthwise very thinly.

2. Heat 3 tbs. butter in a heavy-bottomed saucepan over medium-low heat. Add the artichokes, and sauté for about 5 minutes. Add ⅔ cup broth, and cook, covered, over low heat for 10 minutes.

3. Bring the broth to a simmer.

4. Add the rice to the artichokes, turn the heat to medium-high, and sauté for 2 to 3 minutes, stirring well. Add the broth, 1 cup at a time, and continue cooking, over medium heat, adjusting the recommended amount of liquid as needed, and following the directions for Basic Risotto (p. 83).

5. After 15 minutes add the prosciutto, the parsley, and the pepper, and stir. Taste for salt.

6. When the rice is done, add the cheese and the remaining butter, stir well, and pour onto a heated platter. Serve immediately.

Estimated Cooking Time: 35 minutes
Estimated Total Preparation Time: 1 hour

∽ RISOTTO AL CRESCIONE ∽
Risotto with Watercress For 4

Surprisingly flavorful, this risotto can serve as a light main course or as a delicious side dish with chicken, veal, or roast pork.

*5 to 6 cups homemade chicken
  broth
      or
3 large chicken bouillon cubes,
  dissolved in 5 to 6 cups water
6 tbs. butter
1 large onion, minced
2 bunches watercress, washed
  and chopped*

*2 cups Carolina long grain rice
      or
Italian arborio
1 cup heavy cream
½ cup Gruyère cheese, shredded
freshly ground white pepper
salt*

1. Bring the broth to a simmer.
2. Heat 4 tbs. butter in a heavy-bottomed saucepan over low heat. Add the onion, and sauté until soft and translucent. Add the watercress, and sauté 5 minutes longer.
3. Add the rice, turn the heat to medium-high, and sauté for 1 to 2 minutes, stirring well. Add the broth, 1 cup at a time, and continue cooking, over medium heat, adjusting the recommended amount of liquid as needed, and following the directions for Basic Risotto (p. 83).
4. When the rice is still very al dente (about 1 to 2 minutes before it is done), add the cream, the cheese, the remaining butter, and the pepper. Stir well and taste for salt. Turn the heat off, cover, and let rest 1 to 2 minutes. Then serve immediately in a heated dish.

Estimated Cooking Time: 35 minutes
Estimated Total Preparation Time: 45 minutes

∽ RISOTTO CON FAGIOLI ALLA PIEMONTESE ∽
Risotto with Beans Piedmontese Style   For 4

This is an adaptation of a classic recipe from Novara, which, with Vercelli, is the rice-growing center of Italy.

2 lbs. fresh cranberry beans (also
    called October beans), makes
    about 14 oz. when shelled
1 carrot, thinly sliced
1 celery stalk, chopped
1 28-oz. can Italian-style plum
    tomatoes, broken into pieces
1 large beef bouillon cube

5 oz. bacon
1 medium onion
2 tbs. butter
2 cups Carolina long grain rice
            or
Italian arborio
½ cup red wine
salt

1. In a large saucepan combine the beans, the carrot, the celery, the tomatoes, the bouillon cube, and 6 cups water. Bring the ingredients to a boil, cover, and simmer over medium heat for about 1½ hours.

2. Make a *battuto* by chopping the bacon and the onion together.

3. Heat the butter in a heavy-bottomed casserole. Sauté the *battuto* over medium heat until the onion is soft and translucent. Add the rice, turn the heat to medium-high, and sauté for 1 to 2 minutes, stirring well. Add the wine, and let it evaporate.

4. Strain the vegetables, reserving the liquid. Add the vegetables to the rice, and begin adding the liquid, 1 cup at a time, over medium heat, and following the directions for Basic Risotto (p. 83). If the liquid runs out before the rice is done, add plain water. Taste for salt.

5. When the rice is done, remove it to a heated bowl, and serve immediately.

Estimated Cooking Time: 2 hours
Estimated Total Preparation Time: 2 hours and 45 minutes

∽ RISOTTO CON FUNGHI ∽
Mushroom Risotto   For 4

1 lb. fresh mushrooms
3 tbs. vegetable oil
1 garlic clove, peeled
⅓ cup fresh parsley, minced
salt
5 to 6 cups homemade chicken
   broth
         or
2 large chicken bouillon cubes,
   dissolved in 5 to 6 cups water

2 tbs. butter
1 small onion, minced
2 cups Carolina long grain rice
         or
Italian arborio
½ cup dry white wine
¾ cup cooked ham, chopped
½ cup freshly grated Parmesan
   cheese

1. Trim off the ends of the mushroom stems. If the mushrooms are relatively clean, wipe them thoroughly with a damp paper towel. If there is a lot of soil and dirt clinging to the caps, rinse them thoroughly but quickly in cold water, rubbing them against each other to dislodge the dirt. Dry with paper towels. Slice the mushrooms thinly.

2. Heat the oil in a medium saucepan with the garlic clove over medium heat. Add the mushrooms and 3 tbs. parsley, and sauté for about 3 minutes. Add ¼ tsp. salt, stir, and set aside. Remove the garlic.

3. Bring the broth to a simmer.

4. Heat the butter in a heavy-bottomed saucepan, and sauté the onion over medium heat until soft and translucent.

5. Add the rice, turn the heat to medium-high, and sauté for 1 to 2 minutes, stirring well. Add the wine, stir, and let it evaporate. Add the broth, 1 cup at a time, and continue cooking, over medium heat, adjusting the recommended amount of liquid as needed, and following the directions for Basic Risotto (p. 83).

6. After 15 minutes add the mushrooms and the ham, stir the mixture well, and finish cooking the risotto.

7. When the rice is still very al dente (1 to 2 minutes before it is done), add the remaining parsley and the Parmesan cheese. Stir well, and taste for salt. Turn the heat off, cover, and let rest 1 to 2 minutes. Then serve immediately on a heated platter.

Estimated Cooking Time: 30 minutes
Estimated Total Preparation Time: 1 hour

∽ RISOTTO CON FUNGHI SECCHI ∾
Risotto with Dried Mushrooms   For 4

This risotto with dried mushrooms results in a much richer, stronger taste than the risotto made with fresh mushrooms. It adds a robust touch to winter menus.

1½ oz. Italian or French dried
   mushrooms
3 to 4 cups homemade meat
   broth
            or
1½ large beef bouillon cubes,
   dissolved in 3 to 4 cups water
5 tbs. butter
1 small onion, minced

2 cups Carolina long grain rice
            or
Italian arborio
½ cup red wine
1 cup heavy cream
freshly ground black pepper
½ cup freshly grated Parmesan
   cheese
salt

1. Soak the mushrooms in 2 cups hot water for at least 30 minutes. Drain, reserving the liquid, and cut each into 2 to 3 pieces. Strain the liquid through a sieve lined with cloth or paper towel, and add it to the broth.

2. Bring the broth to a simmer.

3. Heat 3 tbs. butter in a heavy-bottomed saucepan, and sauté the onion over medium heat for 1 to 2 minutes. Add the mushrooms, and cook, covered, with ½ cup broth over low heat for 8 to 10 minutes longer.

4. Add the rice, turn the heat to medium-high, and sauté for 1 to 2 minutes, stirring well. Add the wine, stir, and let it evaporate. Add the broth, 1 cup at a time, and continue cooking, over medium heat, adjusting the recommended amount of liquid as needed, and following the directions for Basic Risotto (p. 83).

5. After about 15 minutes add the cream, the pepper, the Parmesan cheese, and the remaining butter. Stir well, and taste for salt. Turn the heat off, cover, and let rest 2 to 3 minutes, or until the rice is done. Then serve immediately on a heated platter.

Estimated Cooking Time: 35 minutes
Estimated Total Preparation Time: 1 hour and 10 minutes

∽ RISOTTO ALL'INDIVIA AFFUMICATA ∽
Risotto with Grilled Chicory For 4

In Italy radicchio rosso is used as the basis for a similar risotto, but we find that the grilled curly chicory succeeds in giving this risotto a marvelous mellow taste.

2 heads curly chicory
salt
freshly ground black pepper
5 to 6 cups homemade meat
    broth
        or
2 large beef bouillon cubes and
    1 chicken cube, dissolved in
    5 to 6 cups hot water

6 tbs. butter
1 small onion, minced
2 cups Carolina long grain rice
        or
Italian arborio
⅓ cup cognac
¾ cup freshly grated Parmesan
    cheese

1. Remove any hard outer leaves from the chicory. Cut each head vertically into 4 pieces, and wash well. Shake the lettuce vigorously, and pat with paper towels to remove as much moisture as possible. Sprinkle with ¼ tsp. salt and the pepper.

2. Bring the broth to a simmer.

3. Heat 3 tbs. butter in a heavy iron skillet over high heat. Add the chicory, and sear quickly for 2 minutes on each side, pressing it down with a spatula or wooden spoon. Remove the chicory, let cool slightly, and then chop crosswise into thin pieces.

4. Heat 2 tbs. butter in a heavy-bottomed saucepan, and sauté the onion over medium heat until soft and translucent. Add the chicory, and sauté for 2 to 3 minutes more.

5. Add the rice, turn the heat to medium-high, and sauté for 1 to 2 minutes longer, stirring well. Add the cognac, stir, and let it evaporate. Begin adding the broth, 1 cup at a time, over medium heat, adjusting the recommended amount of liquid as needed, and following the directions for Basic Risotto (p. 83).

6. When the rice is still very al dente (1 to 2 minutes before it is done), add the cheese and the remaining butter. Stir well, and taste for salt. Turn the heat off, cover, and let rest 1 to 2 minutes. Then serve the risotto in a heated dish.

Estimated Cooking Time: 35 minutes
Estimated Total Preparation Time: 50 minutes

◇ RISOTTO AL FINOCCHIO ◇
Risotto with Fennel For 4

2 fennel bulbs
4 cups homemade chicken broth
    or
2 large chicken bouillon cubes,
  dissolved in 4 cups water
2 tbs. butter
2 tbs. vegetable oil

2 cups Uncle Ben's long grain rice
    or
Italian arborio
¾ cup dry white wine
½ cup freshly grated Parmesan
  cheese
salt

1. Cut off the green stems, and remove the tough outer part of the fennel bulbs. Wash and dry them, and slice them, crosswise, very thinly.

2. Bring the broth to a simmer.

3. Heat the butter and oil in a heavy-bottomed saucepan over low heat. Add the fennel, and sauté for about 5 minutes.

4. Add the rice to the fennel, turn the heat to medium-high, and sauté for 2 to 3 minutes, stirring well. Add the wine. Stir, and let it evaporate. Add the broth, I cup at a time, and continue cooking, over medium heat, adjusting the recommended amount of liquid as needed, and following the directions for Basic Risotto (p. 83).

5. When the rice is still very al dente (1 to 2 minutes before it is done), add the Parmesan cheese, stir well, and taste for salt. Turn the heat off, cover, and let rest 1 to 2 minutes. Then serve immediately on a heated platter.

Estimated Cooking Time: 25 minutes
Estimated Total Preparation Time: 40 minutes

◇ RISOTTO CON LE MELANZANE ◇
Eggplant Risotto For 4

1 lb. eggplants
salt
5 to 6 cups homemade meat
  broth
    or
3 large beef bouillon cubes,
  dissolved in 5 to 6 cups water
2 tbs. olive oil

2 tbs. vegetable oil
1 garlic clove, mashed
4 tbs. fresh parsley, minced
2 cups Carolina long grain rice
    or
Italian arborio
½ cup freshly grated Parmesan
  cheese

1. Peel the eggplants. Dice, and place in a colander. Sprinkle with 1½ tsp. salt, and let drain for 30 to 40 minutes.

2. Bring the broth to a simmer.

3. Heat the oils together in a heavy-bottomed casserole over medium-high heat. Dry the eggplant, and drop into the oil. Sauté, stirring frequently, for about 5 minutes. Add the garlic and 2 tbs. parsley, and cook the eggplant, covered, for 10 minutes longer over low heat.

4. Add the rice, turn the heat to medium-high, and sauté for 1 to 2 minutes, stirring well. Add 1 cup broth and continue cooking over medium heat, adjusting the recommended amount of liquid as needed, and following the directions for Basic Risotto (p. 83).

5. When the rice is still very al dente (1 to 2 minutes before it is done), add the Parmesan cheese and the remaining parsley. Stir well, and taste for salt. Turn the heat off, cover, and let rest for 1 to 2 minutes. Then serve immediately in a heated dish.

Estimated Cooking Time: 35 minutes
Estimated Total Preparation Time: 1 hour and 25 minutes

∽ RISOTTO CON LE PATATE ∽

Risotto with Potatoes   For 4

Although the idea of rice and potatoes may sound strange, this combination of tastes and textures results in a superb dish.

4 tbs. butter
1 medium onion, minced
4 strips (about 4 oz.) bacon, coarsely chopped
5 to 6 cups homemade meat broth
    or
1½ large chicken bouillon cubes plus 1 large beef cube, dissolved in 5 to 6 cups of water

2 medium potatoes, peeled and cubed
6 to 8 fresh sage leaves, chopped
    or
½ tsp. dried sage, crumbled
2 cups Carolina long grain rice
    or
Italian arborio
½ cup freshly grated Parmesan cheese

1. Heat 3 tbs. butter in a heavy-bottomed saucepan. Add the onion and the bacon, and sauté over medium heat until the onion is soft and translucent.

2. Bring the broth to a simmer.

3. Add the potatoes and the sage to the saucepan, and sauté over medium-low heat for about 5 minutes, stirring from time to time.

4. Add the rice, turn the heat to medium-high, and sauté for 1 to 2 minutes, stirring well. Add the broth, 1 cup at a time, and continue cooking, over medium heat, adjusting the recommended amount of liquid as needed, and following the directions for Basic Risotto (p. 83).

5. When the rice is still very al dente (1 to 2 minutes before it is done), add the cheese and the remaining butter. Stir well, and taste for salt. Turn the heat off, cover, and let rest 1 to 2 minutes. Then serve immediately in a heated dish.

Estimated Cooking Time: 30 minutes
Estimated Total Preparation Time: 45 minutes

∽ RISOTTO CON I PEPERONI ∽
Sweet Red Pepper Risotto For 4

This risotto has a magnificent red color and a very delicate taste.

2 lbs. sweet red peppers
5 to 6 cups homemade meat
  broth
         or
1 large chicken bouillon cube and
  1 large beef cube, dissolved
  in 5 to 6 cups water
6 tbs. butter
1 large onion, minced

½ cup Basic Tomato Sauce I,
  p. 14
2 cups Carolina long grain rice
         or
Italian arborio
½ cup freshly grated Parmesan
  cheese
⅓ cup fresh basil leaves, torn
  into pieces

1. Turn on the broiler.

2. Wash and dry the peppers. Place them on a rack as close as possible to the broiler, and sear on all sides. When the skins of the peppers have loosened and are slightly charred (5 to 10 minutes), remove the peppers from the broiler, and peel. Halve the peppers, remove the seeds, and cut into thin strips.

3. Bring the broth to a simmer.

4. Heat 4 tbs. butter in a heavy-bottomed saucepan. Add half

the onion, and sauté over medium heat until soft and translucent. Add the tomato sauce, and cook for another few minutes. Pour it into a bowl, and set aside.

5. Divide the cooked peppers into two parts. Puree one half in a blender or food processor, and set the rest aside.

6. In the same saucepan you used for the tomato sauce, heat the remaining butter, and sauté the rest of the onion over medium heat until soft and translucent. Add the rice, turn the heat to medium-high, and sauté for 1 to 2 minutes, stirring well. Add the pureed peppers and the tomato sauce, stir well, and begin adding the broth, 1 cup at a time, over medium heat, adjusting the recommended amount of liquid as needed, and following the directions for Basic Risotto (p. 83).

7. When the rice is still very al dente (1 to 2 minutes before it is done), add the remaining peppers, the Parmesan cheese, and the basil. Turn the heat off, cover, and let rest 1 to 2 minutes. Then serve immediately on a heated dish.

Estimated Cooking Time: 35 minutes
Estimated Total Preparation Time: 1 hour and 10 minutes

∽ RISOTTO AL POMODORO ∽
Tomato Risotto   For 4

5 tbs. olive oil
1 28-oz. can Italian-style plum tomatoes
2 garlic cloves, mashed
1 large beef bouillon cube
2 cups homemade meat broth, diluted with 2 cups water
or
1 large beef bouillon cube, dissolved in 4 cups water
2 tbs. butter

1 small onion, minced
2 cups Carolina long grain rice
or
Italian arborio
2 tbs. fresh parsley, coarsely chopped
⅓ cup fresh basil leaves, torn into small pieces
salt
½ cup freshly grated Parmesan cheese

1. In a medium saucepan combine 2 tbs. oil, the tomatoes, the garlic, and the bouillon cube, and cook over medium heat for 25 minutes.

2. Bring the broth to a simmer.

3. Heat 2 tbs. oil and the butter in a heavy-bottomed saucepan, and sauté the onion over medium heat until soft and translucent.

4. Add the rice, stir well, and sauté for 1 to 2 minutes. Add the tomato sauce, and cook, stirring constantly, until most of it has been absorbed.

5. Begin adding the broth, 1 cup at a time, and continue cooking over medium heat, adjusting the recommended amount as needed, and following the directions for Basic Risotto (p. 83).

6. When the rice is done, add the parsley and the basil and stir. Taste for salt, and serve immediately in a heated dish.

7. At the table, add grated cheese and a dash of olive oil to each serving.

Note: If this recipe is doubled, the leftovers can be used to make Deep-Fried Red Rice Balls with Mozzarella (p. 141), which are a great addition to a buffet as well as being a good snack or cocktail fare.

Estimated Cooking Time: 50 minutes
Estimated Total Preparation Time: 1 hour and 10 minutes

∽ RISOTTO CON ZUCCHINE ∽
Risotto with Zucchini   For 4

1¼ lb. zucchini (4 to 5 medium)
5 to 6 cups homemade chicken
 broth
        or
2 large chicken bouillon cubes,
 dissolved in 5 to 6 cups water
4 oz. bacon
1 small onion
1 small garlic clove, peeled

2 tbs. vegetable oil
salt
2 cups Carolina long grain rice
        or
Italian arborio
½ cup fresh parsley, minced
¾ cup freshly grated Parmesan
 cheese
2 tbs. butter

1. Wash the zucchini, scraping off any dirt, and dice them.

2. Bring the broth to a simmer.

3. Make a *battuto* by chopping the bacon, the onion, and the garlic together.

4. Heat the oil in a heavy-bottomed saucepan. Add the *battuto*, and sauté for 2 to 4 minutes over medium heat. Add the zucchini and ¼ tsp. salt, and cook 15 minutes, stirring from time to time.

5. Add the rice, turn the heat to medium-high, and sauté for 1 to 2 minutes, stirring well. Add the broth 1 cup at a time, and continue cooking, over medium heat, adjusting the recommended amount as needed, and following the directions for Basic Risotto (p. 83).

6. After 13 to 14 minutes add the parsley. Two to 3 minutes later add the Parmesan cheese and the butter. Stir well, and taste for salt. Turn the heat off, cover, and let rest 1 to 2 minutes, or until the rice is done. Then serve immediately in a heated dish.

Estimated Cooking Time: 40 minutes
Estimated Total Preparation Time: 1 hour

◇ RISOTTO ALL'ARANCIA ◇
Risotto with Oranges   For 4

This is one of several non-sweet fruit risottos that have recently become popular in Italy. Asparagus Mimosa (p. 27) or Smoked Salmon Toasts (p. 51) would make a good appetizer for this dish, which goes well with a sharp green salad. It's also a nice accompaniment for a roast poultry or ham.

4 cups homemade meat broth
or
1 large chicken bouillon cube
  and 1 large beef cube, dissolved
  in 4 cups water
2 tbs. vegetable oil
1 medium onion, minced

2 cups Uncle Ben's long grain rice
or
Italian arborio
1 cup freshly squeezed orange
  juice
2 tbs. butter
salt
2 large navel oranges, peeled,
  skinned, and cut into cubes

1. Bring the broth to a simmer.
2. Heat the oil in a heavy-bottomed saucepan, and sauté the onion over medium heat until soft and translucent.
3. Add the rice, turn the heat to medium-high, and sauté for 1 to 2 minutes, stirring well. Add the orange juice and the butter, and stir. When the juice is almost all absorbed, add 1 cup broth, and continue cooking, over medium heat, adjusting the recommended amount of liquid as needed, and following the directions for Basic Risotto (p. 83). Taste for salt.

4. When the rice is done, add the orange cubes. Stir them into the mixture, and serve immediately on a heated platter.

Estimated Cooking Time: 25 minutes
Estimated Total Preparation Time: 45 minutes

∾ RISOTTO ALLE FRAGOLE ∾

Risotto with Strawberries For 4

In spite of the strangeness of strawberries in this context, this risotto is a superb combination of rich flavors enhanced by the delicate perfume of the fruit. Most Italians would simply call it *squisito*. A delight for the palate, and not at all sweet, this dish will also be a great conversation piece at the dinner table. Try it with a mushroom antipasto and a salad of sharp greens like watercress or escarole. It also makes a splendid side dish for chicken, veal, or roast pork.

2 pts. strawberries
4 to 5 cups homemade meat
   broth
        or
1 large chicken bouillon cube
   and 1 large beef cube, dissolved
   into 4 to 5 cups water
6 tbs. butter

1 small onion, minced
2 cups long grain Carolina rice
        or
Italian arborio
1 cup dry sherry
1 cup heavy cream
salt

1. Hull the strawberries, and wash them under cold running water using a soft brush to remove any dirt. Puree half the strawberries through a food mill, and break the rest into pieces with a fork. Set aside.

2. Bring the broth to a simmer.

3. Heat 4 tbs. butter in a heavy-bottomed saucepan, and sauté the onion over medium heat until soft and translucent.

4. Add the rice, turn the heat to medium-high, and sauté for 1 to 2 minutes, stirring well. Add ¾ cup sherry, stir, and let evaporate. Add the broth, 1 cup at a time, and continue cooking, over medium heat, adjusting the recommended amount of liquid as needed, and following the directions for Basic Risotto (p. 83).

5. After 10 minutes add the pureed strawberries, and continue cooking.

6. When the rice is still very al dente (1 to 2 minutes before it is done), add the remaining strawberries, the cream, and the remaining butter and sherry. Stir, and taste for salt. Turn the heat off, cover, and let rest 1 to 2 minutes. Then serve immediately on a heated platter.

Estimated Cooking Time: 25 minutes
Estimated Total Preparation Time: 50 minutes

◇ RISOTTO DI BRANZINO ◇
Risotto with Sea Bass   For 4

Delicate without being bland, this is a very subtle seafood dish.

1 small carrot, sliced	2 tbs. olive oil
½ celery stalk, sliced	4 tbs. butter
1 small bay leaf	1 small onion, minced
4 to 5 black peppercorns	2 cups Carolina long grain rice
salt	or
1 1½ to 2 lb. whole sea bass,	Italian arborio
cleaned (with head)	½ cup dry white wine
1 large fish bouillon cube	

1. In a saucepan large enough to hold the fish, combine 6 cups water with the carrot, the celery, the bay leaf, the peppercorns, and 1 tsp. salt. Bring to a boil, and simmer over low heat for 5 to 10 minutes.

2. Add the fish to the stock, and simmer for about 10 minutes. Do not completely cook fish.

3. Remove the fish from the liquid, reserving the stock.

4. Carefully skin, bone, and flake the fish. Set the meat aside.

5. Put the large bone and the head back into the stock. Add the bouillon cube and enough water to make 2 quarts. Bring stock to a boil, and cook, uncovered, until it is reduced to about 5 cups. Strain through a sieve lined with a cloth.

6. Keep the stock at a simmer.

7. Heat the oil and 2 tbs. butter in a heavy-bottomed saucepan

over medium heat. Add the onion, and sauté until soft and trans-lucent.

8. Add the rice, turn the heat to medium-high, and sauté for 1 to 2 minutes, stirring well. Add the wine, stir, and let it evaporate. Begin adding the stock, 1 cup at a time, and continue cooking over medium heat, adjusting the recommended amount of liquid as needed, and following the directions for Basic Risotto (p. 83).

9. After 10 minutes, add the fish, and continue cooking.

10. When the rice is still very al dente (1 to 2 minutes before it is done), add the remaining butter, and taste for salt. Turn the heat off, cover, and let it rest 1 to 2 minutes. Then serve immediately on a heated platter.

Estimated Cooking Time: 1 hour.
Estimated Total Preparation Time: 1 hour and 30 minutes

∽ RISOTTO AL SALMONE ∽
Risotto with Smoked Salmon   For 4

A very special dish that is usually served at formal Italian dinner parties. It is another case of elegance combined with simplicity.

4 to 5 cups homemade fish stock or 2 large fish bouillon cubes, dissolved in 4 to 5 cups water 5 tbs. butter 1 small onion, minced	2 cups Uncle Ben's long grain rice or Italian arborio 1 cup dry white wine 4 oz. smoked salmon, cut into very thin strips 1 cup heavy cream salt

1. Bring the stock to a simmer.

2. Heat 4 tbs. butter in a heavy-bottomed saucepan, and sauté the onion over medium heat until soft and translucent.

3. Add the rice, turn the heat to medium-high, and sauté for 1 to 2 minutes, stirring well. Add the wine, stir, and let it evaporate. Add the stock, 1 cup at a time, and continue cooking, over medium heat, adjusting the recommended amount of liquid as needed, and following the directions for Basic Risotto (p. 83). Uncle Ben's does

not absorb much liquid, so after 12 to 13 minutes add very small amounts of broth. The risotto should be almost dry when you add the cream in step 4. The consistency should always be creamy.

4. When the rice is still very al dente (1 to 2 minutes before it is done), add the salmon, the cream, and the remaining butter. Stir, and taste for salt. Turn the heat off, cover, and let rest 1 to 2 minutes. Then serve immediately on a heated platter.

Note: Scraps of smoked salmon are perfectly adequate for this dish.

Estimated Cooking Time: 25 minutes
Estimated Total Preparation Time: 35 minutes

⬦ RISOTTO DI CALAMARI ⬦
Risotto with Squid
For 4 to 5

This typical dish from the area around Venice does justice to a delicious and unpretentious seafood often overlooked in the United States.

2 lbs. fresh squid
5 to 6 cups homemade fish stock
or
2 large fish bouillon cubes,
dissolved in 5 to 6 cups water
4 tbs. olive oil
1 small onion, minced

1 garlic clove, mashed
2 tbs. fresh parsley, minced
½ cup plus 2 tbs. dry white wine
salt
2 cups Carolina long grain rice
or
Italian arborio

1. Remove the tentacles from the sacs of the squid, and cut them above the eyes, discarding the rest. Rinse under cold running water, and set aside. Peel the sacs by pulling the skin off with your fingers. Remove the cartilage-like bone as well as any gelatinous matter from the sacs, and rinse thoroughly under cold running water. Cut the sacs into thin rings and the tentacles into ½" pieces.

2. Bring the stock to a simmer.

3. Heat the oil in a heavy-bottomed saucepan over medium heat. Add the onion, and sauté until soft and translucent. Add the garlic and the parsley, and sauté 1 to 2 minutes longer.

4. Add the squid, stir, and sauté 1 to 2 minutes. Add ½ cup wine and 1 tsp. salt, and cook for 5 to 8 minutes, or until the wine is evaporated. If the squid give off a lot of liquid, remove them with a slotted spoon, turn the heat to high, and cook briskly until most of the liquid has evaporated.

5. Add the rice, turn the heat to medium-high, and sauté for 1 to 2 minutes, stirring well. Add the stock, 1 cup at a time, and continue cooking, over medium heat, adjusting the recommended amount of liquid as needed, and following the directions for Basic Risotto (p. 83). Taste for salt. Just before serving, sprinkle with the remaining 2 tbs. wine.

Estimated Cooking Time: 35 minutes
Estimated Total Preparation Time: 1 hour and 15 minutes

∽ RISOTTO CON LE COZZE ∽
Risotto with Mussels

For 4 to 5

3 lbs. fresh mussels
3 tbs. cornmeal
4 to 5 cups homemade fish stock
        or
2 large fish bouillon cubes,
    dissolved in 4 to 5 cups water
5 tbs. olive oil

1 small onion, minced
1 garlic clove, mashed
2 cups Carolina long grain rice
        or
Italian arborio
¼ cup fresh parsley, minced
freshly ground black pepper
salt

1. Wash and scrub the mussels thoroughly under cold running water to remove all sand and dirt, discarding any open ones. With a knife scrape off any protruding hair. Soak the mussels in cold water with 1 tbs. cornmeal for 1 hour, changing the water twice and adding 1 tbs. of fresh cornmeal each time. Drain the mussels, rinse in cold water, and place in a large heavy saucepan over medium-high heat. Cover the saucepan, and shake every few minutes so the mussels will open evenly. Remove the mussels from the shells, discarding any that did not open. Halve or quarter the mussels, depending on their size, and set aside. Strain the liquid through a sieve lined with a cloth or a paper towel, and add to the fish stock to make 5 to 6 cups.

2. Bring the stock to a simmer.

3. Heat the oil in a heavy-bottomed saucepan over medium heat. Add the onion, and sauté until soft and translucent. Add the garlic, and stir.

4. Add the rice, turn the heat to medium-high, and sauté for 1 to 2 minutes, stirring well. Add the stock, 1 cup at a time, and continue cooking, over medium heat, adjusting the recommended amount of liquid as needed, and following the directions for Basic Risotto (p. 83).

5. After about 15 minutes, add the mussels, the parsley, and the pepper. Stir well, and taste for salt. When the rice is done, serve immediately on a heated platter.

Note: Mussels must be used the same day they are bought.

Estimated Cooking Time: 30 minutes
Estimated Total Preparation Time: 2 hours

∽ RISOTTO CON LE COZZE ROSSO ∽
Risotto with Mussels and Tomatoes   For 4

In Italian cuisine the combination of seafood and cheese is heresy. However, in Apulia, along the Adriatic coast, cooks often add a touch of pecorino to shellfish dishes.

3 lbs. fresh mussels	1 garlic clove, peeled
3 tbs. cornmeal	salt
4 to 5 cups homemade fish stock	2 cups Carolina long grain rice
or	or
2 large fish bouillon cubes,	Italian arborio
dissolved in 4 to 5 cups water	freshly ground black pepper
5 tbs. olive oil	2 to 3 tbs. freshly grated pecorino
1 lb. ripe tomatoes, peeled,	Romano cheese
seeded, and chopped	

1. Wash and scrub the mussels thoroughly under cold running water to remove all sand and dirt, discarding any open ones. With a knife scrape off any protruding hair. Soak the mussels in cold water with 1 tbs. cornmeal for 1 hour, changing the water twice and adding 1 tbs. of fresh cornmeal each time. Drain the mussels,

rinse in cold water, and place in a large heavy saucepan over medium-high heat. Cover the saucepan, and shake every few minutes so the mussels will open evenly. Remove the mussels from the shells, discarding any that did not open, and put aside. Strain the liquid through a sieve lined with a cloth or a paper towel, and add to the fish stock to make 5 to 6 cups.

2. Bring the stock to a simmer.

3. Heat the oil in a heavy-bottomed saucepan over medium heat. Add the tomatoes, the garlic, and a pinch of salt, and sauté for 10 minutes.

4. Add the rice, turn the heat to medium-high, and sauté for 1 to 2 minutes, stirring well. Add the fish stock combined with the liquid from the mussels, 1 cup at a time, and continue cooking, over medium heat, adjusting the recommended amount of liquid as needed, and following the directions for Basic Risotto (p. 83).

5. After 15 to 16 minutes, add the mussels and the pepper. Stir well, and taste for salt.

6. When the rice is done, pour it onto an oblong heated platter, and sprinkle with the pecorino cheese. Serve immediately.

Note: Mussels must be used the same day they are bought.

Estimated Cooking Time: 30 minutes
Estimated Total Preparation Time: 2 hours

∽ RISOTTO CON LE VONGOLE ∽
Risotto with Clams   For 4

1 10-oz. can whole baby clams
4 to 5 cups homemade fish stock
　　　　　　or
2 large fish bouillon cubes,
　　dissolved in 4 to 5 cups water
2 tbs. butter
2 tbs. olive oil
1 small onion, minced

1 large garlic clove, mashed
2 cups Carolina long grain rice
　　　　　　or
Italian arborio
3 tbs. fresh parsley, minced
freshly ground black pepper
salt

1. Drain the clams, and reserve the liquid. Rinse the clams quickly under cold running water to remove any sand. Strain the liquid through a sieve lined with a cloth or a paper towel, and add to the fish stock. Set the clams aside.

2. Bring the stock to a simmer.

3. Heat the butter and the oil in a heavy-bottomed saucepan over medium heat. Add the onion, and sauté until soft and translucent. Add the garlic, and stir.

4. Add the rice and 2 tbs. parsley. Turn the heat to medium-high, and sauté for 1 to 2 minutes, stirring well. Add the fish stock, 1 cup at a time, and continue cooking, over medium heat, adjusting the recommended amount of liquid as needed, and following the directions for Basic Risotto (p. 83).

5. After 14 to 15 minutes, add the clams, the remaining parsley, and the pepper. Stir well, and taste for salt. When the rice is done, serve immediately.

Estimated Cooking Time: 25 minutes
Estimated Total Preparation Time: 40 minutes

∽ RISOTTO CON GLI SCAMPI ∽

Shrimp Risotto   For 4

1½ lbs. fresh medium shrimp
5 tbs. butter
1½ small onions (mince 1 onion;
　slice ½ onion)
½ carrot, sliced
½ celery stalk, sliced
1 garlic clove, peeled
1 whole sprig parsley plus 2 tbs.
　parsley, minced

¾ cup dry white wine
salt
3 tbs. olive oil
1 tbs. tomato paste
2 cups Uncle Ben's long grain rice
　　　　　　or
Italian arborio
freshly ground white pepper

1. Shell and devein the shrimp, reserving the shells. Keep about ⅓ of the shrimp whole, and cut the rest into 2 to 3 pieces.

2. In a medium saucepan combine 2 tbs. butter, the shrimp shells, the sliced onion, the carrot, the celery, the garlic, and the sprig of parsley. Sauté over medium heat for 3 to 4 minutes. Add the wine, and let it evaporate. Add 2 quarts water and 2 tsp. salt, and bring to a boil. Let boil for 20 to 30 minutes. Strain the stock, return it to the saucepan, and keep it simmering.

3. Heat 2 tbs. butter and 2 tbs. oil in a heavy-bottomed saucepan over medium heat. Add the minced onion, and sauté until soft and translucent. Add the tomato paste, and cook 2 to 3 minutes longer.

4. Add the rice, turn the heat to medium-high, and sauté for 1 to 2 minutes, stirring well. Add the stock, 1 cup at a time, and continue cooking, over medium heat, adjusting the recommended amount of liquid as needed, and following the directions for Basic Risotto (p. 83).

5. After 10 minutes add the cut shrimp, and continue cooking.

6. Heat the remaining oil in a small skillet over medium-high heat, and sauté the whole shrimp for about 5 minutes. Turn off the heat, and keep them warm.

7. When the rice is still very al dente (1 to 2 minutes before it is done), add the remaining butter, the minced parsley, and the pepper. Stir, and taste for salt. Turn the heat off, cover, and let rest 1 to 2 minutes. Then serve the risotto immediately decorated with the sautéed whole shrimp.

Estimated Cooking Time: 55 minutes
Estimated Total Preparation Time: 1 hour and 20 minutes

∾ RISOTTO DI MARE ∾
Risotto with Seafood I   For 4

This is our version of a specialty served in a Roman trattoria that was extracted from a friendly waiter in bits and pieces.

1½ doz. fresh littleneck clams
    or
1 cup canned whole baby clams
1 lb. squid
½ lb. fresh shrimp
    or
½ 12-oz. package frozen raw
    shrimp
½ lb. sea bass fillets
2 scant cups medium bechamel
    sauce (see Bechamel Sauce,
    p. 16)
5 to 6 cups homemade fish stock
    or
2 large fish bouillon cubes
    dissolved in 5 to 6 cups water

2 tbs. olive oil
3 tbs. butter
1 small onion, minced
2 small red chili peppers
2 garlic cloves, mashed
½ cup dry white wine, mixed
    with 1 tsp. tomato paste
salt
2 cups Carolina long grain rice
    or
Italian arborio
2 tbs. fresh parsley, minced

1. Wash and scrub the clams thoroughly under cold running water to remove all sand and dirt, discarding any open ones. Soak the clams in cold water for one hour, changing the water 2 to 3 times. Drain the clams, and place in a heavy saucepan over medium-high heat. Cover the saucepan, and shake it every few minutes so that the clams will open evenly. When they have opened remove them from the shells, and set aside. Discard any clams that do not open. Strain the liquid through a sieve lined with a cloth or a paper towel, and add it to the stock to make 5 to 6 cups. If you use canned clams, drain, and reserve the liquid. Rinse the clams quickly under cold running water to remove any sand. Strain the liquid from the can through a sieve lined with a cloth or paper towel, and add it to the stock to make 5 to 6 cups.

2. Remove the tentacles from the sacs of the squid, rinse under cold running water, and set aside. Cut the sacs above the eyes, discarding the rest. Peel the sacs by pulling the skin off with your fingers. Remove the cartilage-like bone as well as any gelatinous matter from the sacs, and rinse thoroughly under cold running water. Cut the sacs into thin rings and the tentacles into ½" pieces.

3. Shell and devein the shrimp, and cut them in half. If you use frozen shrimp, rinse them quickly in a colander under hot water.

4. Cut the fillets into ½" pieces.

5. Make the bechamel sauce.

6. Bring the stock to a simmer.

7. Heat the oil and butter in a heavy-bottomed saucepan over medium heat. Add the onion, and sauté until soft and translucent. Add the chili peppers and the garlic, and sauté for 1 to 2 minutes longer.

8. Add the squid, stir, and sauté about 2 minutes. Add the wine, the tomato paste, and ¼ tsp. salt, and cook over low heat for about 5 to 8 minutes, or until the wine is evaporated. Add the bass, stir, and sauté 1 minute longer.

9. Add the rice, turn the heat to medium-high, and sauté for 1 to 2 minutes, stirring well. Add the stock, 1 cup at a time, and continue cooking over medium heat, adjusting the recommended amount of liquid as needed, and following the directions for Basic Risotto (p. 83).

10. After 12 to 13 minutes add the shrimp, and continue cooking for 3 to 4 minutes.

11. Add the clams, the parsley, and the bechamel sauce. Stir, and taste for salt. Turn the heat off, cover, and let rest about 2 minutes, or until the rice is done. Then serve immediately on a heated platter.

Estimated Cooking Time: 50 minutes (fresh clams); 45 minutes (canned clams)

Estimated Total Preparation Time: 2 hours and 30 minutes (fresh clams); 1 hour and 15 minutes (canned clams)

∽ RISOTTO DI PESCE ∽

Risotto with Seafood II

For 4

1 lb. small squid
½ lb. fresh small shrimp
            or
½ 12-oz. package frozen raw
    shrimp
½ lb. bass fillets
5 to 6 cups homemade fish stock
            or
3 large fish bouillon cubes,
    dissolved in 5 to 6 cups water
2 tbs. olive oil

4 tbs. butter
2 garlic cloves, peeled
1 small onion, minced
2 cups Carolina long grain rice
            or
Italian arborio
½ cup dry white wine
¼ cup fresh parsley, minced
freshly ground white pepper
salt

1. Remove the tentacles from the sacs of the squid. Rinse under cold running water, and set aside. Cut the sacs above the eyes, discarding the rest. Peel the sacs by pulling the skin off with your fingers. Remove the cartilage-like bone as well as any other gelatinous matter from the sacs, and rinse thoroughly under cold running water. Cut the sacs into thin rings and the tentacles into ½" pieces.

2. Shell and devein the shrimp. If you use frozen shrimp, rinse quickly in a colander under hot water.

3. Cut the bass fillets into ½" pieces.

4. Bring the stock to a simmer.

5. Heat the oil and 2 tbs. butter in a heavy-bottomed saucepan over medium heat. Add the garlic and the onion, and sauté until

the onion is soft and translucent and the garlic barely golden. Discard the garlic.

6. Add the squid to the saucepan, and sauté for 5 to 8 minutes. Add the bass, stir, and sauté 1 minute longer.

7. Add the rice, turn the heat to medium-high and sauté it for 1 to 2 minutes, stirring well. Add the wine, stir, and let it evaporate. Add the stock, 1 cup at a time, and continue cooking, over medium heat, adjusting the recommended amount of liquid as needed, and following the directions for Basic Risotto (p. 83).

8. After 10 to 12 minutes add the shrimp, and continue cooking.

9. When the rice is still very al dente (1 to 2 minutes before it is done), add the remaining butter, the parsley, and the pepper, stir, and taste for salt. Serve on a heated platter.

Estimated Cooking Time: 30 minutes
Estimated Total Preparation Time: 1 hour and 30 minutes

∽ RISO AI QUATTRO FORMAGGI ∽
Rice with Four Cheeses   For 4

salt
2 cups Carolina long grain rice
6 tbs. butter cut into pieces
½ cup light cream
4 1-oz. wedges of imported soft
    cheese (such as La Vache
    Qui Rit)

⅔ cup mozzarella cheese, diced
    (if the mozzarella is dry,
    shred it)
⅔ cup aged sharp Fontina
    cheese, diced
⅔ cup freshly grated Parmesan
    cheese

1. Bring 4 to 5 quarts water with 2 tbs. salt to a boil. Sprinkle the rice into the water. Stir once or twice, and cook over medium-high heat for about 12 minutes, or until *al dente*. Drain in a colander.

2. In the same pot, melt the butter over low heat. Add the cream, stir, and cook 2 to 3 minutes longer. Add the rice and the four cheeses. Stir until all the cheeses are melted. Serve immediately.

Estimated Cooking Time: 25 minutes
Estimated Total Preparation Time: 40 minutes

∼ RISO IN CAGNON ∼

Rice with Cheese For 4

This is a specialty of both Lombardy and Piedmont. We prefer the Lombardian version, which uses Parmesan cheese rather than Fontina.

salt
2 cups Carolina long grain rice
8 tbs. butter

8 to 10 fresh sage leaves
  or
½ tsp. dried sage
¾ cup freshly grated Parmesan
  cheese

1. Bring 4 to 5 quarts water with 2 tbs. salt to a boil. Sprinkle the rice into the water. Stir once or twice, and cook over medium-high heat for about 12 minutes, or until al dente.
2. While the rice is cooking, melt the butter and the sage in a small saucepan over low heat until the butter begins to bubble.
3. Drain the rice in a colander.
4. In a heated serving bowl combine the rice, the melted butter, and the sage, along with the cheese. Mix well. Taste for salt, and serve immediately.

Estimated Cooking Time: 25 minutes
Estimated Total Preparation Time: 35 minutes

∼ RISO ARROSTO CON CARCIOFI ∼

Baked Rice with Artichokes For 4 to 6

This dish makes a lovely presentation. The mint adds an interesting dimension.

juice of one lemon
3 large artichokes
5 tbs. olive oil
2⅓ cups homemade meat broth
  or 1 large chicken bouillon
  cube and ½ large beef cube,
  dissolved in 2⅓ cups water
2 cups Uncle Ben's long grain rice
1 garlic clove, minced

15 to 18 fresh mint leaves, broken
  into small pieces (if fresh mint
  is not available, substitute 2
  tbs. fresh parsley, minced)
salt
½ cup freshly grated pecorino
  Romano cheese
freshly ground black pepper

1. In a bowl mix the lemon juice with 3 cups cold water.

2. Cut off the artichoke stems, leaving about 1". Break off the small leaves at the base, and cut off about 1" from the top. Snap off the hard upper part from the leaves, and peel the tough outer layer from the stems. Cut the artichokes in half lengthwise, and remove the fuzzy choke and prickly leaves around it, being careful not to remove the heart. Cut the artichokes into wedges, and drop into the lemon water. Leave wedges in the water until it is time to cook them.

3. Preheat the oven to 400° F.

4. Drain the artichokes.

5. In a medium skillet place 2 tbs. oil and the artichokes, and sauté over low heat for 5 minutes. Add ⅓ cup broth, cover, and continue cooking over low heat for 15 minutes longer.

6. While the artichokes are cooking, heat 1 tbs. oil in a medium saucepan over medium heat. Add the rice, the garlic, the mint, and ½ tsp. salt. Stir the ingredients, and sauté for about 1 minute. Add ¼ cup cheese, and stir.

7. Remove the rice, and place in a round or oval oven-to-table dish.

8. Arrange the artichokes on top of the rice. Sprinkle with ½ tsp. salt, and drizzle with the remaining oil, pour the remaining broth over the artichokes, and sprinkle with the remaining cheese and the pepper.

9. Bake the rice for about 25 minutes, or until barely done. Let rest for about 5 minutes before serving.

Note: This recipe can be prepared several hours in advance through the first part of step 8 (when the artichokes are spread over the rice). The oil, the broth, and the cheese should be added just before baking.

Estimated Cooking Time: 45 minutes
Estimated Total Preparation Time: 1 hour and 15 minutes

◇ RISO AL PESTO CON PATATE ◇
Rice and Potatoes with Pesto   For 4

The Genoese serve a pasta dish with potatoes and pesto. We like this variation that combines the pesto/potato flavors with rice.

2 cups fresh basil leaves, washed
   and dried
4 garlic cloves, slightly mashed
¼ cup pine nuts
salt
½ cup olive oil
⅓ cup freshly grated Parmesan
   cheese

⅓ cup freshly grated pecorino
   Sardo cheese
       or
¼ cup freshly grated pecorino
   Romano cheese
2 medium potatoes (preferably
   new), peeled and cubed
2 cups Carolina long grain rice
       or
Italian arborio
2 tbs. butter

1. Combine the basil leaves, the garlic, the pine nuts, ½ tsp. salt, and the oil in a food processor, and chop for 60 seconds to make a smooth paste. Stop every 20 seconds to scrape the mixture away from the sides.

2. Add the cheeses, and chop for 5 seconds longer. Set the sauce aside.

3. Drop the potatoes and 2 tbs. salt into 4 quarts boiling water. Bring the water back to a boil, and sprinkle the rice into it. Cook over medium heat for about 14 minutes, or until just tender.

4. Drain the rice and the potatoes, reserving ½ cup of the cooking water.

5. In a heated serving bowl combine the rice and the potatoes, the water, the butter, and the sauce. Toss well, and serve immediately.

Note: Classic pesto is prepared with a mortar and pestle, the recipe for which is given in Linguine al Pesto (p. 177). That version omits the pine nuts but can be used in this recipe with highly satisfying results. If you plan to store the pesto, use this recipe.

Estimated Cooking Time: 25 minutes
Estimated Total Preparation Time: 45 minutes.

∽ RISO DI MARE ARROSTO ∽
Baked Rice with Seafood   For 4 to 6

The idea for this recipe came from a wonderful dish sampled one summer at the celebrated restaurant at the airport on the island of Elba.

1 doz. fresh littleneck clams
1 lb. fresh mussels
3 tbs. cornmeal
1 lb. fresh squid
½ lb. fresh shrimp
4 tbs. olive oil
1 small onion, minced
1 garlic clove, mashed
½ cup dry white wine

2 cups Uncle Ben's long grain rice
2 to 3 cups homemade fish stock
or
1 large fish bouillon cube,
    dissolved in 2 to 3 cups water
salt
3 tbs. fresh parsley, minced
freshly ground black pepper

1. Wash and scrub the clams and the mussels thoroughly under cold running water to remove all sand and dirt, discarding any that do not open. With a knife scrape off any hair protruding from the mussels. Soak the clams and the mussels in cold water with 1 tbs. cornmeal for 1 hour, changing the water twice and adding 1 tbs. of fresh cornmeal each time. Drain, rinse in cold water, and place in a large heavy saucepan, over medium-high heat. Cover the saucepan, and shake every few minutes so that the clams and mussels will open evenly. When they have opened, remove them from the shells. Discard any that do not open. Halve or quarter the mussels depending on the size. Strain the liquid through a sieve lined with a cloth or paper towel, and set aside.

2. Remove the tentacles from the sacs of the squid, and cut them above the eyes, discarding the rest. Rinse under cold running water, and set aside. Peel the sacs by pulling the skin off with your fingers. Remove the cartilage-like bone as well as any other gelatinous matter from the sacs, and rinse thoroughly under cold running water. Cut the sacs into thin rings and the tentacles into ½″ pieces.

3. Shell and devein the shrimp.

4. Preheat the oven to 350° F.

5. Heat the oil in a heavy-bottomed saucepan over medium heat. Add the onion, and sauté until soft and translucent. Add the garlic, and sauté a few seconds longer.

6. Add the squid to the pan, and sauté 3 to 5 minutes. Add the wine, and let it evaporate.

7. Add the rice, and sauté for 1 to 2 minutes. Add the clams, the mussels, the shrimp, and 3 cups liquid consisting of the reserved mussel and clam liquid and fish stock. Stir well.

8. Pour the mixture into a round oven-to-table dish, preferably terracotta, and bake, covered, for about 20 minutes, or until the rice is al dente. Taste for salt. The consistency should be rather moist, almost soupy.

9. Just before serving, add the parsley and the pepper, stirring well.

Estimated Cooking Time: 40 minutes
Estimated Total Preparation Time: 2 hours

∽ POMODORI AL RISO ∽
Baked Tomatoes Stuffed with Rice   For 4

A summer standby of the Roman kitchen both at home and in restaurants. The versatility of this dish is unlimited.

8 ripe medium tomatoes
salt
¾ cup Carolina long grain rice
1 garlic clove, mashed
½ cup olive oil
⅓ cup fresh basil leaves, chopped

1½ tbs. fresh parsley leaves,
* chopped*
¼ tsp. dried oregano
freshly ground black pepper
1 lb. medium baking potatoes

1. Preheat oven to 350° F.

2. Slice the tops off the tomatoes, sprinkle with salt, and set aside. If the tomatoes have stems, leave them on for a prettier presentation.

3. Scoop out the pulp and the seeds from the tomato bottoms, making sure not to break the walls of the tomatoes.

4. Puree the tomato pulp in a food mill, blender, or food processor, or simply mash it with a fork.

5. In a large bowl mix the pulp with the rice, the garlic, ¼ cup oil, 1 tsp. salt, the basil, the parsley, the oregano, and the pepper.

6. Fill each of the tomato bottoms about ⅔ high with the rice mixture, cover with the tops, and place in a shallow baking dish.

7. Peel and cube the potatoes. In a small bowl toss them with 2 tbs. oil, and distribute them around the tomatoes. Sprinkle the potatoes with ¼ tsp. salt.

8. Drizzle the remaining 2 tbs. olive oil over both the tomatoes and potatoes, and bake for 1½ hours.

9. Let cool. Serve at room temperature.

Note: This dish is best when prepared several hours in advance. If you prefer to cook the tomatoes the day before, do not reheat them. Simply let them sit outside the refrigerator until they return to room temperature.

Estimated Cooking Time: 1 hour and 30 minutes
Estimated Total Preparation Time: 2 hours

∾ POMODORI PRIMAVERA ∾
Cold Tomatoes Stuffed with Rice   For 4

A tasty and easy-to-prepare summer dish that offers an intriguing combination of flavors.

8 ripe medium tomatoes
salt
¾ cup Carolina long grain rice
2 tbs. heavy cream
1 cup mayonnaise (see
  Mayonnaise, p. 17)

¾ cup Emmenthal (Swiss)
  cheese, shredded
2 tbs. fresh chives, chopped
½ bunch watercress

1. Slice off the tops of the tomatoes, and scoop out the pulp, reserving it for some other use. Sprinkle the insides of the tomatoes with ½ tsp. salt, and turn them upside down to drain for about 30 minutes.

2. Bring 2 quarts water with 2 tsp. salt to a boil. Sprinkle the rice into the water, stir once or twice, and cook over medium-high heat for about 14 minutes, or until just tender.

3. Drain the rice in a colander, and rinse under cold water. Shake the colander to remove most of the moisture, and set the rice aside.

4. Mix the cream with the mayonnaise.

5. In a bowl combine the rice, the cheese, the chives, and ¾ cup mayonnaise, and stir together.

6. Fill the tomatoes with the rice mixture, place a dollop of the remaining mayonnaise on top, and decorate with sprigs of watercress.

Note: These tomatoes can be prepared several hours in advance.

Estimated Cooking Time: 25 minutes
Estimated Total Preparation Time: 1 hour

∽ PEPERONI ALLA CALABRESE ∽

Peppers Stuffed with Rice and Tuna   For 4

This recipe from Calabria makes a good buffet dish.

4 large green peppers, washed
   and dried
2 anchovy fillets
2 tbs. capers, drained
4 Italian green olives, pitted
4 Italian or Greek black olives,
   pitted
salt

¾ cup Carolina long grain rice
¼ cup fresh parsley, minced
1 6½-oz. can tuna, flaked
4 tbs. olive oil
freshly ground black pepper
½ large chicken bouillon cube,
   dissolved in 1 cup water

1. Preheat the oven to 350° F.

2. Cut the tops off the peppers in such a way that they can be put back in place. Remove all the seeds and filaments. Set aside.

3. Chop together the anchovies, the capers, and the olives.

4. Bring 2 quarts water with 2 tsp. salt to a boil. Sprinkle the rice into the water, stir once or twice, and cook over medium-high heat for 5 minutes. Drain the rice in a colander.

5. In a small mixing bowl combine the rice with the anchovy mixture, the parsley, the tuna, ¼ tsp. salt, the olive oil, and the pepper. Stuff the peppers with the mixture, put the tops back on, and stand the peppers in a shallow baking dish just large enough to contain them. Pour the chicken broth into the bottom of the dish, and bake for about 1 hour, or until the peppers are tender.

6. Serve the peppers at room temperature.

Note: These peppers can be prepared the day before and refrigerated. Remove them from the refrigerator several hours before serving.

Estimated Cooking Time: 1 hour and 15 minutes
Estimated Total Preparation Time: 1 hour and 30 minutes

◇ PEPERONI RIPIENI ALLA PIEMONTESE ◇
Stuffed Peppers Piedmontese Style   For 4

4 large green peppers	5 tbs. olive oil
salt	2 tbs. butter
1 cup Carolina long grain rice	1 large garlic clove, mashed
3 tbs. fresh parsley, minced	8 anchovy fillets, chopped

1. Wash and dry the peppers. Place them on a rack as close as possible to the broiler, and sear on all sides. When the skins of the peppers have loosened and are slightly charred (5 to 10 minutes), remove from the broiler.

2. Bring 3 to 4 quarts water with 1½ tbs. salt to a boil. Sprinkle the rice into the water, stir once or twice, and cook over medium-high heat for about 10 minutes.

3. While the rice is cooking, peel the peppers, and cut them in half lengthwise. Remove all the seeds and filaments, and set aside.

4. Drain the rice in a colander.

5. Place the rice in a bowl. Add the parsley and 3 tbs. oil, and mix well.

6. Divide the rice among the pepper halves, and arrange them in a buttered baking dish.

7. Heat the remaining oil and the butter over very low heat. Add the garlic and the anchovies, stirring and mashing them together with a wooden spoon for about 5 minutes. Do not fry.

8. Pour the sauce over the peppers, and bake for about 30 minutes. Serve warm.

Note: These peppers are equally good at room temperature and can be prepared a day in advance.

Estimated Cooking Time: 50 minutes
Estimated Total Preparation Time: 1 hour and 10 minutes

∽ TIMBALLO DI RISO AL FORMAGGIO ∽
Rice Mold with Cheese   For 4

salt
2 cups Carolina long grain rice
5 tbs. butter
10 fresh sage leaves, broken into
  pieces
        or
¼ tsp. dried sage
⅔ cup cooked country ham, cut
  into slivers, plus 4 very thin
  slices cooked ham

½ cup freshly grated Parmesan
  cheese
4 oz. Fontina cheese, thinly sliced
4 1-oz. wedges of imported soft
  cheese (such as La Vache Qui
  Rit), broken into small pieces

1. Bring 4 to 5 quarts water with 2 tbs. salt to a boil. Sprinkle the rice into the water. Stir once or twice, and cook over medium-high heat for about 12 minutes, or until al dente. Drain the rice in a colander.

2. Preheat the oven to 400° F.

3. In a small skillet heat the butter and the sage and sauté for 1 minute over low heat. Add the ham slivers, stir, and remove the skillet from the fire.

4. In a bowl combine the rice, the ham mixture, and ¼ cup Parmesan cheese. Mix well.

5. Butter a 6″ to 7″ diameter souffle dish, and line the bottom with the thin slices of ham cut into triangles to create a pinwheel shape. Put ⅓ of the rice mixture on top of the ham, and top it with a layer of Fontina cheese. Add a second layer of rice followed by a layer of the soft cheese. Finish with a top layer of rice sprinkled with the remaining Parmesan cheese.

6. Bake the rice for about 15 minutes. Remove from the oven, and let set for about 5 minutes.

7. Slide a knife around the sides of the baking dish, and unmold the timballo onto a round platter.

Estimated Cooking Time: 40 minutes
Estimated Total Preparation Time: 1 hour and 10 minutes

✑ TIMBALLO DI RISO CON SPINACI ✑
Rice Mold with Spinach   For 4

3 lbs. fresh spinach
or
3 10-oz. packages frozen spinach,
  thawed
salt
4 tbs. butter

¼ cup freshly grated Parmesan
  cheese
Risotto with Parmesan Cheese,
  p. 86, with 2 cups Carolina
  long grain rice and 4 to 5 cups
  broth (see step 5, below)

1. Preheat the oven to 400° F.
2. Wash the spinach well, and without shaking the leaves, place it in a saucepan with ½ tsp. salt. Cook, covered, over medium heat for 10 to 12 minutes, or until barely tender. Drain the spinach, and let cool. Squeeze it with your hands to remove as much liquid as possible and chop until fine. If frozen spinach is used, squeeze out as much liquid as possible, and chop until fine.
3. Heat the butter in a medium skillet over medium heat. Add the spinach, and sauté about 5 to 7 minutes, or until dry. Remove from the burner. Let cool slightly, mix with the Parmesan cheese, and set aside.
4. Butter an 8-cup souffle or charlotte mold.
5. Make the risotto, omitting the Parmesan cheese at the end. Undercook by 2 to 3 minutes.
6. Line the bottom and sides of the mold with the risotto, reserving enough to cover the top. Fill the center with the spinach. Cover with a layer of rice, pushing it down as tightly as possible.
7. Bake the mold for 20 minutes. Remove it from the oven, and let set for about 5 minutes.
8. Unmold the rice timballo onto a heated dish, and serve immediately.

Estimated Cooking Time: 1 hour (fresh spinach); 50 minutes (frozen spinach)
Estimated Total Preparation Time: 1 hour and 15 minutes (fresh spinach); 1 hour (frozen spinach)

∽ TIMBALLO DI RISO E MELANZANE ∽
Rice Mold with Eggplant   For 4

When this timballo is unmolded, the layer of eggplant on the top adds a very impressive accent. The unbeatable combination of eggplant, tomatoes, and cheese enhances the flavor of the rice.

2½ lbs. eggplants
salt
2 cups Basic Tomato Sauce II,
    p. 15
¼ cup fresh parsley, minced
2½ cups homemade meat broth
                or
1 large beef bouillon cube,
    dissolved in 2½ cups water

1 cup vegetable oil
2 tbs. butter
1 medium onion, minced
2 cups Carolina long grain rice
½ cup freshly grated pecorino
    Romano cheese

1. Wash and dry the eggplants. Cut crosswise into ¼" slices. Place the slices in a colander, sprinkle with 2 tsp. salt, and let drain for 30 to 40 minutes.

2. Preheat the oven to 400° F.

3. Heat the tomato sauce, and stir in the parsley.

4. Bring the broth to a simmer.

5. Heat the oil in a large skillet over medium-high heat. Dry the eggplant slices thoroughly with paper towels. When the oil is very hot, slide the eggplant slices into the oil in a single layer. Cook until brown, and turn. When browned on both sides, remove slices to brown paper to drain. Continue this process with the rest of the eggplant.

6. Heat the butter in a medium saucepan over medium heat. Add the onion, and sauté until soft and translucent. Add the rice, and stir until well coated with the fat. Add the broth, stir, and cook, covered, over low heat for about 10 minutes, or until very al dente. Add ¼ cup cheese, and toss well.

7. Line the bottom of an 8" diameter souffle dish with a layer of eggplant. Spoon ⅓ of the tomato sauce over the eggplant, and cover with half the rice. Repeat the process, then finish with a layer of eggplant and the remaining sauce. Sprinkle the remaining cheese on the top, and bake for 10 to 15 minutes. Remove from the oven, and let set for about 5 minutes.

8. Slide a knife around the sides of the dish, and unmold the timballo onto a round platter.

Note: This timballo can be served immediately or at room temperature several hours later.

Estimated Cooking Time: 40 minutes
Estimated Total Preparation Time: 1 hour and 30 minutes

∽ ANELLO DI RISOTTO CON FONDUTA ∽
Ring of Risotto with Cheese Fondue   For 4

Italian fonduta, which is exclusively a Piedmontese dish, differs from the Swiss version in that it is made with milk rather than wine. The basic ingredients are Fontina cheese, milk, butter, and egg yolks. When the fonduta is ready, it is usually served in individual soup dishes with bread on the side. The famous white truffles of Piedmont are sliced on top. Fonduta is extremely temperamental and curdles—*impazzisce*, which means goes crazy—very easily, especially if it is not removed from the heat immediately. For this version we've added a little flour to prevent curdling, so even though it's not "pure," it will never embarrass you.

FONDUTA	RICE
14 oz. *Fontina cheese, thinly sliced*	*Risotto with Parmesan Cheese, p. 86, with 2 cups Carolina long grain rice and 4 to 5 cups broth (see step 3, below)*
1 cup *milk*	
2 tbs. *butter*	
1 tbs. *flour*	
3 egg yolks	1½ oz. *white truffles (optional)*

1. In a bowl place the Fontina cheese, cover with ½ cup milk, and let stand for at least 2 hours.

2. Melt the butter in the top part of a double boiler placed directly on a medium-low burner. Add the flour, and cook for 2 to 3 minutes, being careful not to brown it. Add the remaining milk, and stir with a whisk. Place the top part of the double boiler inside the bottom part, filled with hot water, add the Fontina mixture, and continue cooking over medium-low heat, stirring

with the wisk until smooth and creamy. Add the egg yolks, one at a time, stirring well after each addition. Turn the heat off, cover the fonduta, and keep warm.

3. Make the risotto, using a little less liquid than usual and omitting the Parmesan cheese at the end. The risotto should be a little dry.

4. Butter a 6-cup ring mold, and fill it with the hot risotto, pressing the rice in as tightly as possible. Let set for 2 to 3 minutes.

5. Unmold the rice ring onto a round serving dish that is not too shallow. Fill the hollow center with the fonduta, and pour the remaining portion over the rice. Slice the truffles very thinly over the sauce. Serve immediately.

Estimated Cooking Time: 40 minutes
Estimated Total Preparation Time: 3 hours

∽ ANELLO DI RISO CON ZUCCHINE ∽
Rice Ring with Zucchini   For 4

The pungent garlic and vinegar really enhance the taste of the zucchini, making this an unexpectedly impressive dish.

2 lbs. small zucchini, washed and dried	freshly ground black pepper
salt	½ cup red wine vinegar
¾ cup vegetable oil	2 cups Carolina long grain rice
2 garlic cloves, minced	or
⅓ cup fresh basil leaves, torn into small pieces	Italian arborio

1. Cut the zucchini lengthwise into ⅛″ slices. Place in a colander, sprinkle with 1 tsp. salt, and let drain for about 1 hour.

2. Heat the oil in a large skillet until very hot. Dry the zucchini, and slide the slices into the oil in a single layer. Fry quickly over high heat until tender and slightly browned. Remove to a shallow dish. Continue this process with the remaining zucchini.

3. Sprinkle the zucchini with the garlic, the basil, and the pepper. Strain the frying oil to remove any burned particles. Put ⅓ cup back into the pan, cook over medium heat, and add the vine-

gar. Stir for about 30 seconds, then pour over the zucchini, and let it marinate for at least 2 hours.

4. Bring 4 to 5 quarts water with 2 tbs. salt to a boil. Sprinkle the rice into the water, stir once or twice, and cook over medium-high heat for about 14 minutes, until just tender. Drain.

5. In a large bowl combine the rice and half the marinated zucchini.

6. Oil a 6-cup ring mold, and fill it with the rice mixture, pressing it in as tightly as possible. Let set for 2 to 3 minutes.

7. Unmold the rice ring by placing a warm round serving dish over the mold and turning it upside down. Garnish by draping the remaining zucchini slices over the top of the ring.

Note: The zucchini can be prepared the day before. It does not need to be refrigerated. The leftovers are delicious eaten cold as a salad or as a side dish with cold meat.

Estimated Cooking Time: 45 minutes
Estimated Total Preparation Time: 3 hours

∽ ANELLO DI RISOTTO CON SCAMPI ∽
Ring of Risotto with Shrimp and Mushroom Sauce
For 4 to 5

½ lb. fresh mushrooms
1¼ lbs. fresh shrimp
or
1 lb. frozen raw shrimp
Risotto with Parmesan Cheese,
p. 86, with 2 cups Carolina
long grain rice and 4 to 5 cups
broth (see step 3, below)
2 cups homemade fish stock
or
1 large fish bouillon cube,
dissolved in 2 cups water

5 tbs. butter
1½ tbs. flour
3 tbs. Basic Tomato Sauce I,
p. 14
or
2 tbs. tomato paste
1 medium onion, minced
⅓ cup dry white wine
1 tbs. fresh parsley, minced
freshly ground white pepper
salt

1. Trim off the ends of the mushroom stems. If the mushrooms are relatively clean, wipe them thoroughly with a damp paper towel. If there is a lot of soil and dirt clinging to the caps, rinse

thoroughly but quickly in cold water, rubbing them against each other to dislodge the dirt. Dry with paper towels, and cut them in half.

2. Shell and devein the shrimp. If you use frozen shrimp, place in a colander, and thaw by pouring 3 to 4 cups boiling water over them.

3. Make the risotto, using a little less liquid than usual and omitting the butter and Parmesan cheese at the end. The risotto should be a little dry.

4. Butter a 6-cup ring mold, and fill it with the hot risotto, pressing the rice in as tightly as possible.

5. Bring the stock to a simmer.

6. Heat 2 tbs. butter in a small saucepan. Add the flour, and stir with a whisk over medium heat until the flour turns gold. Add the fish broth all at once, and stir briskly with the whisk. Cook for about 5 minutes, stirring until it has thickened. Add the tomato sauce or paste, stir, and turn the heat off.

7. Heat the remaining butter in a medium saucepan, and sauté the onion over medium heat until soft and translucent. Add the mushrooms, and sauté for 3 minutes. Add the shrimp, and sauté 2 minutes more. Add the white wine, the parsley, the pepper, and salt to taste. Cook until the wine is almost evaporated, about 5 minutes.

8. Add the sauce to the shrimp-mushroom mixture, and heat thoroughly.

9. Unmold the rice ring by placing a warm round serving dish over the mold and turning it upside down. Spoon part of the sauce into the hollow center, and serve the rest separately.

Estimated Cooking Time: 50 minutes
Estimated Total Preparation Time: 1 hour and 15 minutes

~ ANELLO DI RISOTTO ALLA PESCATORA ~

Ring of Risotto with Seafood Sauce   For 4 to 5

Appealing to the eye and to the palate, this delicious concoction of seafood flavors provides an impressive focus for a special meal.

2 lbs. fresh mussels as small as can be found	Risotto with Parmesan Cheese, p. 86, with 2 cups Uncle Ben's long grain rice and 3½ to 4 cups broth (see step 3, below)
3 tbs. cornmeal	
1½ doz. fresh littleneck clams	
or	1 recipe Basic Tomato Sauce I, p. 14
¾ cup canned Italian whole baby clams	
	2 tbs. olive oil
1 lb. fresh small shrimp	2 tbs. butter
or	2 tbs. brandy
1 12-oz. package frozen raw shrimp	freshly ground white pepper
	salt

1. Wash and scrub the mussels and the clams thoroughly under cold running water to remove all sand and dirt, discarding any open ones. With a knife scrape off any hair protruding from the mussels. Soak the mussels and the clams in cold water with 1 tbs. cornmeal for 1 hour, changing the water twice and adding 1 tbs. of fresh cornmeal each time. Drain and rinse in cold water, and place in a large heavy saucepan over medium-high heat. Cover the saucepan, and shake every few minutes so that the mussels and clams will open evenly. When they have opened, remove them from the shells. Discard any that do not open. Halve or quarter the mussels depending on the size. Strain the liquid through a sieve lined with a cloth or paper towel, and set aside.

If you use canned clams, drain in a colander, reserving the liquid, and rinse quickly under cold water to remove any sand. Strain the liquid through a sieve lined with a cloth or paper towel, and set aside.

2. Shell and devein the shrimp. If you use frozen shrimp, place in a colander, and thaw by pouring 3 to 4 cups boiling water over them. Set aside.

3. Make the risotto, using a little less liquid than usual and omitting the butter and the Parmesan cheese at the end. The risotto should be a little dry.

4. While the risotto is cooking, heat the tomato sauce over medium-low heat.

5. Butter a 6-cup ring mold, and fill it with the hot risotto, pressing the rice in as tightly as possible.

6. Heat the oil and the butter in a large skillet over high heat. Add the shrimp, and sauté for about 3 minutes. Add the mussels and clams, and sauté 2 minutes longer (if you use frozen shrimp, add them with the other seafood). Add the brandy, and stir. Add the tomato sauce, 3 to 4 tbs. of the shellfish liquid, and the pepper. Taste for salt, and cook 1 to 2 minutes longer.

7. Unmold the rice ring by placing a warm round serving dish over the mold and turning it upside down.

8. Fill the hollow center with part of the seafood sauce, and distribute the remaining sauce around the ring.

Note: Mussels must be used the same day they are bought.

Estimated Cooking Time: 30 minutes
Estimated Total Preparation Time: 2 hours

∽ ANELLO DI RISO ALL'ISOLANA ∽
Savory Rice Ring with Tomatoes   For 4

This unusual combination of flavors is delicious. The tomatoes complement the rice beautifully in addition to adding a magnificent splash of color.

salt	1 tbs. anchovy paste
2 cups Carolina long grain rice	2 lbs. ripe tomatoes, peeled,
6 tbs. olive oil	seeded, and coarsely chopped
1 small onion, minced	1 tbs. fresh marjoram leaves,
¼ cup red wine vinegar	chopped
¼ cup lemon juice	or
½ tsp. Dijon mustard	½ tsp. dried marjoram

1. Bring 4 to 5 quarts water with 2 tbs. salt to a boil. Sprinkle the rice into the water. Stir once or twice and cook over medium-high heat for about 12 minutes, or until al dente.

2. While the rice is cooking, heat 3 tbs. oil in a small skillet over medium heat. Add the onion, and sauté until soft and translucent. Add the vinegar, and let it evaporate. Add the lemon juice, the mustard, and the anchovy paste. Stir well, and remove from the burner.

3. Drain the rice in a colander.

4. In a large bowl combine the rice and the sauce, and mix well. Taste for salt.

5. Oil an 8″ ring mold, and pack very tightly with the rice. Let sit for 5 to 10 minutes.

6. Meanwhile, heat the remaining oil in a medium skillet over medium-high heat. Add the tomatoes, the marjoram, and ½ tsp. salt, and cook, stirring for 7 to 10 minutes.

7. Unmold the rice ring by placing a warm round serving dish over the mold and turning it upside down. Pour the tomatoes into the center. Serve immediately.

Estimated Cooking Time: 25 minutes
Estimated Total Preparation Time: 45 minutes

∽ INSALATA DI RISO FANTASIA ∽

Rice Salad with Ham, Cheese, and Mixed Vegetables
For 4 to 6

Like all the rice salads, this one is great for picnics and summer menus.

salt
1 cup Carolina long grain rice
¾ cup frozen tiny peas
¾ cup cooked ham, diced
⅓ cup Fontina or Emmenthal (Swiss) cheese, diced
⅓ cup celery hearts, diced
½ cup marinated artichoke hearts, quartered

½ cup black Italian or Greek olives, whole
⅓ cup olive oil
2 tbs. red wine vinegar
freshly ground black pepper
1 tbs. oil from marinated artichoke hearts

1. Bring 3 to 4 quarts water with 1½ tbs. salt to a boil. Sprinkle the rice into the water, stir once or twice, and cook over medium-high heat for about 14 minutes, or until just tender.

2. Drain the rice in a colander, and rinse under cold water. Shake the colander to remove most of the moisture, and set the rice aside.

3. Put the peas in a strainer, and thaw by pouring boiling water over them.

4. In a large bowl combine the rice, the peas, the ham, the cheese, the celery hearts, half the artichoke hearts, and half the olives.

5. In a small bowl mix the oil, the vinegar, ½ tsp. salt, the pepper, and 1 tbs. oil from the marinated artichokes. Pour this dressing over the rice mixture, and toss gently.

6. Arrange the rice salad on an oblong platter, mounding it slightly in the center. Decorate it with the remaining olives and artichoke hearts. Serve at room temperature.

Note: This salad can be prepared several hours in advance and stored in the refrigerator. It should be served at room temperature.

Estimated Cooking Time: 25 minutes
Estimated Total Preparation Time: 50 minutes

◇ INSALATA DI RISO TONNATA ◇
Rice Salad with Tuna
For 4 to 6

salt
1 cup Carolina long grain rice
1 6½-oz. can chunk light tuna, drained and flaked
2 tbs. capers, drained
10 Italian green olives, pitted and slivered

16 Italian black olives (10 whole, 6 pitted and slivered)
3 hard-boiled eggs, shelled (1 whole, 2 cut into wedges)
⅓ cup olive oil
3 tbs. red wine vinegar
freshly ground black pepper
8 cherry tomatoes

1. Bring 3 to 4 quarts water with 1½ tbs. salt to a boil. Sprinkle the rice into the water, stir once or twice, and cook over medium-high heat for about 14 minutes, or until just tender.

2. Drain the rice in a colander, and rinse under cold water. Shake the colander to remove most of the moisture.

3. In a large bowl combine the rice, the tuna, the capers, the green olives, and the slivered black olives.

4. In a small bowl mash the whole egg with the oil, the vinegar, ½ tsp. salt, and the pepper. Pour the mixture over the rice. Toss gently, and taste for salt.

5. Arrange the rice salad on an oblong platter, mounding it slightly in the center. Decorate with the remaining black olives, the egg wedges, and the tomatoes. Serve at room temperature.

Note: This salad can be prepared several hours in advance. In that case add the eggs and tomatoes at the last moment. Serve at room temperature.

Estimated Cooking Time: 25 minutes
Estimated Total Preparation Time: 40 minutes

∽ INSALATA DI RISO ALLA MARINARA ∽
Rice Salad with Seafood For 4 to 6

2 lbs. fresh mussels
1 doz. fresh littleneck clams
 or
1 10-oz. can baby clams
3 tbs. cornmeal
½ carrot
½ celery stalk with leaves
½ small onion
1 whole parsley sprig plus ¼ cup, minced
1 small bay leaf

½ cup dry white wine
salt
½ lb. small fresh shrimp, shelled and deveined
 or
6 oz. frozen raw shrimp
1 cup Uncle Ben's long grain rice
⅓ cup olive oil
3 tbs. lemon juice
freshly ground black pepper

1. Wash and scrub the mussels and the clams thoroughly under cold running water to remove all sand and dirt, discarding any open ones. With a knife scrape off any hair protruding from the mussels. Soak the mussels and the clams in cold water with 1 tbs. cornmeal for 1 hour, changing the water twice and adding 1 tbs. of fresh cornmeal each time. Drain the mussels and the clams, rinse in cold water, and place in a large heavy saucepan over medium-high heat. Cover the saucepan and shake every few minutes so the mussels and clams open evenly. When they have opened, remove all but 8 mussels and 4 clams from their shells, discarding any that did not open. Set aside the mussels and the clams in their

half shells. If the shelled mussels are very large, cut them in half. Strain the liquid through a sieve lined with a cloth or paper towel, and set aside.

2. Meanwhile, combine the carrot, the celery, the onion, the parsley sprig, the bay leaf, the wine, ¼ tsp. salt, and 1 quart water in a medium saucepan, and bring to a boil over high heat. Lower the heat, and simmer, covered, for about 10 minutes. Turn the heat to medium-high, add the shrimp, and cook for 4 to 5 minutes. Drain. Keep 8 shrimp whole, and cut the rest in half.

3. Bring 3 to 4 quarts water with 1½ tbs. salt to a boil. Sprinkle the rice into the water, stir once or twice, and cook over medium-high heat for about 14 minutes, or until just tender.

4. Drain the rice in a colander, and rinse under cold water. Shake the colander to remove most of the moisture, and set the rice aside.

5. If you use canned clams, drain in a colander and reserve the liquid. Rinse the clams quickly under cold running water to remove any sand. Strain the liquid through a sieve lined with a cloth or paper towel, and reserve for another use. (It can be frozen.)

6. In a large bowl combine the rice, the mussels, the shrimp, the clams, and the minced parsley, and mix.

7. In a small bowl combine the oil, the lemon juice, the pepper, and 2 tbs. of the mussel liquid. Stir the mixture, and pour over the rice. Toss the rice gently, making sure the ingredients are well mixed.

8. Arrange the rice salad on an oblong serving platter, mounding it slightly in the center. Decorate with the mussels in their half shells and the whole shrimp.

Note: This salad can be prepared several hours in advance and refrigerated. In that case remove the salad from the refrigerator about two hours before serving. Mussels must be used the same day they are bought.

Estimated Cooking Time: 50 minutes
Estimated Total Preparation Time: 2 hours and 15 minutes

∾ INSALATA DI RISO CAMPAGNOLA ∾
Rice Salad Country Style   For 4 to 6

salt
1 cup Carolina long grain rice
3 frankfurters
1 8-oz. jar mixed pickles (mild
   giardiniera), drained and diced
¼ cup sweet gherkins, diced

2 tbs. capers, drained
¼ cup marinated artichoke
   hearts, quartered
2 tbs. fresh parsley, minced
1½ cups mayonnaise (see
   Mayonnaise, p. 17)

1. Bring 3 to 4 quarts water with 1½ tbs. salt to a boil. Sprinkle the rice into the water, stir once or twice, and cook over medium-high heat for about 14 minutes, or until just tender.

2. Drain the rice in a colander, and rinse under cold water. Shake the colander to remove most of the moisture, and set the rice aside.

3. Heat water in a small saucepan, and cook the frankfurters for about 5 minutes. Drain, and cut into ¼" slices.

4. In a large bowl combine the rice, the frankfurters, the pickles, the gherkins, 1 tbs. capers, the artichoke hearts, and 1 tbs. parsley. Mix the ingredients together.

5. Add the mayonnaise. (The mayonnaise should be creamy; if it is too thick, add some lemon juice.) Toss the salad gently, and taste for salt.

6. Arrange the rice salad on an oblong platter, mounding it slightly in the center. Sprinkle with the remaining parsley and capers. Serve at room temperature.

Note: This salad can be prepared several hours in advance.

Estimated Cooking Time: 25 minutes
Estimated Total Preparation Time: 45 minutes

∾ SUPPLI AL LIMONE ∾
Deep-Fried Lemon Rice Balls   Makes 30 to 40

Supplì—some say the name is a bastardization of the French word *surprise*, referring to the hidden mozzarella in the center—are nevertheless typically Roman. Traditionally a first course, the

Romani now eat them on the run at stand-up eating establishments (*tavole calde*). At the Bar Ungaria, a favorite spot in Rome's fashionable district of *Parioli*, you often see moviegoers stopping for a late night hot supplì.

2 quarts milk
2 cups Carolina long grain rice
1 tbs. butter
1 whole egg plus 3 egg yolks
1 cup freshly grated Parmesan
   cheese
1 lemon rind, grated

¼ tsp. nutmeg
salt
6 oz. mozzarella, cut into ¼"
   cubes
1 cup plain dry bread crumbs
2 cups vegetable oil

1. In a large heavy-bottomed saucepan bring the milk to a boil. Sprinkle the rice into the milk, and add the butter. Stir the rice once or twice, and cook over medium-low heat, stirring often, for about 14 minutes, or until just tender.

2. Drain the rice in a colander, and let cool.

3. Beat the whole egg and the yolks together in a large bowl, and combine with the rice. Add the Parmesan cheese, the lemon rind, the nutmeg, and ½ tsp. salt. Mix well, using a wooden spoon or your hands.

4. Take a small fistful of the rice (about 1½ tbs.), and make a hole in the center. Put a piece of mozzarella in the hole, enclose it, and shape the rice into a ball. Roll the ball in the bread crumbs, and place on a tray or cookie sheet. Continue this process with the remaining rice.

5. Refrigerate the balls for at least 1 hour to make sure that they are firm and that the bread crumbs have adhered well.

6. Heat the oil in a deep-frying pan over medium-high heat. When the oil is very hot, add the balls, a few at a time, and fry until golden brown.

7. Lift the balls out with a slotted spoon, and drain on brown paper.

8. Serve the suppli hot or at room temperature. (At room temperature the cheese will be firm rather than melted.)

Note: The suppli can be prepared the day before through step 5.

Estimated Cooking Time: 40 minutes
Estimated Total Preparation Time: 2 hours and 40 minutes

❦ SUPPLI AL RISO ROSSO ❦
Deep-Fried Red Rice Balls with Mozzarella

Makes 30 to 40

This is a great way to use leftover Tomato Risotto. If you are making the risotto for four, double the recipe, and use the remaining cooked rice for these delicious morsels. You could also substitute other leftover risotti, but we find that the red rice goes best.

1 recipe Tomato Risotto,
  chilled (p. 103)
salt
1 whole egg plus 1 egg yolk

6 oz. mozzarella cheese, cut into
  ¼" cubes
1 cup plain dry bread crumbs
2 cups vegetable oil

1. Taste a little of the cold rice, and add salt if necessary.
2. Beat the whole egg and the egg yolk together, and mix with the rice.
3. Take a small fistful of the rice (about 1½ tbs.), and make a hole in the center. Put a piece of mozzarella in the hole, enclose it, and shape the rice into a ball. Roll the ball in the bread crumbs, and place on a tray or cookie sheet. Continue this process with the remaining rice.
4. Refrigerate the balls for at least 1 hour to make sure that they are firm and that the bread crumbs have adhered well.
5. Heat the oil in a deep-frying pan over medium-high heat. When the oil is very hot, add the balls, a few at a time, and fry until golden brown.
6. Lift the balls out with a slotted spoon, and drain on brown paper.
7. Serve hot or at room temperature. (At room temperature the cheese will be firm rather than melted.)

Estimated Cooking Time: 15 minutes
Estimated Total Preparation Time: 2 hours

6 Pasta

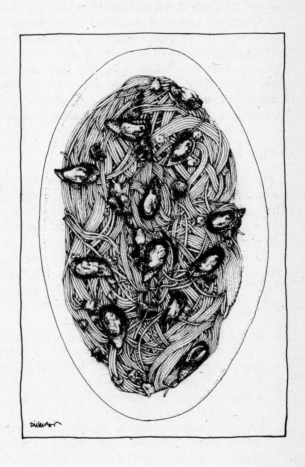

*P*asta, as old as Rome itself, is eaten in Italy in a variety of dried and fresh forms. Machine-made dry pasta, a product of the industrial revolution, has long been a favorite of southern Italy, but until recently it was scorned by northern Italians. Now, however, pasta has not only conquered the northern palate, but the world's. It is found in out-of-the-way Japanese coffee shops as well as American diners and has come a long way from the overcooked, stereotyped, pseudo-Italian "spaghetti and meatballs." With its great variety of shapes and forms, this healthy and nutritious staple lends itself to an infinite number of dishes. The outcome is sometimes rustic, sometimes refined, and always delicious.

Matching the Pasta and the Sauce

For most Italians eating pasta is an almost sensual rite, thus for best results the pasta-sauce match must make a good marriage. Although at times even Italians may argue over which pasta goes best with which sauce in cases where the distinction is ever so subtle, there are some definite dos and don'ts. The main determining factors are pasta size (long or short) and texture (dry and smooth, dry and ridged, or fresh). Listed below are some of the general rules, but keep in mind that every rule has its exceptions, especially in Italy. Some of the obvious exceptions are noted.

1. Butter and Parmesan cheese, the simplest pasta flavorings of all, are suitable for any long pasta, dry or fresh, such as spaghetti, linguine, vermicelli, and tagliolini, as well as for very small short pasta such as elbow macaroni or little shells.

2. Tomato sauce is the most versatile of all sauces and adapts to virtually any type of pasta, dry or fresh.

3. Fresh uncooked tomato sauce with a combination of basil and/or olives, anchovies, capers, garlic, and mozzarella is used mainly with spaghetti. The exceptions to this are Small Elbow Macaroni with Fresh Tomatoes, p. 182, and Rigatini with Mozzarella and Tomatoes, p. 190.

4. Seafood sauces should be combined only with long dry pasta, such as spaghetti, linguine, or vermicelli, and never, or almost never, with short or fresh pasta. Canned tuna, when combined with vegetables or used in pasta salads, is often adapted to

short pasta (Cavatelli with Tuna and Cauliflower, p. 170; Penne Salad, p. 188; and Tortiglioni Salad, p. 192). Yet, strictly speaking, these are not seafood sauces. Salmon and caviar sauces, because they are more refined and elegant, are used with long fresh pasta (Tagliolini with Smoked Salmon, p. 212; Tagliolini with Greek Tarama, p. 210; and Tagliolini with Caviar, p. 211).

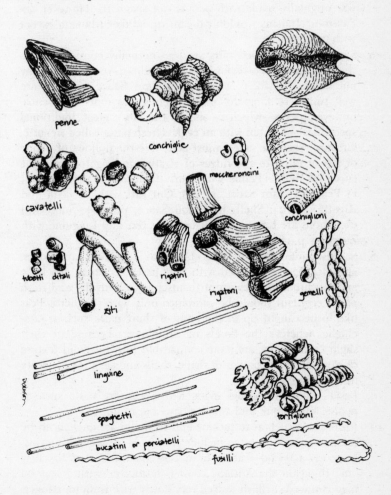

5. Rich clinging sauces that include any combination of butter, onions, ham or bacon, cheeses, cream, and tomatoes are usually mixed with short dry pasta such as penne, rigatini, and tortiglioni. Spaghetti alla Carbonara, p. 149, is perhaps the most obvious exception. It's interesting to note that this dish, which owes its name to the *carbonai* (the men who gather wood to burn into charcoal) from the mountains northeast of Rome, was originally made with penne, not spaghetti. However, today most Italians wouldn't dream of eating carbonara except with spaghetti.

6. Sauces with chopped nuts are also normally combined with short dry pasta (Tortiglioni Michelangelo, p. 191), but creamy nut sauces (Pesto, p. 177, and Walnut Sauce, p. 178) are well suited to long dry pasta, such as linguine. In Genoa, however, pesto—which is one of the city's great traditional specialties—is eaten with an eggless fresh pasta called trenette.

7. Creamy vegetable sauces must penetrate the hollows of penne or ziti or cling to the ridges of rigatini and rigatoni and the curves of shells (Penne with Curly Chicory, p. 183; Rigatini in Pepper Cream Sauce, p. 188; Cut Ziti with Broccoli and Ricotta, p. 193; Shells in Onion Sauce, p. 172). Successful exceptions are Linguine with Leeks, p. 180, and Linguine with Zucchini, p. 181.

8. Sauces containing such vegetables as eggplants, artichokes, and mushrooms are used with long pasta. Whereas artichoke and mushroom sauces adapt themselves to both dry and fresh pasta, eggplant should be combined only with spaghetti. Peas like to be caught up in the curls of short pasta such as conchiglie, whereas the florets of cauliflower, because of their slight crunchiness, are more compatible with the solid texture of cavatelli. Very similar in shape, shells and cavatelli are quite different in texture.

9. Pasta salads are always made with short dry pasta such as penne, tortiglioni, and small elbow macaroni.

10. Fresh pasta such as fettuccine and tagliolini are enchanced by refined sauces that often include cream. As we are writing this, however, a friend visiting from Italy mentions that the new "in" thing on the Adriatic coast is fettuccine with a seafood ragu (minced shellfish cooked very slowly with fresh tomatoes).

Some final advice: We recommend that you follow the recipe combinations here, including the exceptions to the usual rules. Eventually, you'll develop a feel for what works well. If you can't find the suggested pasta shape for a particular recipe, choose something similar as far as such general characteristics as long and thin, short and curly, short and hollow go.

How to Eat Pasta

Most pasta is best eaten in a wide, slightly shallow soup bowl. The rounded shape helps to keep the pasta and the sauce cradled together. Exceptions to this are some of the baked pastas such as lasagne and cannelloni and the rotoli, which are fine eaten on a regular flat dinner plate since the sauce is mainly on top.

Although many people have been taught to eat long pasta by twisting it around a fork held against the inside of a soup spoon, Italians don't eat it that way. In fact, it is considered bad table manners. The correct method is to pick a few strands of long pasta with the fork, hold the fork with the prongs against the bowl, and twist it around until most of the pasta is rolled around the fork. Unavoidably there will be some strands hanging when the pasta is cooked al dente.

Dry Pasta ~

Although pasta is one of the easiest dishes to prepare, it can turn into a disaster if not cooked properly. Abundant salted water and careful timing are essential to success. For one pound of dry pasta, use a six-quart pot, preferably a tall one. Fill it with four to five quarts of water, and bring to a boil. Add two scant tablespoons salt, and stir with a wooden spoon. When the water is bubbling vigorously, drop in the pasta all at once. When you cook spaghetti or other long pasta, push it in with your hand and, with the aid of a wooden spoon or fork, submerge it completely in the water. Stir with a wooden spoon or fork to prevent the strands from sticking together. This is a very important step. Cover the pot briefly to bring the water back to a boil quickly. Remove the cover, and slightly lower the heat to prevent the water from boiling over. Stir the pasta from time to time.

Packages of dry pasta usually provide cooking instructions. The cooking time suggested is invariably too long, and you should automatically subtract several minutes from it. About five to seven minutes before the suggested cooking time on the package, begin trying the pasta to see whether it's done. It should be firm but not rigid or stiff, presenting some resistance to the bite without being hard. If you break it with your fingers and the inner core is still white, it isn't done. When the pasta has reached the point called al dente, stop the cooking by pouring one cup of cold water into the pot. Drain the pasta in a colander immediately, and shake briskly a couple of times to remove all excess water.

Regardless of the sauce you are using, it must be ready when the pasta is done. If the pasta is not tossed with the sauce immediately, it continues to cook while it sits. It's a good idea to reserve one cup of the cooking water in case you need it to dilute the sauce.

When you cook two pounds of pasta, it isn't necessary to double the amount of water. Five to six quarts are sufficient. The estimated cooking time in the following recipes includes the approximately ten minutes it takes to bring the pasta water to a boil.

⌒ SPAGHETTI AL BURRO ⌒
Spaghetti with Butter and Cheese   For 4

Along with spaghetti and tomato sauce, this is one of the two classic ways of preparing spaghetti. It is a particular favorite among children.

1 lb. spaghetti   *½ cup freshly grated Parmesan*
salt   *cheese*
6 tbs. butter, cut into small pieces

1. Drop the spaghetti into 4 to 5 quarts boiling salted water.
2. Drain the spaghetti when al dente.
3. In a heated serving bowl toss the spaghetti with the butter and the Parmesan cheese, and serve.

Estimated Cooking Time: 20 minutes
Estimated Total Preparation Time: 25 minutes

∽ SPAGHETTI AL POMODORO ∽
Spaghetti with Tomato Sauce   For 4

1 lb. spaghetti
salt
2 cups Basic Tomato Sauce I, II,
   or III, pp. 14–16

2 tbs. butter
½ cup freshly grated Parmesan
   cheese

1. Drop the spaghetti into 4 to 5 quarts boiling salted water.
2. While the spaghetti is cooking, heat the tomato sauce over medium-low heat.
3. Drain the spaghetti when al dente.
4. Combine the spaghetti, the sauce, and the butter in a heated serving bowl. Toss gently, and sprinkle the cheese on top. Serve immediately.

Note: Any leftovers can be used for Spaghetti Frittata (p. 167).

Estimated Cooking Time: 20 minutes
Estimated Total Preparation Time: 25 minutes

∽ SPAGHETTI ALLA CARBONARA I ∽
Spaghetti with Eggs and Bacon   For 4

Although Spaghetti alla Carbonara is a classic in Roman and Abruzzese cuisine, every cook has his or her favorite version of this dish. With Bucatini with Tomatoes and Pancetta and Spaghetti with Garlic, Oil, and Hot Chili Pepper, this is often the choice for a late night *spaghettata*.

2 tbs. butter
1 medium onion, minced
½ lb. lean bacon, cut into ½"
   strips (if using slab bacon, cut
   into ¼" cubes)
½ cup dry white wine

1 lb. spaghetti
salt
1 whole egg plus 3 egg yolks
½ cup freshly grated Parmesan
   cheese
freshly ground black pepper

1. Heat the butter in a skillet, and sauté the onion and bacon over medium heat for about 5 minutes.
2. Add the wine, and continue cooking over medium-low heat

until the wine is evaporated and the bacon is cooked but not crisp, 10 to 15 minutes.

3. Drop the spaghetti into 4 to 5 quarts boiling salted water.

4. In a warm serving bowl beat the whole egg and the yolks until creamy. Add the Parmesan cheese, and mix well.

5. Drain the spaghetti when al dente.

6. Add the spaghetti to the egg mixture, a little at a time, mixing thoroughly after each addition to prevent the eggs from scrambling (this is the key step).

7. Add the bacon sauce, toss well, and sprinkle with black pepper. Serve immediately.

Estimated Cooking Time: 25 to 30 minutes
Estimated Total Preparation Time: 40 minutes

∽ SPAGHETTI ALLA CARBONARA II ∽
Spaghetti with Eggs and Italian Bacon For 4

2 tbs. butter
¼ lb. pancetta (Italian bacon), diced
1 lb. spaghetti
salt

1 whole egg plus 2 egg yolks
½ cup freshly grated pecorino Romano cheese
freshly ground black pepper
¼ cup heavy cream

1. Heat the butter in a large skillet, and sauté the pancetta over medium heat until slightly browned. Keep warm.

2. Drop the spaghetti into 4 to 5 quarts boiling salted water.

3. In a bowl beat together the egg, the egg yolks, the pecorino cheese, and the pepper.

4. Drain the spaghetti when very al dente.

5. Add the spaghetti to the skillet along with the egg mixture and the cream. Toss for a minute over low heat, and serve immediately on a heated platter. Taste for salt.

Estimated Cooking Time: 25 minutes
Estimated Total Preparation Time: 35 minutes

∽ SPAGHETTI ALLA CARBONARA DI MAGRO ∽
Spaghetti in Egg Sauce For 4

4 egg yolks
1 lb. spaghetti
salt
6 tbs. butter
½ cup cream

juice of 1 lemon
⅓ cup fresh basil leaves, torn
   into small pieces
¼ tsp. freshly grated nutmeg

1. Put the egg yolks into a large shallow serving bowl, and beat slightly.
2. Drop the spaghetti into 4 to 5 quarts boiling salted water.
3. In a small saucepan or butter warmer, heat the butter and the cream until the cream is warm and the butter begins to melt.
4. Add the cream and butter to the egg yolks a little at a time to prevent the eggs from scrambling.
5. Drain the spaghetti when al dente.
6. Pour the spaghetti into the serving bowl. Toss with the sauce, and sprinkle with the lemon juice, the basil, and the nutmeg. Toss again, taste for salt, and serve immediately.

Estimated Cooking Time: 20 minutes
Estimated Total Preparation Time: 30 minutes

∽ SPAGHETTI ALLA CARRETTIERA ∽
Spaghetti Pushcart Style For 4

Here is one of the many versions of this highly recommended spaghetti dish from southern Italy.

1 lb. spaghetti
salt
6 tbs. olive oil
1 red chili pepper
   or
¼ tsp. red pepper flakes

1 garlic clove, mashed
4 anchovy fillets, chopped
¼ cup black Italian or Greek
   olives, pitted and chopped
½ tsp. dried oregano
3 tbs. fresh parsley, chopped

1. Drop the spaghetti into 4 to 5 quarts boiling salted water.
2. Warm the oil in a large skillet over low heat. Add the red

pepper, and sauté for 1 to 2 minutes. Add the garlic and the anchovies, and mash them gently together with a wooden spoon. Add the olives and the oregano. Stir, and turn the heat off.

3. Drain the spaghetti when al dente.

4. Add the spaghetti and parsley to the sauce. Toss well, taste for salt, and serve.

Estimated Cooking Time: 25 minutes
Estimated Total Preparation Time: 40 minutes

∽ SPAGHETTI CON MOZZARELLA ∽

Spaghetti with Tomato Sauce and Mozzarella　　For 4

1 egg
2 tbs. milk
salt
1 lb. mozzarella cheese, diced
1 lb. spaghetti

2 cups Basic Tomato Sauce III
　(p. 16), pureed
2 tbs. butter
¼ cup freshly grated Parmesan
　cheese

1. Preheat the oven to 425° F.

2. In a small bowl beat the egg with the milk and ½ tsp. salt. Add the mozzarella, stir, and set aside.

3. Drop the spaghetti into 4 to 5 quarts boiling salted water.

4. Heat the tomato sauce over medium-low heat.

5. Drain the spaghetti when very al dente, or 2 to 3 minutes before done.

6. In a large bowl toss the spaghetti with the tomato sauce, the butter, and the Parmesan cheese.

7. Put the spaghetti in a shallow oven-to-table baking dish. Spread the mozzarella mixture over the spaghetti, and bake for 5 to 10 minutes, or until the cheese is melted. Serve immediately.

Estimated Cooking Time: 30 minutes
Estimated Total Preparation Time: 45 minutes

∽ SPAGHETTI ALL'AGLIO, OLIO, E PEPERONCINO ∽
Spaghetti with Garlic, Oil, and Hot Chili Pepper   For 4

1 lb. spaghetti	2 large garlic cloves, peeled
salt	2 red chili peppers, whole
⅓ cup olive oil	2 tbs. fresh parsley, minced

1. Drop the spaghetti into 4 to 5 quarts boiling salted water.
2. Heat the oil in a small saucepan over medium heat. Add the garlic and the red chili peppers, and sauté until the garlic is golden. Remove the garlic and the pepper.
3. Drain the spaghetti when al dente.
4. In a heated bowl combine the spaghetti, the oil, and the parsley, and toss well. Taste for salt, and serve immediately.

Estimated Cooking Time: 20 minutes
Estimated Total Preparation Time: 25 minutes

∽ SPAGHETTI CON LE ACCIUGHE ∽
Spaghetti in Anchovy Sauce   For 4

This is a simple, tasty, not at all fishy dish to which the bread crumbs add a delicious texture.

1 lb. spaghetti	¼ cup olive oil
salt	3 tbs. butter
10 anchovy fillets, minced	2 tbs. plain dry bread crumbs
2 cloves garlic, chopped	

1. Drop the spaghetti into 4 to 5 quarts boiling salted water.
2. Place the anchovies, the garlic, the oil, and the butter in a skillet, and cook over low heat, stirring and mashing, until the ingredients form a fairly smooth sauce. Add the bread crumbs, and cook 2 to 3 minutes longer, allowing the bread crumbs to brown.
3. Drain the spaghetti when very al dente. Add it to the skillet with the anchovy sauce, and toss over low heat until the spaghetti is well coated. Serve immediately.

Estimated Cooking Time: 20 minutes
Estimated Total Preparation Time: 30 minutes

⌒ SPAGHETTI CON LE VONGOLE ⌒
Spaghetti with Baby Clams For 4

2 doz. fresh littleneck clams
        or
1 10-oz. can Italian baby clams
1 lb. spaghetti

salt
⅓ cup olive oil
2 garlic cloves, mashed
¼ cup fresh parsley, minced

1. Wash and scrub the clams thoroughly under cold running water to remove all sand and dirt, discarding any open ones. Soak them in cold water for one hour, changing the water frequently. Drain, and place in a large heavy saucepan over medium-high heat. Cover the saucepan, and shake it every few minutes so the clams open evenly. When they open, remove all but 8 from their shells, and set aside. Discard any clams that do not open. Strain the liquid through a sieve lined with a cloth, and reserve.

If you use canned clams, drain them in a colander, reserving the liquid. Rinse the clams quickly under cold water to remove any sand. Strain the liquid through a cloth or paper towel, and set aside.

2. Drop the spaghetti into 4 to 5 quarts boiling salted water.

3. Heat the oil in a large skillet, and sauté the garlic over medium heat for 1 to 2 minutes. Add the liquid from the clams or the canned clam juice, and boil until it is reduced.

4. Add the clams, and cook for another 1 to 2 minutes.

5. Drain the spaghetti when al dente.

6. Add the spaghetti and the parsley to the skillet, and toss well. Taste for salt, and serve immediately on a heated oblong platter garnished with the reserved clams in the shells.

Estimated Cooking Time: 25 minutes
Estimated Total Preparation Time: 2 hours (fresh clams); 30 minutes
(canned clams)

∽ SPAGHETTI ALLE VONGOLE MACCHIATI ∽
Pink Spaghetti with Clams   For 4

2 doz. fresh littleneck clams
    or
1 10-oz. can Italian baby clams
1 lb. spaghetti
salt
⅓ cup olive oil

2 garlic cloves, mashed
½ red chili pepper, crushed
    or
⅛ tsp. red pepper flakes
⅓ cup Basic Tomato Sauce I,
p. 14

1. Wash and scrub the clams thoroughly under cold running water to remove all sand and dirt, discarding any open ones. Soak them in cold water for one hour, changing the water frequently. Drain the clams, and place them in a large heavy saucepan over medium-high heat. Cover the saucepan, and shake it every few minutes so the clams open evenly. When they are opened, remove all but 8 from the shells, and set aside. Discard any clams that do not open. Strain the liquid through a sieve lined with a cloth, and reserve for later use (it can be frozen).

If you use canned clams, drain them in a colander, and rinse quickly under cold water to remove any sand.

2. Drop the spaghetti into 4 to 5 quarts boiling salted water.

3. Heat the oil in a large skillet, and sauté the garlic and the chili pepper over medium-high heat for 2 to 3 minutes.

4. Add the clams, cook for another 1 to 2 minutes, and turn the heat off.

5. Drain the spaghetti when al dente.

6. Add the spaghetti and the tomato sauce to the skillet, and toss for 1 to 2 minutes over low heat. Taste for salt, and serve immediately on a heated oblong platter garnished with the reserved clams in the shells.

Estimated Cooking Time: 25 minutes
Estimated Total Preparation Time: 2 hours (fresh clams); 30 minutes
                                      (canned clams)

∽ SPAGHETTI CON LE COZZE ∽
Spaghetti with Mussels   For 4

A delicious and decorative seafood dish well worth the time it takes to prepare.

3 lbs. fresh mussels	1 lb. spaghetti
3 tbs. cornmeal	salt
5 tbs. olive oil	¼ cup fresh parsley, minced
2 garlic cloves, mashed	freshly ground black pepper
2 ripe plum tomatoes, peeled, seeded, and cut into thin strips	

1. Wash and scrub the mussels thoroughly under cold running water to remove all sand and dirt, discarding any open ones. With a knife scrape off any protruding hair. Soak the mussels in cold water with 1 tbs. cornmeal for 1 hour, changing the water twice and adding 1 tbs. of fresh cornmeal each time. Drain the mussels, rinse in cold water, and place in a large heavy saucepan over medium-high heat. Cover the saucepan, and shake it every few minutes so the mussels open evenly. When they open, remove all but 12 from their shells, and set aside. Discard any mussels that do not open. Strain the liquid through a sieve lined with a cloth, and set aside.

2. Heat the oil in a large skillet, add the garlic and the tomatoes, and sauté over medium-high heat for about 2 minutes. Add the liquid from the mussels, and cook for 5 minutes longer, or until the liquid is reduced to about 2 tbs. Turn the heat off.

3. Drop the spaghetti into 4 to 5 quarts boiling salted water.

4. Add the shelled mussels, the parsley, ½ tsp. salt, and the pepper to the tomato mixture, and cook for 2 to 3 minutes over medium heat.

5. Drain the spaghetti when al dente.

6. Add the spaghetti to the skillet, and toss well. Serve immediately on a heated oblong platter garnished with the mussels in their shells.

Note: Mussels must be used the same day they are bought.

Estimated Cooking Time: 20 minutes
Estimated Total Preparation Time: 1 hour and 30 minutes

⌣ SPAGHETTI CON TONNO E POMODORO ⌣
Spaghetti with Tuna and Tomato Sauce   For 4

2 tbs. butter
4 tbs. olive oil
1 small onion, minced
1 28-oz. can Italian-style plum
  tomatoes, chopped
2 anchovy fillets, chopped
1 lb. spaghetti

salt
1 6½-oz. can chunk light tuna,
  drained
freshly ground black pepper
½ cup fresh basil leaves, torn
  into pieces

1. Heat the butter and 2 tbs. oil in a large skillet over medium heat. Add the onion, and sauté until soft and translucent. Add the tomatoes and the anchovies, and cook them, uncovered, for about 15 minutes.

2. While the sauce is cooking, drop the spaghetti into 4 to 5 quarts boiling salted water.

3. Add the tuna to the sauce, and stir. Add the pepper, and taste for salt. Keep sauce warm.

4. Drain the spaghetti when al dente.

5. Add the spaghetti to the sauce, and toss quickly and thoroughly. Add the basil, sprinkle with the remaining oil, toss again, and serve immediately on a heated platter.

Estimated Cooking Time: 30 minutes
Estimated Total Preparation Time: 50 minutes

⌣ SPAGHETTI CON I CALAMARI ⌣
Spaghetti with Squid   For 4

2 lbs. fresh squid
4 tbs. olive oil
1 large garlic clove, mashed
salt

½ cup white wine
2 cups Basic Tomato Sauce III,
  p. 16
1 lb. spaghetti

1. Remove the tentacles from the sacs of the squid. Cut them above the eyes, discarding the rest. Rinse under cold running water, and set aside. Pull the skin off the sacs with your fingers,

and remove the cartilage-like bone as well as any gelatinous matter from the sacs. Rinse thoroughly under cold running water. Cut the sacs into thin rings and the tentacles into ½″ pieces.

2. Heat the oil in a medium saucepan over medium heat. Add the squid, the garlic, and ½ tsp. salt, and cook for about 5 minutes longer. Add the tomato sauce, turn the heat to low, and continue cooking for 5 to 10 minutes.

3. While the sauce is cooking, drop the spaghetti into 4 to 5 quarts boiling salted water.

4. Drain the spaghetti when al dente.

5. Toss the spaghetti with the squid sauce on an oblong platter, and serve immediately.

Estimated Cooking Time: 30 minutes
Estimated Total Preparation Time: 1 hour and 15 minutes

ᴖ SPAGHETTI ALLA MARINARA ᴖ
Spaghetti with Seafood
For 4 to 5

An old family recipe that has never failed to win an enthusiastic response.

½ oz. dried mushrooms
1 doz. fresh littleneck clams
      or
¾ cup canned Italian baby clams
1 lb. fresh mussels
      or
¾ cup canned mussels
3 tbs. cornmeal
4 tbs. olive oil

1 lb. ripe tomatoes, peeled,
    seeded, and coarsely chopped
1 garlic clove, minced
1 lb. spaghetti
salt
½ 6½-oz. can chunk light tuna,
    drained and flaked
freshly ground black pepper

1. Soak the mushrooms in 1 cup of warm water for 30 minutes. Drain, and cut into 2 to 3 pieces.

2. Wash and scrub the clams and the mussels thoroughly under cold running water to remove all sand and dirt, discarding any open ones. With a knife scrape off any hair protruding from the mussels. Soak the clams and the mussels in cold water with 1 tbs. cornmeal for one hour, changing the water twice and adding 1 tbs. of fresh cornmeal each time. Drain the clams and the mussels,

rinse in cold water, and place in a large heavy saucepan over medium-high heat. Cover the saucepan, and shake it every few minutes so the mussels and clams open evenly. When they are opened, remove them from the shells, discarding any that do not open. Halve or quarter them depending on the size, and put aside. Strain the liquid through a sieve lined with a cloth, and set aside.

If you use canned shellfish, drain in a colander, and rinse quickly under cold water to remove any sand. Strain the liquid through a sieve lined with a cloth or paper towel, and reserve 2 tbs.

3. Heat the olive oil in a large skillet, and sauté the tomatoes and the garlic over high heat for about 5 minutes. Add the mushrooms, and continue cooking for another 5 minutes.

4. Drop the spaghetti into 4 to 5 quarts boiling salted water.

5. Add the mussels, the clams, the tuna, and 2 tbs. of the shellfish liquid to the sauce. Stir, and cook a few minutes longer. Add salt and pepper to taste.

6. Drain the spaghetti when al dente.

7. Add the spaghetti to the seafood mixture. Toss well, and serve immediately on a heated platter.

Note: Mussels must be used the same day they are bought.

Estimated Cooking Time: 25 minutes
Estimated Total Preparation Time: 2 hours and 15 minutes (fresh shellfish); 1 hour (canned shellfish)

∽ SPAGHETTI CON CARCIOFI ∽
Spaghetti with Artichokes   For 4

2 large or 3 medium artichokes
1 lemon, halved
6 tbs. olive oil
2 garlic cloves, mashed
⅓ cup fresh parsley, chopped
1 large beef bouillon cube, dissolved in ½ cup water

1 lb. spaghetti
salt
2 tbs. butter
½ cup freshly grated Parmesan cheese
freshly ground black pepper

1. Cut off the artichoke stems, leaving about 1". Break off the small leaves at the base, and cut off about 1" from the top. Snap

off the hard upper part of the leaves, and peel the tough outer layer from the stems. Cut the artichokes in half lengthwise, and remove the fuzzy choke and the prickly leaves around it. Rub the halves with a piece of lemon to prevent discoloration. Slice each half crosswise very thinly.

2. Heat the oil in a medium saucepan, preferably enamel or stainless steel to avoid discoloration. Add the artichokes, the garlic, and ¼ cup parsley, and sauté, uncovered, over medium-low heat for about 10 minutes. Add the bouillon, and continue cooking, partially covered, over low heat for 15 to 20 minutes, or until tender. If the sauce becomes too dry, add more water. Add the remaining parsley, stir, and turn the heat off.

3. While the sauce is cooking, drop the spaghetti into 4 to 5 quarts boiling salted water.

4. Drain the spaghetti when al dente.

5. In a large serving bowl toss the spaghetti with the butter, the sauce, the Parmesan cheese, and the pepper. Taste for salt, and serve immediately.

Estimated Cooking Time: 40 minutes
Estimated Total Preparation Time: 1 hour

∽ SPAGHETTI CON LE MELANZANE ∽
Spaghetti with Eggplant   For 4

1 *large eggplant (about 1 lb.)*   1 *lb. spaghetti*
              or   3 *tbs. fresh parsley, minced*
1 *lb. small Italian eggplants*   ½ *cup freshly grated ricotta*
salt   *salata (aged ricotta)*
7 *tbs. olive oil*   *or*
1 *28-oz. can Italian-style plum*   *pecorino Sardo*
   tomatoes, chopped   *freshly ground black pepper*
1 *large garlic clove, mashed*

1. Wash and dry the eggplant. Cut lengthwise into 4 pieces, and cut each piece into ⅓" slices. If you use small eggplants, cut them in half, and then slice. Place the slices in a colander, sprinkle with ¾ tsp. salt, and let drain for 30 to 40 minutes. Dry with paper towels.

2. Heat 5 tbs. oil in a large saucepan over medium-high heat, add the eggplant, and sauté for 15 to 20 minutes, or until brown and soft. Add the tomatoes and the garlic, and cook for another 15 minutes.

3. Drop the spaghetti into 4 to 5 quarts boiling salted water.

4. Add the parsley and the remaining oil to the sauce, stir, and taste for salt.

5. Drain the spaghetti when al dente.

6. Add the spaghetti, the cheese, and the pepper to the sauce. Toss well, and serve on a shallow heated dish.

Estimated Cooking Time: 50 minutes
Estimated Total Preparation Time: 1 hour and 35 minutes

∽ SPAGHETTI CON LE MELANZANE FRITTE ∽
Spaghetti with Fried Eggplant For 4

1 *lb. small Italian eggplants*	1 *lb. ripe Italian plum tomatoes,*
or	*peeled, seeded, and chopped*
1 *large eggplant (about 1 lb.)*	*or*
salt	1 1-*lb. can Italian-style plum*
4 *tbs. olive oil*	*tomatoes, chopped*
1 *small onion, minced*	1 *cup vegetable oil*
1 *garlic clove, mashed*	1 *lb. spaghetti*
	10 *to* 15 *fresh basil leaves, torn*
	into pieces

1. Wash and dry the eggplants. Cut them lengthwise into ⅛″ slices. If you use one large eggplant, cut it crosswise instead. Place the slices in a colander, sprinkle with ¾ tsp. salt, and let drain for 30 to 40 minutes. Dry with paper towels.

2. Heat the oil in a medium saucepan over medium heat. Add the onion, and sauté until soft and translucent. Add the garlic, the tomatoes, and ¼ tsp. salt, and continue cooking, uncovered, for about 10 minutes, or until the sauce is fairly thick.

3. Heat the vegetable oil in a large skillet over medium-high heat. When the oil is very hot, slide in the eggplant slices in a single layer. Turn the slices once, and when browned on both sides, remove and drain on brown paper. Continue this process with the rest of the eggplant.

4. Drop the spaghetti into 4 to 5 quarts boiling salted water.

5. Drain the spaghetti when al dente.

6. Toss the spaghetti with the tomato sauce and half the eggplant slices on an oblong heated platter. Garnish with the remaining eggplant, and sprinkle the basil on top. Serve immediately.

Estimated Cooking Time: 1 hour
Estimated Total Preparation Time: 2 hours

◇ SPAGHETTI CON FUNGHI ◇

Spaghetti with Fresh Mushrooms   For 4

1 lb. mushrooms	4 tsp. lemon juice
1 lb. spaghetti	¼ cup fresh parsley, minced
salt	2 tbs. olive oil
2 tbs. butter	freshly ground black pepper
2 tbs. vegetable oil	

1. Remove the mushroom stems. If the caps are relatively clean, wipe them thoroughly with a damp paper towel. If there is a lot of soil and grit clinging to the caps, rinse thoroughly but quickly in cold water, rubbing them against each other to dislodge the dirt. Dry with paper towels, and slice thinly.

2. Drop the spaghetti into 4 to 5 quarts boiling salted water.

3. Heat the butter and vegetable oil in a large skillet over medium-high heat. Add the mushrooms, 3 tsp. lemon juice, and the parsley, and sauté quickly for about 3 minutes. Be careful not to cook the mushrooms to the point when they give off their liquid; they should be white and crisp. Add salt to taste.

4. Drain the spaghetti when al dente.

5. Add the spaghetti and the olive oil to the skillet. Sprinkle with the remaining lemon juice, and taste for salt and black pepper. Toss quickly, and serve.

Note: The mushroom stems may be used for risottos; in the filling for cannelloni; and in the sauces for pasta rolls and Green Raviolini Baked in a Crust (p. 233).

Estimated Cooking Time: 20 minutes
Estimated Total Preparation Time: 40 minutes

ᵔ SPAGHETTI CON FUNGHI E PISELLI ᵔ
Spaghetti with Peas and Mushrooms For 4

½ lb. mushrooms
6 tbs. butter
1 small onion, minced
1 lb. fresh peas, shelled
    or
8 oz. frozen tiny peas, rinsed
    quickly under hot water

salt
1 lb. spaghetti
½ cup freshly grated Parmesan
    cheese
2 eggs, slightly beaten
freshly ground black pepper

1. Trim off the ends of the mushroom stems. If the mushrooms are relatively clean, wipe them thoroughly with a damp paper towel. If there is a lot of soil and grit clinging to the caps, rinse thoroughly but quickly in cold water, rubbing them against each other to dislodge the dirt. Dry with paper towels, and slice thinly.

2. Heat the butter in a medium skillet, and sauté the onion over medium heat until soft and translucent.

3. If you are using fresh peas, add them with ½ cup water, and cook, covered, over low heat for 15 to 18 minutes, or until the peas are barely tender and fairly dry. Sprinkle with ¼ tsp. salt, and stir. Add the mushrooms, and sauté 5 to 7 minutes longer. If you are using frozen peas, add the mushrooms, and sauté 3 to 5 minutes. Add the peas and ¼ tsp. salt, and sauté 3 to 5 minutes longer.

4. Drop the spaghetti into 4 to 5 quarts boiling salted water.

5. In a large serving bowl combine the Parmesan cheese and the beaten eggs.

6. Add the mushrooms and peas, a little at a time, to the cheese and eggs. Mix well to combine all the ingredients thoroughly.

7. Drain the spaghetti when al dente. Toss with the sauce, taste for salt, and serve immediately with a grinding of black pepper.

Estimated Cooking Time: 40 minutes (fresh peas); 25 minutes (frozen peas)
Estimated Total Preparation Time: 1 hour (fresh peas); 45 minutes (frozen peas)

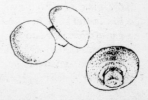

∽ SPAGHETTI CON FUNGHI E FONTINA ∽
Spaghetti with Mushrooms and Fontina Cheese   For 4

1 lb. mushrooms	salt
7 tbs. butter	1 lb. spaghetti
1 medium onion, minced	6 oz. Fontina cheese, diced
½ cup dry vermouth	freshly ground black pepper

1. Trim off the ends of the mushroom stems. If the mushrooms are relatively clean, wipe them thoroughly with a damp paper towel. If there is a lot of soil and grit clinging to the caps, rinse thoroughly but quickly in cold water, rubbing them against each other to dislodge the dirt. Dry with paper towels, and slice thinly.

2. Heat 5 tbs. butter in a large skillet over medium heat. Add the onion, and sauté until soft and translucent.

3. Add the mushrooms to the skillet. Turn the heat to high, and sauté for 5 minutes. Add the vermouth and ½ tsp. salt, and sauté 5 minutes longer, or until the liquid is reduced to about ¼ cup. Keep warm.

4. Drop the spaghetti into 4 to 5 quarts boiling salted water.

5. Drain the spaghetti when al dente.

6. Add the spaghetti, the cheese, and the remaining butter to the sauce, and toss well until the cheese is melted. Taste for salt.

7. Serve immediately with a grinding of black pepper.

Note: The mushroom sauce can be prepared several hours in advance and kept covered. Reheat before adding the spaghetti.

Estimated Cooking Time: 25 minutes
Estimated Total Preparation Time: 45 minutes

∽ SPAGHETTI ALLA BURINA ∽
Spaghetti Peasant Style   For 4

2 green peppers	1 lb. spaghetti
½ lb. small Italian eggplants	½ cup Italian or Greek black
4 tbs. olive oil	olives, pitted and slivered
2 tbs. butter	8 anchovy fillets, chopped
1 garlic clove, minced	8 to 10 fresh basil leaves, torn
1 1-lb. can Italian-style plum	into small pieces
tomatoes, quartered	freshly ground black pepper
salt	

1. Wash and dry the peppers. Place them on a rack as close as possible to the broiler and sear on all sides. When the skins of the peppers have loosened and are slightly charred (5 to 10 minutes), remove the peppers from the broiler, and peel off the skins. Halve the peppers, remove the seeds, and cut into ¼" strips.

2. Wash and dry the eggplants. Cut lengthwise into ¼" strips.

3. Heat 2 tbs. oil and the butter in a large heavy skillet over medium-high heat. Add the eggplant, and sauté for about 5 minutes, or until slightly browned. Add the garlic and the tomatoes, and cook for about 10 minutes. Add the peppers and 1 tsp. salt, and continue cooking for 5 minutes longer.

4. While the sauce is cooking, drop the spaghetti into 4 to 5 quarts boiling salted water.

5. Add the olives, the anchovies, the basil, and the pepper to the sauce. Stir well, and cook for 2 to 3 minutes longer. Taste for salt.

6. Drain the spaghetti when al dente, reserving ¼ cup of the cooking water.

7. Add the spaghetti, the remaining oil, and the cooking water to the sauce. Toss well, and serve immediately.

Estimated Cooking Time: 35 minutes
Estimated Total Preparation Time: 50 minutes

∽ SPAGHETTI ESTIVI ∽
Summer Spaghetti   For 4

1½ lbs. ripe plum tomatoes,
   peeled and quartered
salt
pinch of sugar
1 garlic clove, mashed
1 lb. spaghetti

4 tbs. olive oil
¼ cup fresh basil leaves, torn
   into pieces
3 tbs. lemon juice
freshly ground black pepper

1. Place the tomatoes, ½ tsp. salt, and the sugar in a small saucepan, and cook over medium heat for 20 to 25 minutes, or until soft and fairly dry. Puree through a food mill into a bowl. Add the garlic and stir.

2. Drop the spaghetti into 4 to 5 quarts boiling salted water.

3. Drain the spaghetti when al dente.

4. In a large serving bowl combine the spaghetti, the tomato puree, the oil, the basil, and the lemon juice. Sprinkle with pepper. Toss well, and serve.

Note: The tomato puree can be prepared the day before and refrigerated. Warm slightly before using.

Estimated Cooking Time: 35 minutes
Estimated Total Preparation Time: 45 minutes

∽ SPAGHETTI ALLA PUTTANESCA ∾
Spaghetti Hooker Style I For 4

The folklore associated with this recipe claims that members of the oldest profession used to attract most of their customers with the cooking aromas from this spaghetti. Interestingly enough, both this recipe and the following one were given to us by male friends.

1 lb. spaghetti	2 tbs. Italian or Greek black
salt	olives, slivered
1 cup Basic Tomato Sauce II,	4 anchovy fillets, chopped
p. 15, at room temperature	1 red chili pepper, chopped
4 medium ripe tomatoes,	2 tbs. fresh basil leaves, torn into
preferably plum, cubed	small pieces
5 tbs. olive oil	1 tbs. fresh sage leaves, chopped
1 clove garlic, minced	(optional)
1 tbs. capers, drained	

1. Drop the spaghetti into 4 to 5 quarts boiling salted water.
2. In a serving bowl mix all the remaining ingredients.
3. Drain the spaghetti when al dente.
4. Add the spaghetti to the serving bowl. Toss, and serve.

Note: This dish is also excellent when prepared a few hours ahead of time and served cold.

Estimated Cooking Time: 20 minutes
Estimated Total Preparation Time: 40 minutes

∽ SPAGHETTI ALLA MALAFEMMINA ∽
Spaghetti Hooker Style II   For 4

6 tbs. olive oil
1 small onion, minced
1 clove garlic, mashed
4 anchovy fillets, cut into small
  pieces
2 tbs. capers, drained and
  chopped
3 tbs. Italian or Greek black
  olives, pitted and chopped

½ 6½-oz. can chunk light tuna,
  drained and crumbled
2 tbs. Italian-style pickles (mild
  giardiniera), chopped
2 tbs. fresh parsley, minced
1 lb. spaghetti
salt
1 tbs. lemon juice

1. Heat the oil in a large skillet, and sauté the onion over low heat for about 5 minutes.

2. Add the garlic and the anchovies, and mash together gently with a wooden spoon.

3. Add the capers, the olives, the tuna, the pickles, and the parsley, stirring continuously and mashing for a few minutes until the ingredients become a thick paste.

4. Drop the spaghetti into 4 to 5 quarts boiling salted water.

5. Add ½ cup water from the cooking pasta to the sauce, and continue stirring to combine the ingredients thoroughly.

6. Drain the spaghetti when al dente.

7. Add the spaghetti and the lemon juice to the sauce. Toss well, and serve.

Estimated Cooking Time: 30 minutes
Estimated Total Preparation Time: 45 minutes

∽ FRITTATA DI SPAGHETTI ∽
Spaghetti Frittata   For 4

2 cups leftover Spaghetti with
  Tomato Sauce, p. 149
½ cup Basic Tomato Sauce I, II,
  or III, pp. 14–16

6 eggs
¾ cup freshly grated Parmesan
  cheese
5 tbs. butter

1. Mix the spaghetti with the tomato sauce.

2. In a large bowl beat the eggs with a whisk, add the cheese and the spaghetti, and mix well.

3. Heat 4 tbs. butter in a medium skillet over medium heat. Pour in the egg mixture, turn the heat to low, and cook for about 10 minutes.

4. Loosen the frittata from the pan (the cheese sometimes causes it to stick), and turn it onto a dish, cooked side down.

5. Add the remaining butter to the pan, and slide in the frittata, soft side down. Cook this side for 3 to 4 minutes, or until well set, pressing down with a spatula to make sure that there is no liquid egg in the center.

6. Turn the frittata onto a platter, and let sit for at least 10 minutes before serving.

7. Serve the frittata cut into wedges.

Note: You can use any kind of leftover seasoned spaghetti for this frittata.

Estimated Cooking Time: 15 minutes
Estimated Total Preparation Time: 30 minutes

∽ BUCATINI ALL'AMATRICIANA ∽
Bucatini with Tomatoes and Pancetta   For 4

This most popular fare of Roman trattorias has antique origins in Amatrice, a small town in the mountainous region northeast of Rome. The original version did not include the tomatoes, which are a staple in Roman cuisine today. Although not easy to eat because the bucatini are slippery and hard to roll around a fork, resulting in unavoidable splatters, the wonderful combination of tastes is too good to change. Just remember to use a big napkin!

1 tbs. butter
1 tbs. olive oil
¼ lb. pancetta (Italian bacon), diced
2 red chili peppers, seeded and chopped
                or
½ tsp. red pepper flakes

1 recipe Basic Tomato Sauce III, p. 16
1 lb. bucatini (perciatelli)
salt
¼ cup freshly grated Parmesan cheese
¼ cup freshly grated pecorino Romano cheese

1. Heat the butter and oil in a medium skillet, and sauté the pancetta over medium heat for about 2 minutes. Do not let it brown.

2. Add the chili peppers. Stir well, and pour in the tomato sauce. Cook over medium-low heat for about 20 minutes, stirring from time to time.

3. Drop the bucatini into 4 to 5 quarts boiling salted water.

4. Drain the bucatini when al dente.

5. Pour the bucatini back into the pot. Add the sauce and the two cheeses, and toss well. Serve immediately in a heated bowl.

Note: The Amatriciana sauce can be prepared the day before. Reheat before adding the bucatini and the cheeses.

Estimated Cooking Time: 30 minutes
Estimated Total Preparation Time: 45 minutes

∽ BUCATINI AI FUNGHI ∽
Bucatini in Mushroom Sauce   For 4

½ oz. Italian or French dried
  mushrooms
½ lb. fresh mushrooms
4 tbs. butter
1 lb. bucatini (perciatelli)
salt
¼ cup cognac

1 cup heavy cream
3 1-oz. imported soft cheese
  wedges (such as La Vache
  Qui Rit)
½ cup freshly grated Parmesan
  cheese

1. Soak the dried mushrooms in 1 cup warm water for about 30 minutes. Drain, reserving the liquid, and chop coarsely. Strain the liquid through a sieve lined with a cloth or paper towel, and set aside.

2. Trim off the ends of the mushroom stems. If the mushrooms are relatively clean, wipe them thoroughly with a damp paper towel. If there is a lot of soil and dirt clinging to the caps, rinse thoroughly but quickly in cold water, rubbing them against each other to dislodge the dirt. Dry with paper towels, and slice thinly.

3. Heat 2 tbs. butter in a skillet, and sauté the dried mushrooms over low heat for about 10 minutes. Add ½ cup of the mushroom

liquid, and cook for 10 to 15 minutes more, until the mushrooms are soft and most of the liquid has evaporated.

4. Drop the bucatini into 4 to 5 quarts boiling salted water.

5. Add the fresh mushrooms to the skillet, and sauté with the dried mushrooms for 2 to 3 minutes over medium-high heat. Add the cognac, and continue cooking until the liquor has evaporated. Turn the heat off.

6. Drain the bucatini when very al dente.

7. Heat the mushrooms and the cream in the pasta pot. Add the bucatini, the cheese wedges, the Parmesan cheese, and the remaining butter. Toss well for 1 to 2 minutes, until the cheeses are melted and the ingredients are thoroughly blended. Serve immediately on a heated platter.

Estimated Cooking Time: 40 minutes
Estimated Total Preparation Time: 1 hour

∽ CAVATELLI CON TONNO E CAVOLFIORE ∽
Cavatelli with Tuna and Cauliflower   For 4

1 *medium cauliflower (about*	2 *garlic cloves, mashed*
1½ to 2 lbs.)	6 *anchovy fillets, minced*
salt	½ *6½-oz. can chunk light tuna,*
1 *lb. cavatelli*	*drained and flaked*
6 *tbs. olive oil*	*freshly ground black pepper*

1. Remove and discard the cauliflower leaves, and carefully separate the florets, discarding the thick core. Rinse the florets under cold water.

2. Drop the florets and 2 tbs. salt into 2 to 3 quarts boiling water, and cook over medium heat for 8 to 10 minutes, or until just tender. Drain, and set aside.

3. Drop the cavatelli into 4 to 5 quarts boiling salted water.

4. Heat the oil in a large skillet over low heat. Add the garlic and the anchovies, and sauté for 1 to 2 minutes without letting them brown. Add the tuna and cauliflower, and sauté until warm.

5. Drain the cavatelli when al dente.

6. Add the cavatelli to the cauliflower mixture. Toss well,

sprinkle with pepper, and taste for salt. Serve immediately on a round dish.

Note: This dish is also good at room temperature, several hours later. If it becomes too dry, add a little more oil.

Estimated Cooking Time: 25 minutes
Estimated Total Preparation Time: 45 minutes

∽ CONCHIGLIETTE CON PISELLI ∽
Small Shells with Peas

For 4

5 tbs. butter	pinch of sugar
¼ lb. pancetta, chopped	salt
2 tbs. scallions, thinly sliced	1 lb. small shells
1 lb. fresh peas, shelled	¼ lb. boiled or baked ham, diced
or	½ to ¾ cup freshly grated
1 cup frozen tiny peas, rinsed	Parmesan cheese
quickly under hot water	freshly ground black pepper

1. Heat 2 tbs. butter in a skillet over medium heat. Add the pancetta and the scallions, and sauté for 3 to 5 minutes or until the scallions are soft and translucent but not browned. If you are using fresh peas, add them with the sugar and ¾ cup water, and cook, covered, over low heat for 18 to 20 minutes, or until tender. Turn the heat off, and taste for salt. If you are using frozen peas, add them to the scallion and pancetta mixture, and cook for 2 to 3 minutes, then turn the heat off and taste for salt.

2. While the sauce is cooking, drop the shells into 4 to 5 quarts boiling salted water.

3. Drain the shells when al dente.

4. Pour the shells into the skillet with the pancetta, the scallions and the peas, and turn the heat on low. Add the remaining 3 tbs. butter, the ham, and ½ cup grated Parmesan cheese. Toss for 1 minute. Add the pepper to taste. Toss again, and serve immediately sprinkled with extra grated cheese.

Estimated Cooking Time: 40 minutes (fresh peas); 25 minutes (frozen peas)
Estimated Total Preparation Time: 1 hour (fresh peas); 40 minutes (frozen peas)

⌇ CONCHIGLIE CON SUGO DI CIPOLLE ⌇
Shells in Onion Sauce   For 4

6 tbs. butter
1½ lbs. onions (about 5 cups),
   thinly sliced
½ cup dry vermouth
½ large beef bouillon cube

1 lb. shells
salt
½ cup freshly grated pecorino
   Sardo cheese
freshly ground black pepper

1. Melt 4 tbs. butter in a heavy-bottomed saucepan over low heat. Add the onions, cover, and cook for 30 minutes.

2. Uncover the saucepan, add the vermouth and the ½ bouillon cube, and continue cooking over low heat for another 15 minutes. Keep warm.

3. While the sauce is cooking, drop the shells into 4 to 5 quarts boiling salted water.

4. Drain the shells when al dente.

5. Add the shells, the remaining butter, and the cheese to the sauce. Toss well, taste for salt, and serve in a heated bowl with a grinding of black pepper.

Estimated Cooking Time: 1 hour
Estimated Total Preparation Time: 1 hour and 15 minutes

⌇ CONCHIGLIONI RIPIENI ⌇
Jumbo Shells Filled with Ricotta   For 4 to 6

This always popular dish comes from one of the best kitchens in Rome. The hostess gave a special and most elegant dinner simply to introduce us to this family treasure.

2 tbs. butter
1 small onion
1½ lbs. ricotta
¾ cup freshly grated Parmesan
   cheese
1 cup cooked ham, shredded
¼ cup fresh parsley, minced
¼ cup heavy cream

salt
1 12-oz. package jumbo shells
2 cups Basic Tomato Sauce II,
   p. 15
3 tbs. fresh basil leaves, torn into
   pieces
                     or
1 tsp. dry sweet basil

1. Heat the butter in a small skillet, and sauté the onion over medium-low heat until soft and translucent.

2. In a large bowl place the ricotta, the Parmesan cheese, the ham, the parsley, the onion, the cream, and ½ tsp. salt and, with a wooden spoon, blend the ingredients thoroughly.

3. Drop the shells into 4 to 5 quarts boiling salted water.

4. Preheat the oven to 400° F.

5. Drain the shells when very al dente (3 to 4 minutes before end of usual cooking time).

6. Rinse the shells quickly under cold running water, and lay them on a dish towel spread over a flat surface.

7. Butter a large oven-to-table baking dish (about 10″ x 13″). Loosely stuff each shell with a spoonful of the ricotta mixture. Arrange the stuffed shells in the baking dish in one layer.

8. Warm the tomato sauce with the basil, and spoon over the shells.

9. Bake the shells for 15 to 20 minutes. Let settle for 5 minutes before serving.

Note: This pasta can be prepared a day in advance through step 7.

Estimated Cooking Time: 45 minutes
Estimated Total Preparation Time: 1 hour and 30 minutes

❖ GEMELLI AL FUNGHETTO ❖

Gemelli with Dried Mushroom Sauce   For 4

This is our version of a sensational pasta dish served at a little trattoria in Rome near Piazza Barberini. The dish combines the woodsy taste of the mushrooms with the smooth richness of a tomato-flavored cream sauce.

*4 oz. Italian or French dried
  mushrooms
6 tbs. butter
½ cup dry white wine
salt
1 lb. gemelli
      or
1 lb. small elbow macaroni*

*1½ cups heavy cream
4 tbs. tomato paste
½ cup freshly grated Parmesan
  cheese*

1. Soak the mushrooms in 2 cups warm water for about 30 minutes. Drain, reserving the liquid, and cut into 2 to 3 pieces.

Strain the liquid through a sieve lined with a cloth or paper towel, and set aside.

2. Heat 4 tbs. butter in a small saucepan, and sauté the mushrooms over low heat. Add the wine, and cook, uncovered, about 10 minutes, until it has evaporated. Add 1 cup of the mushroom liquid and ¼ tsp. salt, and simmer, uncovered, over low heat for about 30 minutes, until the mushrooms are very soft. The sauce should be thick but not dry.

3. Drop the gemelli into 4 to 5 quarts boiling salted water.

4. Heat the cream in a large skillet over low heat. Add the tomato paste, and mix thoroughly.

5. Drain the gemelli when al dente.

6. Add the gemelli and the remaining butter to the cream and tomato sauce. Toss well, and taste for salt.

7. Pour the gemelli into a shallow heated dish. Spoon the mushroom sauce on top, and serve immediately with the cheese on the side.

Estimated Cooking Time: 50 minutes
Estimated Total Preparation Time: 1 hour and 30 minutes

∽ FUSILLI ALLE OLIVE ∽
Fusilli with Olives

For 4

2 garlic cloves, mashed
1 red chili pepper, seeded and
    crushed
¼ cup fresh basil leaves, torn into
    pieces
                    or
1 tsp. dried sweet basil
½ cup olive oil
1 lb. fusilli
salt

1 1-lb. can Italian-style plum
    tomatoes, drained and coarsely
    chopped
3 tbs. canned tomato sauce
½ cup Italian green olives,
    pitted and coarsely chopped
½ cup Italian or Greek black
    olives, pitted and coarsely
    chopped
1 tbs. capers, drained
¼ cup fresh parsley, chopped

1. Place the garlic, the chili pepper, the dried basil (if fresh basil is not available), and the oil in a small bowl, and let them stand for about 2 hours.

2. Drop the fusilli into 4 to 5 quarts boiling salted water.

3. Heat 2 tbs. of the oil mixture in a medium skillet. Add the tomatoes, the tomato sauce, and ¼ tsp. salt, and sauté over high heat for about 5 minutes.

4. Drain the fusilli when al dente.

5. In a serving bowl combine the tomatoes, the fusilli, the olives, the capers, the parsley, the basil (if fresh basil is used), and the remaining oil mixture. Toss well, taste for salt, and serve.

Estimated Cooking Time: 20 minutes
Estimated Total Preparation Time: 2 hours and 20 minutes

∽ FUSILLI CON PEPERONI E PIGNOLI ∽

Fusilli with Sweet Peppers and Pine Nuts   For 4

A most unusual and pleasurable combination of flavors and textures, not to speak of color, this recipe comes from a Roman lawyer friend who is well known for her inventiveness in the kitchen.

1 *lb. fusilli*	2 *large sweet yellow or red*
salt	*peppers, washed, dried, seeded,*
4 *tbs. olive oil*	*and cut lengthwise into strips*
3 *tbs. butter*	½ *cup pine nuts*

1. Drop the fusilli into 4 to 5 quarts boiling salted water.

2. Heat the olive oil and 2 tbs. butter in a large skillet, and sauté the peppers over high heat for a few minutes, until slightly colored but still crisp. Turn the heat off.

3. In a small frying pan heat the remaining butter, and sauté the pine nuts over low heat for about 2 to 3 minutes, until lightly colored.

4. Drain the fusilli when al dente.

5. Add the fusilli to the skillet with the peppers. Toss, and taste for salt. Sprinkle the pine nuts on top. Serve immediately in a heated bowl.

Estimated Cooking Time: 25 minutes
Estimated Total Preparation Time: 35 minutes

∽ FUSILLI AL TONNO ∽
Fusilli with Tuna and Butter   For 4

A childhood favorite from Efrem's mother's closest friend—and rival in the kitchen—this is a great last-minute meal.

1 lb. fusilli
6 tbs. butter cut into small pieces
10 oz. chunk light tuna in oil
    (about 1 ½ cans), drained and
    flaked

½ cup freshly grated Parmesan
    cheese
¼ cup parsley, minced
freshly ground black pepper

1. Drop the fusilli into 4 to 5 quarts boiling salted water.
2. In a serving bowl mix the butter and the tuna.
3. Add all but 2 tbs. of the cheese to the tuna and butter, and mix well without creaming.
4. Drain the fusilli when al dente.
5. Add the fusilli and the parsley to the tuna mixture. Toss well, sprinkle with the remaining Parmesan and a grinding of black pepper, and serve.

Note: This dish is also good when prepared a few hours ahead of time and served cold. If it is to be served cold, add 2 tbs. of the cooking water to the tuna mixture.

Estimated Cooking Time: 25 minutes
Estimated Total Preparation Time: 30 minutes

∽ LINGUINE AL PESTO I ∽
Linguine with Basil Sauce (Mortar and Pestle) For 4

The controversy continues over whether pesto is best with or without pine nuts. This version and the following one, which uses a food processor, are without. If you wish to try pesto with pine nuts, see Rice and Potatoes with Pesto, p. 120.

2 cups fresh basil leaves, washed and dried
4 garlic cloves, slightly mashed
salt
⅓ cup freshly grated Parmesan cheese

⅓ cup freshly grated pecorino Sardo cheese
or
¼ cup freshly grated pecorino Romano cheese
½ cup olive oil
1 lb. linguine
2 tbs. butter

1. Place the basil leaves, the garlic, and the salt in a mortar, and mash with the pestle using a circular motion. Gradually add the cheeses until an evenly mixed paste is formed.
2. Add the oil a little at a time, stirring constantly with a wooden spoon until the mixture reaches a creamy consistency.
3. Drop the linguine into 4 to 5 quarts boiling salted water.
4. Drain the linguine when al dente, reserving 2 tbs. of the cooking water.
5. In a serving bowl toss the linguine with the butter, the basil sauce, and the 2 tbs. cooking water. Taste for salt. Serve immediately on a heated platter.

Note: The best mortars for making pesto are made of marble or stone. Pesto keeps for months in the refrigerator. When you prepare it for storing, omit the garlic and the cheeses and add them just before using. Store, covered with a layer of olive oil, in a jar. For storing, however, we recommend the version with the pine nuts (p. 120).

Estimated Cooking Time: 20 minutes
Estimated Total Preparation Time: 60 minutes

∾ LINGUINE AL PESTO II ∾
Linguine with Pesto (Food Processor) For 4

1 lb. linguine
salt
2 cups fresh basil leaves, washed
   and dried
4 garlic cloves, slightly mashed
½ cup olive oil
⅓ cup freshly grated Parmesan
   cheese

⅓ cup freshly grated pecorino
   Sardo cheese
       or
¼ cup freshly grated pecorino
   Romano cheese
2 tbs. butter

1. Drop the linguine into 4 to 5 quarts boiling salted water.
2. Place the basil leaves, the garlic, ½ tsp. salt, and the oil in a food processor, and chop for 60 seconds to make a smooth paste. Stop every 20 seconds to scrape the mixture from the sides.
3. Add the cheeses, and process for 5 seconds longer.
4. Drain the linguine when al dente, reserving 2 tbs. of the cooking water.
5. In a heated bowl toss the linguine with the butter, the basil sauce, and the 2 tbs. cooking water. Taste for salt. Serve immediately on a heated platter.

Note: For storage, see note for previous recipe.

Estimated Cooking Time: 20 minutes
Estimated Total Preparation Time: 40 minutes

∾ LINGUINE CON LE NOCI ∾
Linguine with Walnuts For 4

Unlike the cuisine of other regions of Italy, Genoese cooking uses nuts extensively. This flavorful dish is in the pesto tradition.

1 lb. linguine
salt
¾ cup walnuts
1 garlic clove, slightly mashed

1 cup heavy cream
3 tbs. butter cut into pieces
1 cup freshly grated Parmesan
   cheese

1. Drop the linguine into 4 to 5 quarts boiling salted water.
2. Put the walnuts and garlic in a processor, and chop for 15 to 20 seconds. Add the cream, and process for another 10 seconds.

Add 2 tbs. of the cooking water and ½ tsp. salt, and process 1 or 2 seconds longer.

3. Remove the sauce to a serving bowl, and mix with the butter and the cheese.

4. Drain the linguine when al dente.

5. Add the linguine to the serving bowl, toss, and serve.

Estimated Cooking Time: 20 minutes
Estimated Total Preparation Time: 25 minutes

◇ LINGUINE CON CARCIOFI E PISELLI ◇
Linguine with Artichokes and Peas For 4

2 large artichokes	3 tbs. cured ham, slivered
½ lemon	salt
4 tbs. butter	1 lb. linguine
2 tbs. olive oil	1 cup heavy cream
½ chicken bouillon cube,	½ cup freshly grated Parmesan
dissolved in ½ cup water	cheese
1 lb. fresh peas	
or	
8 oz. frozen tiny peas	

1. Cut off the stems of the artichokes leaving about 1". Break off the small leaves at the base, and cut off about 1" from the top. Snap off the hard upper part of the leaves, and peel the tough outer layer from the stems. Cut the artichokes in half lengthwise, and remove the choke, as well as the prickly leaves around it. Rub the halves with the lemon to prevent discoloration. Cut each half into very thin lengthwise slices.

2. Heat 2 tbs. butter and the oil in a heavy skillet, preferably enamel, over medium heat. Add the artichokes, and sauté for 3 to 5 minutes. Add the bouillon, and cook, covered, over low heat for about 5 minutes if you are using fresh peas. Add the peas, and continue cooking 15 minutes longer. If you are using frozen peas, cook artichokes and bouillon for about 20 minutes, then add the peas.

3. Add the ham, raise the heat to medium, and cook 5 minutes longer. Taste for salt.

4. Drop the linguine into 4 to 5 quarts boiling salted water.

5. Add the cream to the artichoke mixture, and cook for 3 to 4 minutes, until the cream has thickened.

6. Drain the linguine when al dente.

7. Add the linguine, the remaining butter, and the cheese to the sauce, toss well, and serve immediately on a heated platter.

Estimated Cooking Time: 40 minutes
Estimated Total Preparation Time: 1 hour and 15 minutes (fresh peas); 1 hour (frozen peas)

∽ LINGUINE CON I PORRI ∽

Linguine with Leeks   For 4

6 *leeks*	*salt*
5 *tbs. butter*	*freshly ground black pepper*
2 *tbs. vegetable oil*	1 *lb. linguine*
1 *cup homemade chicken broth*	½ *cup freshly grated Parmesan*
or	*cheese*
1 *large chicken bouillon cube,*	
dissolved in 1 cup water	

1. Cut off the root ends and all but 2″ of the green parts of the leeks. Slit them in half lengthwise, and wash thoroughly under running cold water. Dry, and slice very thinly crosswise.

2. Heat 3 tbs. butter and the oil in a large skillet, and sauté the leeks over medium-high heat for about 5 minutes. Add the chicken broth, and cook, covered, over low heat for about 30 minutes. The sauce will become slightly brown and very thick. Add salt and pepper to taste.

3. While the sauce is cooking, drop the linguine into 4 to 5 quarts boiling salted water.

4. Drain the linguine when al dente.

5. Add the linguine, the remaining butter, and the Parmesan cheese to the sauce, and toss well. Taste for salt, and serve immediately on a heated bowl.

Estimated Cooking Time: 50 minutes
Estimated Total Preparation Time: 1 hour

∽ LINGUINE CON LE ZUCCHINE ∽

Linguine with Zucchini   For 4

This tasty and colorful preparation makes a wonderful choice for a buffet. We always enjoyed it this way in the house of a close Roman friend, whose home region—Emilia—is a synonym for good food. The chili peppers add more color than heat.

4 tbs. olive oil
1 medium onion, minced
2 lbs. zucchini, washed, dried,
  and cut into matchsticks
salt
1 cup heavy cream
6 oz. mozzarella cheese, shredded
  or diced

3 red chili peppers, whole
2 egg yolks
2 tbs. freshly grated Parmesan
  cheese
2 tbs. butter
1 lb. linguine

1. Heat the oil in a heavy-bottomed saucepan, and sauté the onion over medium heat until soft and translucent.

2. Add the zucchini and 1 tsp. salt, and continue cooking, uncovered, over medium heat for about 20 minutes, or until the zucchini are tender.

3. In a large bowl combine the cream, the mozzarella, the chili peppers, the egg yolks, and the Parmesan cheese. Mix well. Add the butter and ¾ of the zucchini, and mix again.

4. Drop the linguine into 4 to 5 quarts boiling salted water.

5. Drain the linguine when al dente.

6. Add the linguine to the sauce, toss well, and serve immediately on a heated oblong platter garnished with the remaining zucchini.

Estimated Cooking Time: 30 minutes
Estimated Total Preparation Time: 50 minutes

∽ MACCHERONCINI AL POMODORO CRUDO ∽
Small Elbow Macaroni with Fresh Tomatoes   For 4

This is a refreshing and light summer dish particularly satisfying to enthusiastic tomato growers.

6 to 8 ripe plum tomatoes, peeled, quartered, and seeded	salt
½ cup fresh basil leaves	6 tbs. olive oil
1 lb. small elbow macaroni	freshly ground black pepper

1. Chop the tomatoes and the basil together coarsely.
2. Drop the macaroni into 4 to 5 quarts boiling salted water.
3. Put the tomato-basil mixture in a serving bowl with the oil, ½ tsp. salt, and the pepper.
4. Drain the macaroni when al dente.
5. Add the macaroni to the tomato mixture, toss, and serve.

Note: This dish is equally good when prepared a few hours ahead of time and served cold.

Estimated Cooking Time: 20 minutes
Estimated Total Preparation Time: 25 minutes

∽ PENNE ALL'ARRABIATA ∽
Penne with Red Chili Pepper   For 4

The name of the recipe—"in anger," or full of heat and fire—is self-explanatory.

4 tbs. olive oil	2 to 4 red chili peppers
1 small onion, chopped	or
1 28-oz. can Italian-style plum tomatoes	1 tsp. red pepper flakes
	salt
⅓ cup white wine	1 lb. penne
	2 tbs. fresh parsley, minced

1. Heat the oil in a heavy saucepan, and sauté the onion over medium heat until soft and translucent.

2. Add the tomatoes, the wine, the chili peppers, and ½ tsp. salt, and cook over medium-high heat for about 25 minutes.

3. Puree the sauce in a food processor or through a food mill. Return it to the pot, and simmer over low heat until the penne are ready.

4. Drop the penne into 4 to 5 quarts boiling salted water.

5. Drain the penne when al dente.

6. In a heated bowl toss the penne with the sauce, and sprinkle the parsley on top. Serve immediately.

Estimated Cooking Time: 40 minutes
Estimated Total Preparation Time: 50 minutes

◇ PENNE ALL'INDIVIA ◇
Penne with Curly Chicory   For 4

In Italy this dish is made with radicchio rosso, a winter lettuce from the Treviso area near Venice, prized for its deep red color, pleasant bitterness, and firm texture. We have found that in the United States, where radicchio rosso is seldom available, curly chicory is the best substitute.

3 tbs. butter
1 medium onion, minced
3 tbs. vegetable oil
1 lb. curly chicory, washed and cut into ½" pieces
salt
freshly ground black pepper
½ cup dry white wine

8 ripe plum tomatoes, peeled and pureed
               or
8 canned Italian-style tomatoes, pureed
1 cup heavy cream
1 lb. penne
¾ cup freshly grated Parmesan cheese

1. Heat the butter in a large skillet, and sauté the onion over medium heat until soft and translucent.

2. Add the oil, the chicory, ½ tsp. salt, and the pepper, and stir well. Cook for 5 minutes. Add the wine, stir, and cook until evaporated. Add the pureed tomatoes and 2 cups water, and simmer, covered, over medium-low heat for about 45 minutes, stirring from time to time. If the sauce gets too dry, add a little more water.

3. Add the cream to the sauce, stir, and cook for 10 minutes longer.

4. Drop the penne into 4 to 5 quarts boiling salted water.

5. Drain the penne when al dente.

6. Add the penne to the sauce, and toss well. Add the Parmesan cheese. Toss, and taste for salt. Serve immediately in a heated dish.

Estimated Cooking Time: 1 hour and 25 minutes
Estimated Total Preparation Time: 2 hours

∽ PENNE ALLA NAPOLETANA ∽

Penne Neapolitan Style   For 4

6 tbs. olive oil
1 garlic clove, minced
1 red chili pepper, seeded and
  chopped
10 anchovy fillets, chopped
1 tbs. capers, drained and
  chopped
¼ cup Italian or Greek black
  olives, pitted and sliced

4 fresh plum tomatoes, chopped
  or
4 canned plum tomatoes,
  chopped
⅓ cup canned tomato sauce
1 lb. penne
salt
¼ cup plain dry bread crumbs

1. Heat 4 tbs. olive oil in a large skillet, and sauté the garlic and the chili pepper over medium heat until the garlic is golden.

2. Turn the heat to low. Add the anchovies, mash gently with a wooden spoon until the ingredients form a paste. Add the capers and the olives, and stir for 1 to 2 minutes longer. Add the tomatoes and the tomato sauce, stir, and let simmer over low heat for about 5 minutes. Turn the heat off.

3. Drop the penne into 4 to 5 quarts boiling salted water.

4. Heat the remaining oil in a small skillet, add the bread crumbs, and sauté until golden brown. Turn the heat off.

5. Drain the penne when al dente.

6. Add the penne to the sauce in the large skillet, toss well, and

taste for salt. Sprinkle with the bread crumbs, and serve immediately on a heated platter.

Estimated Cooking Time: 35 minutes
Estimated Total Preparation Time: 1 hour

ᔛ PENNE CON I CAPPERI ᔛ
Penne in Spicy Tomato Sauce with Capers   For 4

⅓ cup olive oil
1 large garlic clove, minced
1 large red chili pepper
    or
¼ tsp. red pepper flakes
1 28-oz. can Italian-style plum
   tomatoes, chopped

1 lb. penne
salt
1 3½-oz. jar imported capers,
   drained
2 tbs. butter

1. Heat the oil in a heavy-bottomed skillet over medium-low heat. Add the garlic and the chili pepper, and cook for 2 to 3 minutes. Add the tomatoes. Turn the heat to medium-high, and cook until the sauce is thick, 25 to 30 minutes.
2. Drop the penne into 4 to 5 quarts boiling salted water.
3. Add the capers to the sauce, and continue cooking over very low heat.
4. Drain the penne when very al dente.
5. Add the penne and the butter to the sauce, toss thoroughly, and cook over low heat for 1 to 2 minutes more. Serve immediately on a heated platter.

Estimated Cooking Time: 45 minutes
Estimated Total Preparation Time: 1 hour

ᔛ PENNE ALLA VODKA ᔛ
Penne in Vodka Cream Sauce   For 4

Loved by our families and invariably a great hit with guests, this is a unique and elegant version of vodka sauce without tomatoes.

It was shared with us by a dear friend whose dinner invitations no one would ever refuse.

4 tbs. butter
1 medium onion, minced
1 lb. penne
salt
⅓ cup vodka
1 red chili pepper, seeded and chopped

6 oz. Italian prosciutto, slivered
or
6 oz. cured ham, slivered
1 cup heavy cream
½ cup freshly grated Parmesan cheese

1. Heat the butter in a large skillet, and sauté the onion over low heat until soft and translucent.
2. Drop the penne into 4 to 5 quarts boiling salted water.
3. In a small saucepan warm the vodka.
4. Add the chili pepper and the prosciutto to the onion, pour on the heated vodka, and flame.
5. When the flame burns out, add the cream, and stir the sauce until thickened and heated through. Turn off the heat.
6. Drain the penne when al dente.
7. Add the penne to the cream mixture, turn the heat on low, and stir well. Add the Parmesan cheese, stir again, and taste for salt. Serve immediately in a heated dish.

Note: Be careful when flaming the vodka. Do not shake the pan, which can intensify the flames. If it is necessary to stop the flames, cover briefly with a top.

Estimated Cooking Time: 20 minutes
Estimated Total Preparation Time: 30 minutes

∾ PENNE ALLA VODKA ROSSE ∾
Penne in Pink Vodka Sauce

For 4

1 red chili pepper, halved
or
¼ tsp. red pepper flakes
½ cup vodka
1 lb. penne
salt

1 recipe Basic Tomato Sauce II, p. 15
1 garlic clove, mashed
½ cup heavy cream
1 tsp. fresh parsley, minced

1. Soak the red chili pepper in the vodka for at least one hour. Take out the chili (or drain the chili flakes), reserving the vodka.

2. Drop the penne into 4 to 5 quarts boiling salted water.

3. Heat the tomato sauce with the garlic and the vodka over low heat. Turn the heat to medium-high, and let the vodka evaporate. Add the cream, and heat through. Stir in the parsley.

4. Drain the penne when al dente.

5. Add the penne to the sauce, stir well, and taste for salt. Serve immediately in a heated dish.

Estimated Cooking Time: 20 minutes
Estimated Total Preparation Time: 1 hour and 20 minutes

∽ PENNE AL BASILICO E PANNA ∽

Penne with Basil and Cream   For 4

5 tbs. butter
½ cup (about 4 oz.) bacon,
    coarsely chopped
1 large garlic clove, peeled
½ red chili pepper, seeded and
    chopped
        or
⅛ tsp. red pepper flakes
1 lb. penne

salt
¼ cup cognac
½ cup (about 4 oz.) cooked ham,
    coarsely chopped
1 cup heavy cream
⅓ cup fresh basil leaves, chopped
½ cup freshly grated Parmesan
    cheese

1. Heat 2 tbs. butter in a large skillet. Add the bacon, the garlic, and the chili pepper, and sauté over medium heat for about 5 minutes.

2. Drop the penne into 4 to 5 quarts boiling salted water.

3. Add the cognac to the bacon mixture, and cook until evaporated. Add the ham and the cream, and cook over low heat for 4 to 5 minutes. Remove the garlic.

4. Drain the penne when al dente.

5. Add the penne, together with the remaining butter, the basil, and the Parmesan cheese to the skillet. Toss well, and taste for salt. Serve immediately in a heated dish.

Estimated Cooking Time: 20 minutes
Estimated Total Preparation Time: 40 minutes

∽ PENNE IN INSALATA ∾
Penne Salad
For 4 to 5

2 green peppers
1 lb. penne
salt
1 cup mayonnaise (see
    Mayonnaise, p. 17)
¼ cup Italian green olives, pitted
    and slivered

¼ cup Italian or Greek black
    olives, pitted and slivered
1 6½-oz. can chunk light tuna,
    drained and flaked
freshly ground black pepper
8 cherry tomatoes, halved
2 hard-boiled eggs, cut into
    wedges

1. Wash and dry the peppers. Place on a rack as close as possible
to the broiler, and sear on all sides. When the skins of the peppers
have loosened and are slightly charred (5 to 10 minutes), remove
the peppers from the broiler, peel, and cut into strips.

2. Drop the penne into 4 to 5 quarts boiling salted water.

3. Drain the penne when al dente, and rinse under cold water.
Shake well to remove any excess liquid.

4. Combine the penne and the mayonnaise in a serving bowl,
and mix thoroughly. Add the peppers, the olives, the tuna, ½ tsp.
salt, and the pepper to taste. Mix well, making sure that all the
ingredients are coated with the mayonnaise. Taste for salt.
Arrange the salad on a round platter, and garnish with the tomato
halves and the egg wedges.

Estimated Cooking Time: 25 minutes
Estimated Total Preparation Time: 45 minutes

∽ RIGATINI ALLA CREMA DI PEPERONI ∾
Rigatini in Pepper Cream Sauce
For 4

This simple and unusual sauce is exquisite in both taste and
color. It was shared with us by a friend whose highly refined sense
of aesthetics dominates everywhere, including the kitchen.

2 tbs. olive oil
4 tbs. butter
1 lb. red or green sweet peppers,
    washed, dried, and cut into
    strips

1 medium onion, minced
salt
1 lb. rigatini
1 cup heavy cream
½ cup freshly grated Parmesan
    cheese

1. Heat the oil and 2 tbs. butter in a large skillet over medium heat. Add the peppers, the onion, and ¼ tsp. salt, and cook, covered, over medium-low heat for about 40 minutes, or until the peppers are soft. Turn the heat off.

2. Drop the rigatini into 4 to 5 quarts boiling salted water.

3. Put the peppers and onion through a food mill, and return the puree to the skillet. Keep warm over low heat.

4. Drain the rigatini when very al dente.

5. Add the cream to the pepper and onion puree, and stir well. Add the rigatini, the Parmesan cheese, and the remaining butter. Toss the ingredients for 1 to 2 minutes, and taste for salt. Serve immediately in a heated dish.

Estimated Cooking Time: 1 hour
Estimated Total Preparation Time: 1 hour and 15 minutes

∽ RIGATINI AI QUATTRO FORMAGGI ∽
Rigatini with Four Cheeses   For 4

1 lb. rigatini	⅔ cup Gruyère cheese, diced
salt	⅔ cup Gouda cheese, diced
6 tbs. butter	⅔ cup mozzarella, diced (if the
⅔ cup freshly grated Parmesan	mozzarella is dry, shred it)
cheese	

1. Drop the rigatini into 4 to 5 quarts boiling salted water.

2. A few minutes before the pasta is done, melt the butter over very low heat.

3. Drain the rigatini when al dente.

4. Place the rigatini in a heated serving bowl. Add the warm butter and the Parmesan cheese, and toss well. Add the remaining cheeses. Toss thoroughly, and serve immediately.

Estimated Cooking Time: 20 minutes
Estimated Total Preparation Time: 35 minutes

⌁ RIGATINI ALLA CAPRESE ⌁
Rigatini with Mozzarella and Tomatoes For 4

1 lb. rigatini
salt
½ cup olive oil
1½ lbs. ripe tomatoes, peeled,
   seeded, and diced

1 lb. mozzarella (preferably
   fresh), diced
½ cup fresh basil leaves, torn
   into small pieces
freshly ground black pepper

1. Drop the rigatini into 4 to 5 quarts boiling salted water.
2. Drain the rigatini when al dente.
3. In a large serving bowl toss the rigatini with the oil. Add the tomatoes, the mozzarella, the basil, and the pepper. Taste for salt.

Note: This dish can also be served at room temperature. Cook the pasta, and toss with the oil, the mozzarella, and the basil several hours in advance. It is preferable to add the tomatoes just before serving. However, if you take this dish on a picnic, you can prepare it all in advance.

Estimated Cooking Time: 20 minutes
Estimated Total Preparation Time: 30 minutes

⌁ RIGATONI ALLA "PENTOLA" ⌁
Rigatoni with Spinach and Ricotta For 4

This dish was a specialty at one of our favorite trattorias in Rome. The portion was always so large and the combination so satisfying that we rarely ate anything else. Spinach and ricotta are not an unusual accompaniment to pasta, but the addition of Italian bacon in this dish makes for a truly sensational taste.

6 tbs. butter
1 10-oz. package frozen
   leaf spinach, partially thawed
   and chopped
salt
2 tbs. onion, minced

¼ lb. pancetta, diced
   or
¼ lb. bacon, cut into ¼″ strips
1 lb. rigatoni
⅔ cup fresh ricotta
½ cup freshly grated Parmesan
   cheese

1. Heat 2 tbs. butter in a small skillet over medium heat. Add the spinach and ½ tsp. salt, and sauté for 8 to 10 minutes, or until almost dry.

2. Heat the remaining butter in another skillet, and sauté the onion and the bacon over medium heat for about 10 minutes.

3. Drop the rigatoni into 4 to 5 quarts boiling salted water.

4. While the pasta is cooking, cream the spinach and the ricotta in a heated serving bowl.

5. Drain the rigatoni when al dente.

6. Add the rigatoni to the serving bowl, and mix well, until the rigatoni are well coated. Add the onion and bacon and the Parmesan cheese, and toss. Taste for salt, and serve immediately.

Estimated Cooking Time: 30 minutes
Estimated Total Preparation Time: 45 minutes

∽ TORTIGLIONI ALLA MICHELANGELO ∽

Tortiglioni Michelangelo   For 4

This recipe has no connection with *the* Michelangelo but is the specialty of a Roman friend by the same name. The walnuts give an unusual texture and rich flavor to the tomato-cream sauce.

1 *small onion*	1 *28-oz. can Italian-style plum*
1 *small carrot*	*tomatoes, chopped*
½ *stalk celery*	*salt*
4 *tbs. butter*	1 *lb. tortiglioni*
1 *red chili pepper, seeded and*	1 *cup heavy cream*
chopped	1 *cup walnuts, chopped (avoid*
or	*any pieces with very dark skins)*
¼ *tsp. red pepper flakes*	½ *cup freshly grated Parmesan*
	cheese

1. Make a *battuto* by chopping the onion, the carrot, and the celery together until fine.

2. Heat the butter in a large skillet. Add the *battuto* and the chili pepper, and sauté 4 to 5 minutes over medium heat. Add the tomatoes and 1 tsp. salt and cook, uncovered, for 20 minutes more.

3. Drop the tortiglioni into 4 to 5 quarts boiling salted water.

4. Add the cream and the walnuts to the tomato sauce, and heat for 2 to 3 minutes.

5. Drain the tortiglioni when al dente.

6. Add the tortiglioni to the sauce, and toss. Add the Parmesan

cheese, toss again, and taste for salt. Serve immediately in a heated round dish.

Estimated Cooking Time: 40 minutes
Estimated Total Preparation Time: 1 hour

∽ TORTIGLIONI CON LE ALICI ∽
Tortiglioni in Anchovy Sauce   For 4

1 lb. tortiglioni
salt
6 tbs. butter
1 2-oz. can anchovy fillets,
    drained and chopped

6 oz. mozzarella (preferably
    fresh), diced
½ cup freshly grated Parmesan
    cheese

1. Drop the tortiglioni into 4 to 5 quarts boiling salted water.
2. Melt 4 tbs. butter in a large skillet over medium-low heat. Add the anchovies, and stir with a wooden spoon, gently mashing them to form a paste.
3. Drain the tortiglioni when al dente, reserving ¼ cup of the cooking water.
4. Add the tortiglioni, the remaining butter, the mozzarella, and the Parmesan cheese to the skillet. Toss for 1 to 2 minutes, until the ingredients are thoroughly mixed and the mozzarella has melted. Taste for salt. Serve immediately in a heated dish.

Estimated Cooking Time: 30 minutes
Estimated Total Preparation Time: 40 minutes

∽ TORTIGLIONI ESTIVI ∽
Tortiglioni Salad   For 4

1 lb. tortiglioni
salt
1 cup mayonnaise (see
    Mayonnaise, p. 17)
¼ cup heavy cream
½ cup Basic Tomato Sauce I,
    p. 14

½ 6½-oz. can chunk light tuna,
    drained and flaked
10 to 12 Italian or Greek black
    olives, pitted or slivered
¼ cup freshly grated Parmesan
    cheese
freshly ground black pepper

1. Drop the tortiglioni into 4 to 5 quarts boiling salted water.
2. In a small bowl combine the mayonnaise, the cream, and the tomato sauce. Mix thoroughly.
3. Drain the tortiglioni when al dente.
4. In a serving bowl combine the tortiglioni, the mayonnaise mixture, the tuna, the olives, and the cheese. Toss well, and taste for salt. Sprinkle with pepper, and serve.

Note: This dish can be prepared several hours ahead and served at room temperature.

Estimated Cooking Time: 20 minutes
Estimated Total Preparation Time: 30 minutes

∽ ZITI CON BROCCOLI E RICOTTA ∽
Cut Ziti with Broccoli and Ricotta　　　　For 4

A sensational way to use a favorite winter vegetable.

1 large bunch fresh broccoli
　　or
1 lb. frozen broccoli pieces
⅓ cup olive oil
2 garlic cloves, mashed
¼ tsp. red chili pepper flakes
　(optional)
salt

1 lb. cut ziti or other short pasta
　such as penne
2 cups (about 1 lb.) fresh ricotta
¼ cup freshly grated pecorino
　Romano cheese
¼ cup freshly grated Parmesan
　cheese

1. Wash the broccoli well in cold water. Remove the stems, and discard about ½″ from the bottom. Peel off the outer skin and cut the stems into 1″ pieces. Cut each piece lengthwise into matchsticks. Cut the florets lengthwise into pieces.
2. Heat the olive oil in a large skillet, and sauté the broccoli, the garlic, the chili pepper, and ½ tsp. salt over low heat, covered, until tender, 15 to 20 minutes.
If you use frozen broccoli, cut them into sticks when still frozen, and drop them into the hot olive oil with the garlic, the chili

pepper, and ½ tsp. salt. Sauté for 1 to 2 minutes over high heat. Lower the heat, cover, and cook for another 10 minutes, or until soft.

3. Drop the ziti into 4 to 5 quarts boiling salted water.

4. Add the ricotta to the broccoli, mix well, and heat through. Turn the heat off.

5. Drain the ziti when al dente, reserving ⅓ cup of the cooking water.

6. Add the cooking water to the broccoli-ricotta mixture with the pasta and the cheeses. Toss well, and taste for salt. Serve immediately in a heated shallow dish.

Estimated Cooking Time: 35 minutes (fresh broccoli); 25 minutes (frozen broccoli)
Estimated Total Preparation Time: 50 minutes (fresh broccoli); 35 minutes (frozen broccoli)

✧ ZITI CON PANNA ACIDA ✧
Ziti in Sour Cream Sauce   For 4

Sour cream is a relatively new ingredient in Italian cooking. It works wonderfully well with homemade tomato sauce.

1 lb. ziti
salt
1 cup Basic Tomato Sauce III,
   p. 16
¼ lb. prosciutto, diced or
   shredded

1 tbs. fresh sage leaves, chopped
   or
1 tsp. dried sage
½ cup sour cream
2 tbs. butter
½ cup freshly grated Parmesan
   cheese

1. Drop the ziti into 4 to 5 quarts boiling salted water.

2. In a large skillet bring the tomato sauce to a simmer over low heat. Add the prosciutto, the sage, and the sour cream, and heat for 2 to 3 minutes.

3. Drain the ziti when very al dente.

4. Add the ziti, the butter, and the Parmesan cheese to the sauce, and toss until the pasta is well coated. Taste for salt. Serve immediately in a heated dish.

Estimated Cooking Time: 20 miuntes
Estimated Total Preparation Time: 30 minutes

◇ TIMBALLO DI RIGATINI E MELANZANE ◇
Baked Rigatini Mold with Eggplant　　　　For 4

2½ lbs. small Italian eggplants
salt
1 cup vegetable oil
1 lb. rigatini
3 cups Basic Tomato Sauce II,
　p. 15
2 cloves garlic, mashed

1 lb. mozzarella, thinly sliced
1 cup freshly grated pecorino
　Romano cheese
10 to 12 leaves fresh basil, broken
　into small pieces, plus a few
　sprigs

1. Preheat the oven to 400° F.
2. Cut the eggplants lengthwise into ¼″ to ⅛″ thick slices. Place the slices in a colander, sprinkle with 2 tsp. salt, and let drain for at least 30 minutes. Dry with paper towels.
3. Heat the oil in a large skillet over medium-high heat. When the oil is very hot, slide in the eggplant in a single layer. Turn it once, and when browned on both sides remove onto brown paper to drain. Continue this process with the rest of the eggplant.
4. Drop the rigatini into 4 to 5 quarts boiling salted water.
5. Heat the tomato sauce in a small saucepan with the garlic.
6. Drain the rigatini when underdone, about 2 to 3 minutes before al dente.
7. Add 1 cup sauce to the rigatini, and toss.
8. Butter a 9-inch souffle dish. Place ⅓ of the rigatini on the bottom. Spoon ⅓ of the tomato sauce over the pasta, and top with a layer of eggplant, a layer of mozzarella, ⅓ cup pecorino cheese, and half of the basil. Repeat the process two more times, ending with the pecorino cheese.
9. Bake for 20 minutes.
10. Let the timballo rest for 5 to 8 minutes, then umold it onto a large round platter. Garnish with sprigs of fresh basil.

Estimated Cooking Time: 45 minutes
Estimated Total Preparation Time: 1 hour and 45 minutes

∾ TIMBALLO DI RIGATONI CON ZUCCHINE ∾
Baked Rigatoni Mold with Zucchini   For 4 to 6

2 scant cups medium bechamel
    sauce (see Bechamel Sauce,
    p. 16)
2 lbs. zucchini
1 cup vegetable oil
salt
1 lb. rigatoni

3 tbs. butter
1 cup fresh ricotta
1 cup freshly grated Parmesan
    cheese
¼ cup fresh parsley, minced, plus
    a few sprigs

1. Make the bechamel sauce.
2. Wash and dry the zucchini. Cut into sticks the size of a little finger.
3. Heat the oil in a large skillet over medium-high heat. When the oil is very hot, slide in the zucchini sticks in a single layer. Fry them quickly, until tender and slightly browned. Remove onto brown paper to drain. Continue this process with the remaining zucchini. Sprinkle them with ½ tsp. salt.
4. While the zucchini are frying, drop the rigatoni into 4 to 5 quarts boiling salted water.
5. Drain the rigatoni when underdone, 2 to 3 minutes before al dente.
6. Preheat the oven to 400° F.
7. In a bowl combine the rigatoni, the butter, the bechamel sauce, the ricotta, and ½ cup Parmesan cheese, and toss well.
8. Butter an 8-cup souffle dish. Place ⅓ of the rigatoni mixture on the bottom. Top it with half the zucchini, pressing them down. Sprinkle the zucchini with half the parsley and 2 tbs. Parmesan cheese. Repeat the layers, ending with the rigatoni. Sprinkle the remaining Parmesan cheese on top.
9. Bake for 20 minutes.
10. Let the timballo rest for 5 to 8 minutes, then unmold it onto a large round platter. Garnish with sprigs of parsley.

Estimated Cooking Time: 1 hour
Estimated Total Preparation Time: 1 hour and 30 minutes

∽ POMODORI RIPIENI DI TUBETTI ∽
Tomatoes Stuffed with Tubetti   For 4

8 firm ripe tomatoes
salt
pinch of sugar
¾ cup tubetti or other small
   tubular pasta

2 tbs. fresh parsley, chopped
½ tsp. dried oregano
½ cup fresh basil leaves, torn
   into small pieces
4 tbs. olive oil

1. Preheat the oven to 375° F.
2. Slice the tops off the tomatoes, setting them aside. Scoop out the pulp, and reserve. Sprinkle the inside of the tomatoes with salt, and turn them upside down to drain for about 30 minutes.
3. Chop the pulp, discarding the seeds, and put into a small saucepan with a pinch of salt and a pinch of sugar. Cook for 15 minutes over medium heat, until most of the liquid has evaporated.
4. Place the tomatoes upside down on a rack over a baking pan to catch any juice, and bake for about 5 minutes. Remove from the oven.
5. Drop the pasta into 2 quarts boiling water with 1 tbs. salt. Cook the pasta for about 10 minutes; it will be underdone and very al dente. Drain the pasta.
6. In a bowl combine the pasta, the parsley, the oregano, the basil, the cooked pulp, and 3 tbs. olive oil. Taste for salt.
7. Place the remaining oil in a baking dish just large enough to hold the tomatoes.
8. Fill the tomatoes with the pasta mixture. Replace the tops, and put the tomatoes into the baking dish. Bake for 20 minutes.
9. Remove the tomatoes from the oven, and let set for 5 to 10 minutes before serving.

Estimated Cooking Time: 50 minutes
Estimated Total Preparation Time: 2 hours

Fresh Egg Pasta ∽

Pasta all'uovo differs from most factory-made pasta in that it contains eggs. In Italy it is considered more desirable and elegant than dry pasta; it is also more nutritious because of the eggs.

Although manufactured pasta all'uovo—egg noodles—such as

fettuccine and tagliatelle is sometimes available, it resembles only vaguely the homemade product. The best-tasting pasta is fresh, and you can make it at home by hand or by machine. For the most part, making pasta by hand in today's hectic world has become a rare amateur's hobby, so we've omitted this traditional process in favor of the very popular machine method. With a hand or an electric rolling machine such as the Bialetti, the process is the same. You knead the dough by hand and then roll it through the machine. The electric machine has the advantage of being speedy and effortless, and because of the special covering on the rollers, the pasta made from it has a slightly better texture.

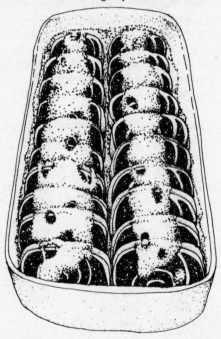

Another kind of electric pasta machine that is becoming popular does everything for you—mixes, kneads, and cuts out the dough. Both Bialetti and Simac make these machines. All you have to do is measure the ingredients into the machine, and in about eight minutes your pasta will be ready! The advantage is that practically all you do is put the water for the pasta on the stove, combine the flour and eggs in the machine, and by the time the water comes to a boil, your pasta is ready to be cooked. However, there is a small price to be paid for such magic: the resulting pasta lacks texture and elasticity. Although not as speedy, the electric rolling machine nevertheless saves you time and effort, and from our experience we feel that the superior quality of pasta is worth the eight minutes you put into the kneading.

Unbleached all-purpose flour is the closest supermarket version of Italian flour. Although some experts advocate the use of durum and/or semolina flours, these are used primarily to make commercial fresh pasta. Both semolina and durum flour come from durum wheat which, because of its hardness, undergoes several grinds, semolina being one of the coarsest and durum flour one of the finest. Commercial fresh pasta makers often use a combination of semolina, durum flour, and regular all-purpose flour. Because of the high gluten content of semolina and durum flour, the resulting product is a strong pasta that will resist stretching, will not get sticky, and will cook evenly after many hours of shelf life. Durum flour is not available in supermarkets. Semolina is found in some supermarkets and Italian specialty stores. Pastas made from these flours require fewer eggs.

Egg pasta can be kept for a long time either dried or frozen. Dry pasta thoroughly, and store it in closed containers, preferably tin boxes. Over time, however, dried pasta loses some of its taste. Frozen pasta, on the other hand, is almost indistinguishable from fresh pasta. If you freeze pasta, dry it only slightly, as if you were using it immediately. Freeze fettuccine, tagliolini, and pappardelle in sealed plastic bags; the pasta will separate when dropped into boiling water and stirred with a fork. Place lasagne and stuffed pastas in a box between layers of lightly floured waxed paper. Ravioli and tortelli can be frozen by first placing them on a cookie sheet in one layer, chilling them in the freezer for about 20 minutes, and then removing them into plastic bags. This is particularly convenient for storing large quantities.

All the dishes in this section are based on fresh egg pastas, for which the recipes are given here. A limited variety of fresh pasta is also available in specialty shops and some supermarkets. You can substitute equivalent amounts of such pasta, but the dishes will suffer some loss in texture and flavor.

Most recipes for fresh egg pasta that you may have come across call for a combination of whole eggs, flour, salt, water, and sometimes oil. Although everyone in Emilia—the region that is identified with fresh egg pasta—would agree that oil and water are definitely to be left out, there is a controversy about the eggs. In some localities of Emilia such as Guastalla, fresh pasta had been made, for generations, with only egg yolks, giving optimum results in texture and color. Although claimed to be the best, it is, unfortunately, practically impossible to handle. Our recipe, which uses a combination of eggs and egg yolks, yields a fresh pasta that is not only beautiful to look at for its natural golden color, but presents a better texture than pasta made only with whole eggs. It is slightly harder to knead, but the effort is well worth the result.

The best surface for mixing and kneading fresh pasta dough is a large flat table, preferably one with a wooden or formica top.

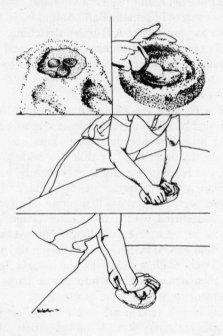

∽ PASTA ALL'UOVO ∽
Basic Fresh Egg Pasta

Makes about 15 oz. fresh pasta

2 cups unbleached all-purpose
   flour
2 large whole eggs

2 large egg yolks
½ tsp. salt

1. Place the flour on a flat surface in a mound. Make a well in the center, and put the eggs and the egg yolks into it. Sprinkle all over with the salt. Beat the eggs with a fork as if you were scrambling them, and slowly combine with the flour from the inner part of the well. Support the well from the outside with one hand to prevent it from collapsing. When enough flour has been absorbed by the eggs to form a paste, work in the remaining flour with your hands. If the dough becomes sufficiently dry before all the flour has been incorporated, discard whatever flour is left.

2. When the flour has been absorbed, knead the dough for about 8 minutes by pushing it away from you with the heel of your palm, then folding it over. Repeat this process, turning the dough from time to time. The dough should be firm yet elastic. Shape it into a ball, and wrap with waxed paper or plastic wrap.

3. Take ¼ of the dough, and flatten it with your hands.

4. Set the rollers on your pasta maker at their widest opening, and pass the dough through. If it is still a little sticky, sprinkle it lightly with flour, fold it, and pass it through the rollers 3 or 4 more times.

5. Turn rollers down one notch, and pass the dough through once. Perform this process once through each successive notch

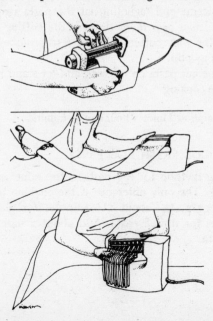

until the desired thickness is reached. On a scale from 6 to 0 you should choose:

Notch 3 for tagliolini (you need a thicker dough)

Notch 2 for fettuccine, pappardelle, and lasagne (you need a slightly thinner dough)

Notch 2 or 1½ for cannelloni, ravioli, and tortellini (you need a thin dough). On a scale from 8 to 10 you should choose notches 5, 3, and 2 or 1, respectively. Preferences differ about the proper thickness of the dough for the filled pasta. We suggest that you experiment with the machine a few times until you find what works best for you. Sometimes a difference of ½ to 1 notch may be necessary.

6. Sprinkle the work surface with flour, lay the rolled pasta strip on it, and if you are making stuffed pasta, such as ravioli, cut and stuff the dough very quickly before it loses its elasticity; otherwise it will start breaking at the edges, making it difficult to seal the pasta. Repeat the process with the remaining dough. Remember to roll out the second strip only when you are ready to stuff it. For flat pasta roll out all the strips then cut the desired shapes using a fluted wheel for lasagne (2″ x 8″ strips) and pappardelle (1″ x 4″ strips), and a regular knife for cannelloni (3½″ x 5″ rectangles). To make fettuccine and tagliolini, let the pasta strips dry for 10 to 15 minutes, then pass them through the cutting rollers of the machine; use the wide cutters to make fettuccine and the narrow ones to make tagliolini.

7. Spread the cut pasta on a towel, and let stand for at least 10 minutes before cooking.

Estimated Preparation Time: 1 hour and 30 minutes

HOW TO COOK FRESH EGG PASTA

The cooking method for egg pasta is the same as that for dry pasta (p. 147). The only difference is the cooking time, which is minimal for egg pasta—about 1½ minutes for plain pasta and 4 to 5 minutes for stuffed pasta. Add about 2 more minutes for frozen egg pasta.

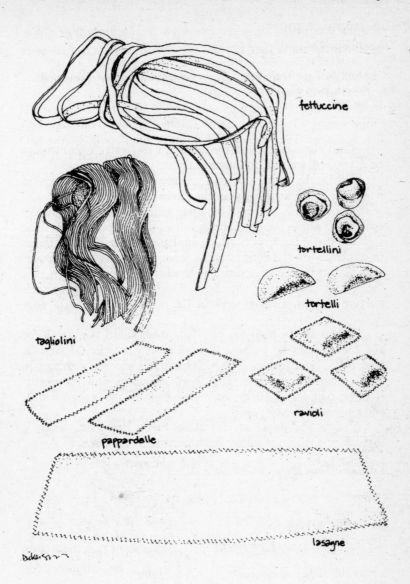

fettuccine

tortellini

tortelli

tagliolini

ravioli

pappardelle

lasagne

Dickerson

∾ PASTA VERDE ∾
Basic Spinach Egg Pasta

Makes about 1 lb. fresh pasta

½ 10-oz. package frozen leaf
spinach, partially thawed
¼ tsp. salt

2 cups unbleached all-purpose
flour
1 whole egg
2 egg yolks

1. Cook the spinach with the salt and 1 tbs. water, over medium heat, covered, for 5 to 10 minutes. Drain.

2. When the spinach is cool, squeeze it with your hands to remove as much liquid as possible. Chop it very fine.

3. Place a mound of flour on a flat surface. Make a well in the center, and put in the egg, the egg yolks, and the spinach. Beat the eggs and the spinach with a fork until thoroughly blended. Begin to combine with the flour from the inner part of the well. Support the well from the outside with one hand to prevent it from collapsing. When enough flour has been absorbed into the egg-spinach mixture to form a paste, work in the remaining flour with your hands.

4. When all the flour has been absorbed, knead the dough for about 8 minutes by pushing it away from you with the heel of your palm, then folding it over. Repeat this process, turning the dough from time to time. The dough should be firm yet elastic. If the dough is still sticky, add more flour. Shape it into a ball, and wrap with waxed paper.

5. Follow the directions for Basic Fresh Egg Pasta, steps 3 through 7, p. 200, for rolling out the pasta by machine.

Estimated Total Preparation Time: 2 hours

∾ PASTA ROSSA ∾
Basic Tomato Egg Pasta

Makes about 15 oz. fresh pasta

2 cups unbleached all-purpose
flour
2 large whole eggs

2 egg yolks
2½ tbs. tomato paste

1. Place a mound of flour on a flat surface. Make a well in the center, and put in the eggs and tomato paste. Beat the eggs and

the tomato paste with a fork until thoroughly blended. Begin to combine with the flour from the inner part of the well. Support the well from the outside with one hand to prevent it from collapsing. When enough flour has been absorbed into the egg-tomato mixture to form a paste, work in the remaining flour with your hands.

2. When all the flour has been absorbed, knead the dough for about 8 minutes by pushing it away from you with the heel of your palm, then folding it over. Repeat this process, turning the dough from time to time. The dough should be firm yet elastic. If the dough is still sticky, add a little more flour. Shape it into a ball, and wrap in waxed paper.

3. Follow the directions for Basic Fresh Egg Pasta, steps 3 through 7, p. 200, for rolling out the pasta by machine.

Estimated Total Preparation Time: 1 hour and 30 minutes

∽ FETTUCCINE AL GORGONZOLA E MASCARPONE ∽
Fettuccine with Gorgonzola and Cream Cheese　For 4

Torta di Gorgonzola e Mascarpone is a delectable cheese composed of mild Gorgonzola alternating with layers of a plain but rich white cheese that resembles American cream cheese. Although this combination of Gorgonzola and cream cheese does not exactly duplicate the original taste, it is equally delicious. The resulting sauce is thick and smooth and coats the fettuccine beautifully.

3 oz. mild Gorgonzola softened	15 oz. fettuccine (see Basic
or	Fresh Egg Pasta, p. 200)
3 oz. Danish creamy blue cheese	salt
½ cup plus 2 tbs. light cream	⅓ cup freshly grated Parmesan
2 oz. cream cheese, softened	cheese
4 tbs. butter	

1. In a bowl cream the Gorgonzola with 2 tbs. cream and the cream cheese.
2. Heat the butter in a large skillet over low heat. Add the ½

cup light cream and the cream cheese-Gorgonzola mixture. Incorporate the cheese by mashing and stirring with a wooden spoon.

3. Drop the fettuccine into 4 to 5 quarts of boiling salted water. When they are done, drain quickly.

4. Add the fettuccine to the skillet with the Parmesan cheese. Toss gently, and taste for salt. Serve immediately on a heated platter.

Estimated Cooking Time: 20 minutes
Estimated Total Preparation Time: 35 minutes, not including the pasta

∽ FETTUCCINE TRICOLORE ∽

Red, Yellow, and Green Fettuccine   For 6

The lovely combination of colors in this dish makes a spectacular presentation.

12 tbs. butter	7½ oz. red fettuccine (½ Basic
salt	Tomato Egg Pasta, p. 204)
7½ oz. yellow fettuccine (½	1 cup freshly grated Parmesan
Basic Fresh Egg Pasta, p. 200)	cheese
8 oz. green fettuccine (½ Basic	
Spinach Egg Pasta, p. 204)	

1. In a large skillet heat the butter over low heat.

2. Drop the fettuccine into 5 to 6 quarts of boiling salted water. When they are done, drain quickly.

3. Add the fettuccine to the skillet with ¾ cup Parmesan cheese. Toss well.

4. Pour the fettuccine onto a heated serving platter, and sprinkle with the remaining Parmesan cheese. Serve immediately.

Estimated Cooking Time: 15 minutes
Estimated Total Preparation Time: 2 hours and 30 minutes, including the pasta

∽ FETTUCCINE AI FUNGHI ∽
Fettuccine with Mushroom Sauce   For 4

1 oz. Italian or French dried
   mushrooms
½ lb. fresh mushrooms
1 tbs. tomato paste
2 tbs. olive oil
4 tbs. butter
1 garlic clove, mashed
¼ tsp. dried rosemary, chopped
3 to 4 ripe plum tomatoes, peeled,

3 to 4 ripe plum tomatoes, peeled,
   seeded, and chopped
     or
3 to 4 canned Italian-style plum
   tomatoes, seeded and chopped
salt
2 tbs. fresh parsley, minced
15 oz. fettuccine (see Basic Fresh
   Egg Pasta, p. 200)
½ cup freshly grated Parmesan
   cheese

1. Soak the dried mushrooms in 1 cup warm water for at least 30 minutes. Drain, reserving ½ cup liquid, and cut each into 2 to 3 pieces. Strain the liquid through a sieve lined with a cloth or paper towel, and set aside.

2. Trim off the ends of the fresh mushroom stems. If the mushrooms are relatively clean, wipe them thoroughly with a damp paper towel. If there is a lot of soil and dirt clinging to the caps, rinse them thoroughly but quickly in abundant cold water, rubbing them against each other to dislodge the dirt. Dry with paper towels, and slice thinly.

3. Dissolve the tomato paste in the mushroom liquid.

4. Heat the oil and 2 tbs. butter in a large skillet. Add the dried mushrooms, the garlic, and the rosemary, and sauté over low heat, covered, for about 10 minutes. Add the tomatoes, the diluted tomato paste, and ½ tsp. salt, and cook for 20 minutes longer. The sauce should be thick, but add some water if it seems too dry. Add the fresh mushrooms and the parsley, and cook for 5 minutes longer.

5. Drop the fettuccine into 4 to 5 quarts boiling salted water. When they are done, drain quickly.

6. Add the fettuccine and the remaining butter to the sauce. Toss quickly, taste for salt, and serve on a heated platter sprinkled with the Parmesan cheese.

Estimated Cooking Time: 45 minutes
Estimated Total Preparation Time: 1 hour and 15 minutes, not including the pasta

⌒ FETTUCCINE AL POMODORO ⌒
Fettuccine with Tomato Sauce For 4

1 *recipe Basic Tomato Sauce III,*   *salt*
   p. 16   *2 tbs. butter*
15 *oz. fettuccine (see Basic*   ½ *cup freshly grated Parmesan*
   Fresh Egg Pasta, p. 200)   *cheese*

1. In a saucepan heat the tomato sauce over medium-low heat.
2. Drop the fettuccine into 4 to 5 quarts of boiling salted water. When they are done, drain.
3. In a heated serving bowl toss the fettuccine with the tomato sauce and the butter. Taste for salt. Sprinkle with ¼ cup Parmesan cheese. Serve the remaining Parmesan cheese separately.

Estimated Cooking Time: 15 minutes
Estimated Total Preparation Time: 20 minutes, not including the pasta

⌒ FETTUCCINE AI TARTUFI ⌒
Fettuccine with Truffle Sauce For 4

½ *cup olive oil*   15 *oz. fettuccine (see Basic*
1 *small garlic clove, crushed*   *Fresh Egg Pasta, p. 200)*
2 *small anchovy fillets, chopped*   *salt*
3 *oz. black truffles, grated*

1. Barely heat the oil in a small saucepan over very low heat. Add the garlic and the anchovies, stirring and mashing with a wooden spoon to form a thick sauce. Add the truffles, and continue stirring until all the ingredients are thoroughly blended. Be careful not to let the sauce boil.
2. Drop the fettuccine into 4 to 5 quarts boiling salted water. When they are done, drain.
3. Toss the fettuccine with the sauce, taste for salt, and serve in a heated dish.

Note: Canned black truffles are available in most specialty stores.

Estimated Cooking Time: 20 minutes
Estimated Total Preparation Time: 30 minutes, not including the pasta

∽ FETTUCCINE ALLA SANREMESE ∾
Fettuccine San Remo   For 4

½ lb. fresh mushrooms
4 tbs. vegetable oil
1 large onion, minced
6 ripe plum tomatoes, peeled,
seeded, and cut into strips
or
6 canned Italian-style plum
tomatoes, seeded and cut into
strips
¼ tsp. dried oregano

5 to 6 fresh basil leaves, torn
into small pieces
or
¼ tsp. dried sweet basil
salt
2 large garlic cloves, sliced thinly
2 oz. Roquefort cheese, softened
15 oz. fettuccine (see Basic
Fresh Egg Pasta, p. 200)
2 tbs. butter

1. Trim off the ends of the mushroom stems. If the mushrooms are relatively clean, wipe them thoroughly with a damp paper towel. If there is a lot of soil and dirt clinging to the caps, rinse them thoroughly but quickly in cold water, rubbing them against each other to dislodge the dirt. Dry with paper towels, and slice thinly.

2. Heat 3 tbs. oil in a large skillet over medium heat. Add the onion, and cook for about 5 minutes. Add the tomatoes, and cook 5 minutes longer. Add the mushrooms, the oregano, the dried basil, and ¼ tsp. salt, and cook for another 5 minutes. If you use fresh basil, add it now.

3. Heat the remaining oil in a small skillet, add the garlic, and sauté over low heat until soft and light in color. Add the cheese, and stir until thoroughly blended.

4. Drop the fettuccine into 4 to 5 quarts boiling salted water. When they are done, drain.

5. Add the fettuccine, the cheese and garlic mixture, and the butter to the tomato sauce. Toss gently, and taste for salt. Serve immediately on a heated platter.

Estimated Cooking Time: 35 minutes
Estimated Total Preparation Time: 1 hour, not including the pasta

∽ FETTUCCINE VERDI ALLA PANNA ∽
Green Fettuccine in Cream Sauce For 4

6 tbs. butter	salt
1 cup heavy cream	¾ cup freshly grated Parmesan
1 lb. green fettuccine (see Basic	cheese
Spinach Egg Pasta, p. 204)	

1. Heat the butter and the cream in a large skillet over low heat until the cream has thickened.
2. Drop the fettuccine into 4 to 5 quarts boiling salted water. When they are done, drain.
3. Add the fettuccine to the skillet with the butter and cream. Sprinkle with ½ cup Parmesan cheese. Toss well, and taste for salt. Serve immediately in a heated dish with the remaining Parmesan cheese sprinkled on top.

Estimated Cooking Time: 15 minutes
Estimated Total Preparation Time: 20 minutes, not including the pasta

∽ TAGLIOLINI AL CAVIALE GRECO ∽
Tagliolini with Greek Tarama For 4

This exquisite and unique concoction comes from a Roman artist friend who is renowned for his masterpieces in the studio and the kitchen.

½ lb. fresh mushrooms	1 cup heavy cream
6 tbs. butter	15 oz. tagliolini (see Basic Fresh
1 small onion, minced	Egg Pasta, p. 200)
4 tbs. tarama (Greek fish roe)	salt

1. Remove the mushroom stems. If the caps are relatively clean, wipe them thoroughly with a damp paper towel. If there is a lot of soil and dirt clinging to the caps, rinse them thoroughly but quickly in cold water, rubbing them against each other to dislodge the dirt. Dry with paper towels, and slice thinly.
2. Heat 4 tbs. butter in a large skillet, and sauté the onion over medium-low heat until soft and translucent. Set aside.

3. Place the tarama in a food processor, and process with the plastic blade for about 10 seconds. Gradually add the cream through the feed tube, and process 1 or 2 seconds longer. You can also beat the tarama and cream, by hand or with an electric beater, until the mixture is creamy. Set aside.

4. Add the mushrooms to the skillet with the onions, and sauté for 2 to 3 minutes.

5. Drop the tagliolini into 4 to 5 quarts boiling salted water. When they are done, drain.

6. Add the tagliolini, the remaining butter, and the tarama mixture to the skillet with the mushrooms and onions. Toss gently for a minute over low heat, taste for salt, and serve immediately on a heated platter.

Note: Greek tarama is less expensive than real caviar and is available in Greek food stores and specialty shops.

The mushroom stems may be used for risottos; in the filling for cannelloni; and in the sauces for the Pasta Roll with Cooked Ham and Fontina (p. 215) and the Green Raviolini Baked in a Crust (p. 233).

Estimated Cooking Time: 15 minutes
Estimated Total Preparation Time: 30 minutes, not including the pasta

⌒ TAGLIOLINI AL CAVIALE ⌒
Tagliolini with Caviar
For 4

6 tbs. butter
1 tbs. lemon juice
2 tbs. vodka
1 cup heavy cream
1 2-oz. jar Danish caviar

freshly ground black pepper
15 oz. tagliolini (see Basic Fresh
    Egg Pasta, p. 200)
salt

1. Melt the butter with the lemon juice in a large skillet over low heat. Add the vodka and the cream, and cook for a few minutes to thicken, stirring gently. Add the caviar and pepper to taste. Stir, and heat through. Turn the heat off.

2. Drop the tagliolini into 4 to 5 quarts boiling salted water. When they are done, drain.

3. Add the tagliolini to the skillet, toss well, and taste for salt. Serve immediately on a heated platter.

Estimated Cooking Time: 15 minutes
Estimated Total Preparation Time: 20 minutes, not including the pasta

∽ TAGLIOLINI AL LIMONE ∽
Tagliolini in Lemon and Cream Sauce
For 4

1 cup medium bechamel sauce
  (see Bechamel Sauce, p. 16)
¾ cup heavy cream
rind of 1 lemon, grated

15 oz. tagliolini (see Basic Fresh
  Egg Pasta, p. 200)
salt
4 tbs. butter
1½ tbs. lemon juice

1. Make the bechamel sauce.
2. Add the cream and the lemon rind to the bechamel, and cook over low heat for 2 to 3 minutes, stirring gently.
3. Drop the tagliolini into 4 to 5 quarts boiling salted water. When they are done, drain.
4. Place the tagliolini, the sauce, the butter, and the lemon juice in a heated serving dish. Toss well. Taste for salt, and serve immediately.

Estimated Cooking Time: 20 minutes
Estimated Total Preparation Time: 25 minutes, not including the pasta

∽ TAGLIOLINI AL SALMONE ∽
Tagliolini with Smoked Salmon
For 4

½ cup butter
1 cup heavy cream
15 oz. tagliolini (see Basic Fresh
  Egg Pasta, p. 200)

salt
4 oz. smoked salmon bits
1 lemon, cut into 4 to 6 wedges
freshly ground black pepper

1. Heat the butter and the cream in a large skillet over low heat, and cook until the cream has thickened.
2. Drop the tagliolini into 4 to 5 quarts boiling salted water. When they are done, drain.

3. Add the tagliolini and the salmon to the skillet with the butter and cream. Toss the tagliolini carefully, making certain to coat them thoroughly with the sauce. Serve immediately on a heated platter. Serve lemon wedges on the side.

4. The pasta may be garnished with a sprinkling of lemon juice and freshly ground black pepper.

Note: It isn't necessary to use perfect slices of smoked salmon for this dish. Stores will often sell scraps of salmon at a greatly reduced price, and they will work perfectly in this recipe.

Estimated Cooking Time: 15 minutes
Estimated Total Preparation Time: 20 minutes, not including the pasta

∽ ROTOLO DI PASTA CON SPINACI ∽
Pasta Roll with Spinach and Ricotta Filling   For 4 to 6

The "rotolo" is one of the most successful "piatti." It always prompts enthusiastic applause at a buffet or sit-down dinner. Although this recipe may look formidable compared with some of the other pastas, it is in fact the easiest stuffed pasta to prepare.

FILLING
1 lb. fresh spinach
    or
1 10-oz. package frozen leaf
  spinach, partially thawed
salt
1 lb. fresh ricotta
1 8-oz. package cream cheese,
  softened
1 cup freshly grated Parmesan
  cheese
1 egg yolk
¼ tsp. freshly grated nutmeg

PASTA
4 strips thin fresh pasta of equal
  length (see Basic Fresh Egg
  Pasta, p. 200)
salt

SAUCE
2 cups Basic Tomato Sauce II,
  p. 15
½ cup heavy cream

¼ cup freshly grated Parmesan
  cheese
2 tbs. butter

1. Wash the spinach well, and without shaking the leaves, place it in a saucepan with ¼ tsp. salt. Cook, covered, over medium heat for about 15 to 20 minutes, or until tender. If frozen spinach is

used, cook with ¼ tsp. salt, covered, over low heat for 5 to 8 minutes. Drain the spinach, and let cool. Squeeze it with your hands to remove as much liquid as possible, and chop until fine.

2. In a large bowl, cream the ricotta, the cream cheese, and the Parmesan cheese with a wooden spoon. Add the spinach, the egg yolk, and the nutmeg, and mix well. Taste for salt.

3. Roll out the pasta strips, and place them on a flat, lightly floured surface, overlapping each other by about ¼" along the long sides. Do not let the strips sit; they will dry out. Dust a rolling pin with flour, and roll over the overlapping edges to seal the pieces together, forming a rectangular sheet about 16" to 18" by 15" to 17". Spread the filling over the pasta sheet leaving a border of about 2" on the long side near you and about ½" on the other 3 sides. Fold the 2" border over the filling, and roll up the pasta, making a uniform sausage-like shape slightly flat on the top. Press together the borders at the long ends to seal the roll, and wrap in a dishcloth, tying the two ends with string.

4. Bring about 4 quarts water with 1½ tbs. salt to a boil in an oblong pan large enough to hold the pasta roll (a fish poacher would be excellent). Gently immerse the roll so that it lies horizontally, and let it cook, over medium-high heat, for about 15 minutes.

5. Remove the roll from the water. As soon as it can be handled, unwrap it, and let it cool on a board.

6. Preheat the oven to 400° F.

7. Heat the tomato sauce over medium heat. Add the cream, and cook 1 to 2 minutes longer, until warm.

8. Cut the roll into ¾" slices, discarding the ends. Spread a little tomato-cream sauce on the bottom of an oven-to-table baking dish, and place the pasta slices in it, overlapping them slightly. Cover with the rest of the sauce. Sprinkle with the Parmesan cheese, and dot with the butter.

9. Bake for 15 to 20 minutes. Let rest 5 to 10 minutes before serving.

Note: The roll and the sauce can be prepared the day before. Store the roll in plastic wrap, and refrigerate it. Assemble the roll in the baking dish a couple of hours before serving. Add the cream to the sauce just before assembling the dish for baking.

Estimated Cooking Time: 1 hour and 20 minutes
Estimated Total Preparation Time: 3 hours and 30 minutes

⌖ ROTOLO DI PASTA CON PROSCIUTTO ⌖
Pasta Roll with Cooked Ham and Fontina   For 4 to 6

SAUCE
½ oz. Italian or French dried
 mushrooms
1 lb. fresh mushrooms
4 tbs. butter
1 small onion, minced
3 tbs. Marsala or sherry
salt
2 cups medium bechamel sauce,
 made with 4 tbs. butter, 3 tbs.
 flour, and 2 cups homemade
 meat broth or 1 large beef
 bouillon cube dissolved in
 2 cups water (see Bechamel
 Sauce, p. 16)
freshly ground black pepper

FILLING
2 cups thick bechamel sauce,
 made with 6 tbs. butter, 4 tbs.
 flour, 2 cups milk, and a pinch
 of salt (see Bechamel Sauce,
 p. 16)
1 lb. cooked ham, thinly sliced
8 oz. Fontina cheese, thinly sliced

PASTA
4 strips thin fresh pasta (see Basic
 Fresh Egg Pasta, p. 200)
salt

¼ cup freshly grated Parmesan
 cheese
2 tbs. butter

1. To prepare the sauce, soak the dried mushrooms in 1 cup warm water for at least 30 minutes.

2. While the dried mushrooms are soaking, trim off the ends of the fresh mushroom stems. If the mushrooms are relatively clean, wipe them thoroughly with a damp paper towel. If there is a lot of soil and dirt clinging to the caps, rinse thoroughly but quickly in abundant cold water, rubbing them against each other to dislodge the dirt. Dry with paper towels. Slice the mushrooms thinly.

3. Drain the dried mushrooms, reserving the liquid, and chop them coarsely. Strain the liquid through a sieve lined with a cloth or paper towel, and set aside.

4. Heat 4 tbs. butter in a wide saucepan, preferably enamel or stainless steel, over medium heat. Add the onion and the dried mushrooms, and sauté until the onion is soft and translucent. Add the Marsala, and continue cooking until evaporated. Add the fresh mushrooms, and sauté for 10 to 15 minutes, until the moisture has evaporated. Add the mushroom liquid and ¼ tsp. salt, and cook 5 minutes longer.

5. While the mushrooms are cooking, prepare the medium bechamel sauce.

6. Stir the bechamel sauce into the mushroom mixture, add the pepper, and taste for salt. Set aside.

7. Prepare the thick bechamel sauce for the filling.

8. Roll out the pasta strips, and place them on a flat, lightly floured surface, overlapping each other by about ¼" along the long sides. Do not let the strips sit; they will dry out. Dust a rolling pin with flour, and roll over the overlapping edges to seal the pieces together, forming a rectangular sheet about 16" to 18" by 15" to 17". Arrange the ham slices on the pasta sheet leaving a border of about 2" on the long side near you and about ½" on the other 3 sides. Spread half the bechamel sauce over the ham. Top it with a layer of Fontina cheese, and spread the remaining bechamel on top. Fold the 2" border over the filling, and roll up the pasta, making a uniform sausagelike shape slightly flat on the top. Press together the borders at the long ends to seal the roll, and wrap in a dishcloth, tying the two ends with string.

9. Bring about 4 quarts water with 1½ tbs. salt to a boil in an oblong pan large enough to hold the pasta roll (a fish poacher would be excellent). Gently immerse the roll so that it lies horizontally, and let it cook, over medium-high heat, for about 15 minutes.

10. Remove the roll from the water. As soon as it can be handled, unwrap it, and let it cool on a board.

11. Preheat the oven to 400°F.

12. Cut the roll into ½" slices, discarding the ends. Spread a little sauce on the bottom of an oven-to-table baking dish, and place the pasta slices in it, overlapping them slightly. Cover with the sauce. Sprinkle with the Parmesan cheese, and dot with 2 tbs. butter.

13. Bake the pasta roll for about 20 minutes. Let it rest for 5 to 10 minutes before serving.

Note: The roll and the sauce can be prepared the day before. Store the roll in plastic wrap, and refrigerate it. Assemble the roll and the sauce a few hours before serving.

Estimated Cooking Time: 1 hour and 30 minutes
Estimated Total Preparation Time: 3 hours and 20 minutes

∽ CANNELLONI AI FORMAGGI ∽
Cannelloni with Cheese   For 4

FILLING
1 lb. fresh ricotta
1 8-oz. package cream cheese
1 cup (6 oz.) coarsely grated
   Fontina cheese
   or
1 cup (6 oz.) coarsely grated
   Edam cheese
1 cup freshly grated Parmesan
   cheese
¼ tsp. freshly grated nutmeg
salt

PASTA
2 strips very thin fresh pasta, cut
   into 3½″ x 5″ rectangles (½
   Basic Fresh Egg Pasta, p. 200)
salt

6 tbs. butter heated until foamy
½ cup freshly grated Parmesan
   cheese

1. Preheat the oven to 425° F.
2. In a bowl combine all the cheeses and the nutmeg. Mix well with a wooden spoon, and taste for salt.
3. Butter a rectangular oven-to-table baking dish.
4. Drop half of the pasta rectangles into 4 to 5 quarts boiling salted water. Cook for about 1 minute. Remove with a skimmer or slotted spoon, rinse quickly under cold water, and spread in one layer on a dish towel. Repeat the process.
5. Place a pasta rectangle on a flat surface. Put about 2 tbs. of the cheese filling along one of the long edges, covering about ⅓ of the rectangle. Starting with the filled end, roll up the rectangle carefully, and place it in the baking dish seam side down. Repeat the process with the remaining rectangles, placing them side by side in the baking dish in one layer.
6. Pour the butter over the cannelloni, and sprinkle with the Parmesan cheese.
7. Bake for 10 to 12 minutes. Serve immediately.

Note: This dish can be prepared a day in advance through step 5. In that case, refrigerate overnight, and remove several hours ahead. Bake for 15 minutes.

Estimated Cooking Time: 25 minutes
Estimated Total Preparation Time: 2 hours

There are other interesting fillings for cannelloni; several samples follow.

ᴄ CANNELLONI AI FUNGHI ᴄ
Cannelloni with Mushrooms   For 4

A most unusual and delectable combination that is a Funghi family tradition—as it should be!

3 cups medium bechamel sauce, made with 6 tbs. butter, 4½ tbs. flour, 3 cups milk, and ½ tsp. salt—for the filling and topping (see Bechamel Sauce, p. 16)

FILLING
1½ cups bechamel sauce
1 cup Emmenthal (Swiss) cheese, shredded
1½ lbs. fresh mushrooms
4 tbs. butter
1 medium onion, minced
¼ cup brandy

2 tbs. fresh parsley, minced
¼ tsp. freshly grated nutmeg
¼ tsp. white pepper
salt

PASTA
2 strips very thin fresh pasta, cut into 3½" x 5" rectangles (½ Basic Fresh Egg Pasta, p. 200)
salt

1½ cups bechamel sauce
½ cup freshly grated Parmesan cheese
2 tbs. butter

1. Make the bechamel sauce. Remove about 1½ cups, and set aside.

2. Add the Emmenthal cheese to the remaining 1½ cups bechamel, and stir until the cheese is melted. Set aside.

3. Trim off the ends of the mushroom stems. If the mushrooms are relatively clean, wipe them thoroughly with a damp paper towel. If there is a lot of soil and dirt clinging to the caps, rinse them thoroughly but quickly in cold water, rubbing them against each other to dislodge the dirt. Dry with paper towels, and cut into thin slices.

4. Heat the butter in a medium skillet, and sauté the onion over medium-low heat until soft and translucent. Add the mushrooms, turn the heat to high, and sauté for about 5 minutes more. Add the brandy, and cook until evaporated. Add the parsley, the nutmeg, the pepper, and the salt, stir, and cook for 5 minutes longer, or until all the liquid has evaporated. Turn the heat off.

5. In a large bowl combine the mushrooms with the bechamel and cheese mixture.

6. Preheat the oven to 400° F.

7. Follow steps 3 to 5 of Cannelloni with Cheese (p. 217).

8. Spread the bechamel over the cannelloni, sprinkle with the Parmesan cheese, and dot with the butter.

9. Bake for about 15 minutes, or until slightly browned on top. Allow the cannelloni to settle for a few minutes before serving.

Note: This dish can be prepared a day in advance through step 7. In that case refrigerate it overnight and remove several hours ahead. Bake for 20 minutes.

Estimated Cooking Time: 50 minutes
Estimated Total Preparation Time: 2 hours and 15 minutes

∽ CANNELLONI DI SPINACI ∽

Cannelloni with Spinach and Ricotta   For 4

FILLING
2 lbs. fresh spinach
or
2 10-oz. packages frozen leaf
  spinach, partially thawed
salt
1 lb. fresh ricotta
1 cup freshly grated Parmesan
  cheese
1 egg plus 1 egg yolk, slightly
  beaten
¼ tsp. freshly grated nutmeg

SAUCE
2 scant cups thin bechamel sauce,
  made with 3 tbs. butter, 1 tbs.

flour, 2 cups light cream, and a
  pinch of salt (see Bechamel
  Sauce, p. 16)
1 tbs. tomato paste
salt

PASTA
2 strips very thin fresh pasta, cut
  into 3½″ x 5″ rectangles (½
  Basic Fresh Egg Pasta, p. 200)
salt

⅓ cup freshly grated Parmesan
  cheese
2 tbs. butter

1. Wash the spinach well, and without shaking the leaves, place it in a saucepan with ½ tsp. salt. Cook, covered, over medium heat, for 15 to 20 minutes, or until tender. If frozen spinach is used, cook it with ½ tsp. salt, covered, over low heat for 5 to 8 minutes. Drain the spinach, and let cool. Squeeze it with your hands to remove as much liquid as possible, and chop until fine.

2. In a large bowl combine the spinach, the ricotta, the Parmesan cheese, the egg and egg yolk, and the nutmeg. Taste for salt, and mix well with a wooden spoon.

3. Make the bechamel sauce. Add the tomato paste, and cook 4 to 5 minutes longer. Taste for salt, and set aside.

4. Preheat the oven to 400° F.

5. Cover a rectangular oven-to-table baking dish with a thin layer of the sauce.

6. Follow steps 3 to 5 of Cannelloni with Cheese (p. 217).

7. Spread the sauce over the cannelloni, sprinkle with the Parmesan cheese, and dot with the butter.

8. Bake the cannelloni for about 15 minutes. Allow to set for a few minutes before serving.

Note: This dish can be prepared a day in advance through step 7. In that case, refrigerate overnight, and remove several hours ahead. Bake for 20 minutes.

Estimated Cooking Time: 50 minutes
Estimated Total Preparation Time: 2 hours and 15 minutes

∽ RAVIOLI DI MAGRO ∽
Ravioli Filled with Swiss Chard and Ricotta   For 4

FILLING
1 lb. Swiss chard
salt
2 tbs. butter
⅓ cup fresh ricotta
¼ cup freshly grated Parmesan
   cheese
1 egg yolk
pinch of nutmeg
freshly ground black pepper

PASTA
2 strips thin fresh pasta (½
   Basic Fresh Egg Pasta, p. 200)
salt

SAUCE
1 cup Basic Tomato Sauce II,
   p. 15, pureed to creamy
   consistency

4 tbs. butter
½ cup freshly grated Parmesan
   cheese

1. Remove the white stalks from the chard, and reserve for another use.

2. Wash the chard well, and without shaking the leaves, place in a large saucepan with ¼ tsp. salt. Cook, covered, over medium heat for about 15 minutes, or until tender. Drain, and let cool.

Squeeze with your hands to remove as much liquid as possible, and chop until fine.

3. Heat the butter in a small saucepan, add the chard, and sauté over medium heat for about 5 minutes, until it is dry. Set aside.

4. In a medium bowl cream the ricotta and the Parmesan cheese with a wooden spoon. Add the chard, the egg yolk, the nutmeg, and the pepper, and mix thoroughly. Taste for salt.

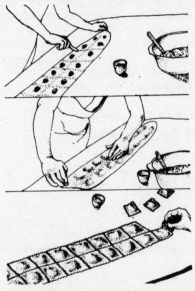

5. Place one strip of the pasta on a flat, lightly floured surface; cover the other strip with a dish towel to prevent it from drying out. Using a teaspoon and a rubber spatula, take a little of the filling at a time, and shape it into small balls. Place the balls about ¾" from the edge of the pasta strip and 1½" apart, making 2 rows. This should give you about 4 dozen ravioli measuring 1" x 1½". With a finger dipped in cold water, trace a grid around the balls. Place the second strip of pasta on top of the first, and retrace the grid, pressing down with your fingers to seal the edges. With a pastry wheel cut the double layer of pasta into rectangular ravioli shapes along the grid. Put the cut-out ravioli on a flat, lightly floured platter or tray in one layer.

6. Heat the tomato sauce over low heat.

7. While sauce is heating, drop the ravioli into 4 to 5 quarts

boiling salted water. If they are fresh, they will be done in 4 to 5 minutes. If they are frozen, it will take 6 to 7 minutes.

8. Drain the ravioli, and place in a shallow heated serving bowl. Cover with the hot tomato sauce, the butter, and ¼ cup Parmesan cheese. Toss gently, and sprinkle with the remaining cheese. Serve immediately.

Note: The stalks of the chard can be boiled for 15 to 20 minutes, until tender, sprinkled with Parmesan cheese, dotted with butter, and quickly baked in a hot oven for 10 to 15 minutes. Boiled, they can also be eaten as a salad seasoned with oil and lemon juice.

Estimated Cooking Time: 40 minutes
Estimated Total Preparation Time: 2 hours and 30 minutes

∾ RAVIOLI DI RICOTTA ∾
Ravioli Filled with Ricotta   For 4

FILLING
1 cup fresh ricotta
⅓ cup freshly grated Parmesan
   cheese
1 egg yolk
salt
pinch of freshly grated nutmeg
   (optional)

SAUCE
6 tbs. butter
2 to 3 sprigs fresh sage
         or
½ tsp. dried sage

½ cup freshly grated Parmesan
   cheese

PASTA
2 strips very thin fresh pasta (½
   Basic Fresh Egg Pasta, p. 200)
salt

1. In a bowl cream the ricotta and the Parmesan cheese with a wooden spoon. Add the egg yolk, ¼ tsp. salt, and the nutmeg. Mix thoroughly, and taste for salt.

2. Follow step 5 of Ravioli Filled with Swiss Chard and Ricotta (p. 220).

3. Drop the ravioli into 4 to 5 quarts boiling salted water. If they are fresh, they will be done in 4 to 5 minutes. If they are frozen, it will take 6 to 7 minutes.

4. Meanwhile heat the butter in a small skillet over medium heat until golden and bubbling. Add the sage and heat for 1 minute longer.

5. Drain the ravioli. Put them in a shallow heated serving bowl. Drizzle the butter and sauce on top, and sprinkle with Parmesan cheese. Serve immediately.

Estimated Cooking Time: 15 minutes
Estimated Total Preparation Time: 2 hours and 15 minutes

∽ TORTELLI CON PATATE ∽
Tortelli Filled with Potatoes For 4

Tortelli, a small stuffed pasta, can be served with many fillings and garnished with a variety of sauces. We include several versions of this delightful pasta. This one is our version of a Sardinian dish that we were introduced to in Ierzu, a small mountainous town on the eastern side of the island. Although the combination of ingredients is entirely unexpected, the result is exquisite.

FILLING
1 large or 2 small Idaho potatoes
salt
¾ cup dry ricotta cheese, grated
1 small garlic clove, mashed
1½ tbs. fresh mint leaves,
*   chopped*

PASTA
2 strips very thin fresh pasta (½
*   Basic Fresh Egg Pasta, p. 200)*
salt

SAUCE
1½ cups Basic Tomato Sauce II,
*   p. 15*

1. Boil the unpeeled potatoes in a deep saucepan covered by 2 to 3 inches of water with ¼ tsp. salt. When the potatoes are soft or you can pierce them with a fork, drain and peel.
2. Pass the potatoes through a food mill into a bowl while they are still warm. Add the ricotta, and mix thoroughly with a wooden spoon. Add the garlic and the mint, and mix well.
3. Place one strip of the pasta on a flat, lightly floured surface. Take a round pastry cutter or a glass about 2¾" in diameter, and cut out circles of dough. Using a teaspoon and a rubber spatula,

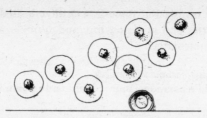

take a little of the filling at a time, shape it into small balls, and place them in the center of each circle. With a finger dipped in cold water, moisten the edge of the upper half of the circle. Fold the circle in half, and press the edges together to seal them. Re-

peat the process with the rest of the circles. Put the cut-out tortelli on a flat, lightly floured platter or tray in one layer. Pass the second strip of dough through the machine and repeat the procedure.

4. Heat the tomato sauce in a small saucepan over medium heat.

5. Drop the tortelli into 4 to 5 quarts boiling salted water. If they are fresh, they will be done in 4 to 5 minutes. If they are frozen, it will take 6 to 7 minutes.

6. Drain the tortelli. Place on a platter with the sauce, toss gently, and serve immediately.

Note: To prevent the pasta from drying out, divide the dough into two batches, and keep half wrapped in waxed paper until you're ready to use it. Roll out and cut the first strip, stuff it, and then roll out the second strip.

Estimated Cooking Time: 15 minutes
Estimated Total Preparation Time: 2 hours and 30 minutes

∽ TORTELLI DI RICOTTA E PREZZEMOLO ∽
Tortelli Filled with Ricotta and Parsley For 4

The parsley gives the tortelli filling a wonderfully fresh taste. Like all the tortelli, these freeze well.

FILLING
1 cup fresh ricotta
1 cup freshly grated Parmesan
  cheese
¼ cup fresh parsley (preferably
  Italian parsley), chopped
1 egg yolk
salt
¼ tsp. freshly grated nutmeg

PASTA
2 strips very thin fresh pasta (½
  Basic Fresh Egg Pasta, p. 200).
  See note for Tortelli Filled
  with Potatoes
salt

SAUCE
6 tbs. butter
1 cup heavy cream
2½ tbs. tomato paste

½ cup freshly grated Parmesan
  cheese

1. In a bowl cream the ricotta and Parmesan cheese with a wooden spoon. Add the parsley, the egg yolk, ¼ tsp. salt, and the nutmeg. Mix thoroughly and taste for salt.

2. Follow step 3 of Tortelli Filled with Potatoes (p. 223) with 2 strips of very thin fresh pasta.

3. Drop the tortelli into 4 to 5 quarts boiling salted water. If they are fresh, they will be done in 4 to 5 minutes. If they are frozen, it will take 6 to 7 minutes.

4. While the tortelli are cooking, heat the butter and cream in a large skillet over low heat. Add the tomato paste, stir gently, and cook for 1 to 2 minutes longer.

5. Drain the tortelli. Place them in the skillet with the sauce. Add ¼ cup Parmesan cheese, and toss gently. Serve in a shallow heated bowl sprinkled with the remaining Parmesan.

Estimated Cooking Time: 15 minutes
Estimated Total Preparation Time: 2 hours and 15 minutes

∿ TORTELLI DI RICOTTA E SPINACI ∿
Tortelli Filled with Ricotta and Spinach   For 4

FILLING
1 lb. fresh spinach
    or
1 10-oz. package frozen spinach,
    partially thawed
salt
1 cup fresh ricotta
½ cup freshly grated Parmesan
    cheese
1 egg yolk
¼ tsp. freshly grated nutmeg

PASTA
2 strips very thin fresh pasta (½
    Basic Fresh Egg Pasta, p. 200).
    See note for Tortelli Filled
    with Potatoes
salt

SAUCE
6 tbs. butter
1 cup heavy cream
½ cup freshly grated Parmesan
    cheese

1. Wash the spinach well, and without shaking the leaves, place it in a saucepan with ¼ tsp. salt. Cook, covered, over medium heat, for 15 to 20 minutes, or until tender. If frozen spinach is used, cook it with ¼ tsp. salt, covered, over low heat for 5 to 8 minutes. Drain, and let cool. Squeeze it with your hands to remove as much liquid as possible, and chop until fine.

2. In a bowl cream the ricotta and the Parmesan cheese using a wooden spoon. Add the spinach, the egg yolk, and the nutmeg. Mix thoroughly, and taste for salt.

3. Follow step 3 of Tortelli Filled with Potatoes (p. 223) with 2 strips of very thin fresh pasta.

4. Drop the tortelli into 4 to 5 quarts boiling salted water. If they are fresh, they will be done in 4 to 5 minutes. If they are frozen, it will take 6 to 7 minutes.

5. While the tortelli are cooking, heat the butter and cream in a large skillet over low heat.

6. Drain the tortelli. Place in the skillet with the butter and cream. Sprinkle with the cheese, toss gently, and serve immediately in a shallow heated dish.

Estimated Cooking Time: 35 minutes (fresh spinach); 25 minutes (frozen spinach)
Estimated Total Preparation Time: 2 hours and 35 minutes

∿ TORTELLI DI ZUCCA ∿
Tortelli Filled with Squash For 4

If you want a light and somewhat unusual pasta filling, here's a tasty one popular in Emilia.

FILLING
1 lb. butternut squash
¾ cup freshly grated Parmesan
  cheese
¼ tsp. freshly grated nutmeg
salt

PASTA
2 strips very thin fresh pasta (½
  Basic Fresh Egg Pasta, p. 200).
  See note for Tortelli Filled
  with Potatoes
salt

SAUCE
6 tbs. butter
8 to 10 fresh sage leaves
  or
½ tsp. dried sage

½ cup freshly grated Parmesan
  cheese

1. Heat the oven to 350° F.
2. Halve or quarter the squash, and remove the seeds. Wrap the squash in aluminum foil, and bake for about 1½ hours, or until tender. Let cool.
3. Remove the pulp, put it into a bowl, and mash with a fork. Add the cheese, the nutmeg, and ¼ tsp. salt, and mix thoroughly.
4. Follow step 3 of Tortelli Filled with Potatoes (p. 223) with 2 strips of very thin fresh pasta.
5. Drop the tortelli into 4 to 5 quarts boiling salted water. If they are fresh, they will be done in 4 to 5 minutes. If they are frozen, it will take 6 to 7 minutes.
6. While the tortelli are cooking, melt the butter and the sage in a small skillet over low heat.
7. Drain the tortelli. Place them on a heated serving platter. Drizzle the butter and sage on top, and sprinkle with the Parmesan cheese. Serve immediately.

Estimated Cooking Time: 1 hour and 45 minutes
Estimated Total Preparation Time: 3 hours and 45 minutes

∽ TORTELLI VERDI AL GORGONZOLA ∽
Green Tortelli with Gorgonzola Sauce For 4

FILLING
¾ lb. fresh spinach
  or
¾ 10-oz. package frozen spinach,
  partially thawed
salt
1 cup fresh ricotta
½ cup freshly grated Parmesan
  cheese
¼ tsp. freshly grated nutmeg

PASTA
2 strips thin fresh green egg pasta
  (½ Basic Spinach Egg Pasta,
  p. 204). See note for Tortelli
  Filled with Potatoes
salt

SAUCE
6 tbs. butter
4 oz. Gorgonzola cheese
  or
4 oz. Danish creamy blue cheese

⅓ cup freshly grated Parmesan
  cheese

1. Wash the spinach well, and without shaking the leaves, place it in a saucepan with ¼ tsp. salt. Cook, covered, over medium heat for 15 to 20 minutes, or until tender. If frozen spinach is used, cook it with ¼ tsp. salt, covered, over low heat for 5 to 8 minutes. Drain the spinach, and let cool. Squeeze it with your hands to remove as much liquid as possible, and chop until fine.

2. In a bowl cream the ricotta and the Parmesan cheese with a wooden spoon. Add the spinach and the nutmeg, and mix thoroughly. Taste for salt.

3. Follow step 3 of Tortelli Filled with Potatoes (p. 223) with 2 strips of thin fresh green egg pasta.

4. Melt the butter and the Gorgonzola cheese in a large skillet over low heat.

5. Drop the tortelli into 4 to 5 quarts boiling salted water. If they are fresh, they will be done in 4 to 5 minutes. If they are frozen, it will take 6 to 7 minutes.

6. Drain the tortelli. Add them to the skillet with the Parmesan cheese. Toss well, and serve immediately on a heated platter.

Estimated Cooking Time: 35 minutes (fresh spinach); 25 minutes
(frozen spinach)
Estimated Total Preparation Time: 2 hours and 35 minutes

❧ LASAGNE CON CARCIOFI ❧
Baked Lasagna with Artichokes   For 4 to 6

6 large artichokes
          or
2 10-oz. packages frozen artichoke
    bottoms, partially defrosted
1 lemon, halved
5 tbs. butter
½ large chicken bouillon cube
    dissolved in 2 tbs. water
salt
thick bechamel sauce, made with
    6 tbs. butter, 5 tbs. flour, and
    4 cups homemade meat broth
    —or 2 large beef bouillon cubes
    dissolved in 4 cups water (see
    Bechamel Sauce, p. 16)
1 small onion, stuck with a clove

1 celery stalk
1 small carrot, halved
2 sprigs parsley
1 bay leaf
2 1-oz. imported soft cheese
    wedges (such as La Vache
    Qui Rit), softened and broken
    into pieces
¾ cup freshly grated Parmesan
    cheese
½ cup heavy cream
2 egg yolks
4 strips of thin fresh pasta, cut
    into 2" x 8" strips with a fluted
    pastry wheel (see Basic Fresh
    Egg Pasta, p. 200)

1. If you're using fresh artichokes, cut off and discard the stems. Break off the small leaves at the base, and cut off about 1" from the top. Snap off the hard upper part of the leaves. Cut the artichokes in half lengthwise, and remove the fuzzy choke as well as the prickly leaves around it. Rub the halves with a piece of lemon to prevent discoloration. Cut each half lengthwise into very thin slices.

2. Heat 3 tbs. butter in a medium saucepan, preferably enamel or stainless steel, over medium heat. Add the artichokes, and sauté over low heat, covered, for about 5 minutes. Add the bouillon and ½ cup water, and cook for 20 minutes longer, or until tender. Taste for salt. If frozen artichoke bottoms are used, heat 3 tbs. butter in a medium saucepan over medium-low heat. Add the artichokes and the bouillon and cook for 5 to 8 minutes. Taste for salt.

3. Make the bechamel sauce. Add the onion stuck with the clove, the celery, the carrot, the parsley, and the bay leaf to the sauce, and simmer over medium heat for 20 to 25 minutes. Turn the heat off. Remove the vegetables and herbs. Add the cheese wedges, and mix until melted. Add ½ cup Parmesan cheese and the cream, and mix well. Remove the sauce from the heat, and add the egg yolks, one at a time, stirring well after each addition. Taste for salt.

4. Preheat the oven to 400° F.

5. Drop half the lasagne into 4 to 5 quarts boiling salted water. If the lasagne are fresh, cook them 1 minute; if they are frozen, cook them for about 2 minutes. Remove with a skimmer or slotted spoon, rinse quickly under cold water, and spread in one layer on a dish towel. Cook the remaining lasagne in the same manner.

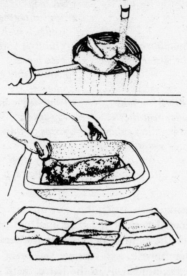

6. Spread a little bechamel sauce on the bottom of an oven-to-table baking dish. Make an overlapping layer of pasta strips, and top it with half the artichokes and ⅓ of the bechamel sauce. Repeat the layers ending with the lasagne. Spread the remaining sauce on top, sprinkle with the last ¼ cup Parmesan cheese, and dot with the remaining 2 tbs. butter.

7. Bake the lasagne for 15 to 20 minutes, or until slightly browned on top. Allow to settle for a few minutes before serving.

Note: This dish can be prepared a day in advance through step 6 and refrigerated. Remove it from the refrigerator several hours before baking.

Estimated Cooking Time: 1 hour and 15 minutes (fresh artichokes); 1 hour (frozen artichokes)
Estimated Total Preparation Time: 2 hours, not including the pasta (fresh artichokes); 1 hour and 15 minutes (frozen artichokes)

✧ LASAGNE AL MASCARPONE ✧
Baked Lasagna with Cream Cheese and Prosciutto
For 4 to 5

2 8-oz. packages cream cheese,
    softened
¼ cup milk
¾ cup freshly grated Parmesan
    cheese
2 egg yolks
6 oz. Italian prosciutto, cut into
    very thin strips
        or
6 oz. cured ham, cut into very
    thin strips

freshly ground black pepper
salt
2 scant cups medium bechamel
    sauce (see Bechamel Sauce,
    p. 16)
4 strips of thin fresh pasta, cut
    into 2" x 8" strips with a fluted
    pastry wheel (see Basic Fresh
    Egg Pasta, p. 200)
2 tbs. butter

1. In a bowl cream the cream cheese with a wooden spoon. Add the milk, and continue until you have a smooth cream. Add ½ cup Parmesan cheese, the egg yolks, the prosciutto, and the black pepper, and mix thoroughly. Taste for salt.

2. Make the bechamel sauce.

3. Preheat the oven to 400° F.

4. Drop half the lasagne into 4 to 5 quarts boiling salted water. If the lasagne are fresh, cook them 1 minute; if they are frozen, cook them for about 2 minutes. Remove them with a skimmer or slotted spoon, rinse quickly under cold water, and spread in one layer on a dish towel. Cook the remaining lasagne in the same manner.

5. Spread a little bechamel sauce on the bottom of an oven-to-table baking dish. Make an overlapping layer of pasta strips, and top it with half the cheese mixture. Repeat the layers ending with the lasagne. Add the remaining bechamel sauce, sprinkle with the remaining Parmesan cheese, and dot with the butter.

6. Bake the lasagne for 15 to 20 minutes, or until slightly browned on top. Allow to settle for a few minutes before serving.

Note: This dish can be prepared a day in advance through step 5 and refrigerated. Remove it from the refrigerator several hours before baking.

Estimated Cooking Time: 35 minutes
Estimated Total Preparation Time: 1 hour and 20 minutes

⌁ PASTICCIO DI PAPPARDELLE E INDIVIA ⌁
Baked Pappardelle and Curly Chicory For 4 to 6

Another adaptation of a radicchio rosso recipe, this is a specialty of a Venetian-style restaurant in Rome. We always enjoyed it with a wonderful glass of Venegazzu'.

4 tbs. butter
2 tbs. vegetable oil
1 large onion, minced
2 lbs. curly chicory, washed and
  cut into ½" pieces
salt
¼ tsp. ground white pepper
½ cup dry white wine

2 scant cups medium bechamel
  sauce (see Bechamel Sauce,
  p. 16)
½ cup cream
4 thin strips of fresh pasta, cut
  into 1" x 4" strips with a fluted
  pastry wheel (see Basic Fresh
  Egg Pasta, p. 200)
1 cup freshly grated Parmesan
  cheese

1. Heat the butter and oil in a large saucepan, and sauté the onion over medium-low heat until soft and translucent.
2. Add the chicory, ½ tsp. salt, and the pepper, and cook for 5 minutes over medium heat. Add the wine, stir, and cook until evaporated. Add 2 cups water, and simmer, covered, over low heat for about 45 minutes, stirring from time to time.
3. Preheat the oven to 400° F.
4. Make the bechamel sauce. Add it to the chicory, along with the cream and ¾ cup Parmesan cheese.
5. Drop the pappardelle into 4 to 5 quarts boiling salted water. If they are fresh, cook 1 minute; if they are frozen, cook for about 2 minutes.
6. Drain the pappardelle.
7. Add the pappardelle to the chicory and bechamel mixture, and toss. Place the mixture in a buttered oven-to-table baking dish, sprinkle with the remaining Parmesan cheese, and bake for 10 minutes. Allow the pappardelle to settle for a few minutes before serving.

Note: This dish can be prepared a day in advance. Remove it from the refrigerator several hours before baking.

Estimated Cooking Time: 1 hour and 15 minutes
Estimated Total Preparation Time: 1 hour and 45 minutes, not including the preparation of the pasta

∽ TIMBALLO DI RAVIOLINI VERDI ∽
Green Raviolini Baked in a Crust   For 4

Timballo, a poetic word for drum, is a culinary term for a cake-like dish usually composed of a pastry shell filled with a pasta, rice, meat, or vegetable preparation. Generally timballi are reserved for very elegant occasions.

CRUST
2 cups sifted all-purpose flour
¼ tsp. salt
5 oz. (10 tbs.) chilled butter, cut
into small pieces
2 egg yolks
2 tbs. chilled water

RAVIOLINI
  FILLING
1 lb. fresh spinach
        or
1 10-oz. package frozen spinach,
partially thawed
salt
2 tbs. butter
½ small onion, minced
4 oz. Italian prosciutto, shredded
        or
4 oz. country ham, shredded
¼ cup freshly grated Parmesan
cheese
pinch of nutmeg

PASTA
2 strips of thin fresh green pasta
(½ Basic Spinach Egg Pasta,
p. 204)
salt

SAUCE
1½ oz. dried mushrooms
2 cups medium bechamel sauce
(see Bechamel Sauce, p. 16)
6 tbs. butter
4 oz. beef marrow, chopped
¼ cup Marsala or sherry
1 cup homemade meat broth
        or
½ large beef bouillon cube
dissolved in 1 cup water

¾ cup freshly grated Parmesan
cheese

1 egg yolk, lightly beaten

1. To prepare the crust, place the flour, the salt, the butter, the egg yolks, and the water in a large mixing bowl. Mix the ingredients quickly with your fingertips until they are blended. Do not knead the dough. Form it into a ball.

If you use a food processor, place the flour, the salt, and the butter in the container, and process 10 seconds. Add the 2 egg yolks and the water through the feed tube while the machine is running, and continue processing for 30 to 50 seconds longer, until a ball of dough is formed. Wrap the dough in waxed paper, and chill in the refrigerator for about 2 hours.

2. To prepare the raviolini, wash the spinach well, and without

shaking the leaves, place it in a saucepan with ¼ tsp. salt. Cook, covered, over medium heat for about 15 minutes, or until just tender. If you use frozen spinach, cook it with ¼ tsp. salt, covered, over low heat for 4 to 6 minutes. Drain, and let cool. Squeeze it with your hands to remove as much liquid as possible, and chop until fine.

3. Heat the butter in a small saucepan over medium heat. Add the onion, and sauté until very soft, about 15 minutes. Add the spinach, and sauté about 5 minutes longer, or until dry. Remove from the burner.

4. In a medium bowl combine the spinach, the prosciutto, the cheese, and the nutmeg. Mix thoroughly, and taste for salt.

5. Make the pasta strips. Place the first strip on a flat, lightly floured surface; keep the second strip covered with a dish towel to prevent it from drying out too quickly. Using a teaspoon and a rubber spatula, take a little of the filling at a time, and shape it into small balls. Place the balls about ½" from the edge of the pasta strip and 1" apart, making 2 rows. With a finger dipped in cold water, trace a grid around the balls of filling. Place the second strip of pasta on top of the first, and retrace the grid, pressing down with your fingers to seal the edges. With a pastry wheel cut the double layer of pasta into square ravioli shapes, about 1" by 1", along the grid. Put the cut-out raviolini on a flat, lightly floured platter or tray in one layer.

6. To prepare the sauce, soak the mushrooms in 1 cup hot water for about 20 minutes to soften. Drain, reserving the liquid, and chop coarsely. Strain the liquid through a sieve lined with a paper towel to remove any sand and dirt.

7. While the mushrooms are soaking, prepare the bechamel sauce.

8. Heat 2 tbs. butter in a medium saucepan over medium heat. Add the mushrooms, and sauté for 1 to 2 minutes. Add the marrow and the Marsala, and cook until the Marsala has evaporated. Add the mushroom liquid and the broth, and simmer, covered, over low heat for 20 to 30 minutes, or until most of the liquid has evaporated. Add the bechamel sauce, mix well, and set aside.

9. Preheat the oven to 375° F.

10. Drop the raviolini into 4 to 5 quarts boiling salted water. If the raviolini are fresh, cook for 2 minutes. If they are frozen, cook for about 4 minutes. Drain the raviolini.

11. In a bowl toss the raviolini with the remaining 4 tbs. butter and half the Parmesan cheese.

12. Divide the dough for the crust into two parts, one twice as large as the other. On a flat floured surface roll out the larger piece into a circle ⅛" thick. With this sheet line an 8" springform. Press the dough well against the bottom and sides, making sure that it reaches over the top of the form. Roll out the smaller piece of dough for the top.

13. Place ⅓ of the raviolini on the bottom of the crust. Spread ⅓ of the sauce on top, and sprinkle with ⅓ of the remaining Parmesan cheese. Repeat the process twice. Cover the top with the second circle of dough, and pinch the border all around to seal the timballo. Brush the top with the egg yolk.

14. Bake the timballo for about 40 minutes. Allow to settle for about 10 minutes before unmolding it onto a round platter. Serve immediately.

Note: The raviolini can be prepared two days ahead. Refrigerate them, dusted with flour, in a closed tin box in layers separated by plastic wrap. The sauce can be prepared the day before and refrigerated. Warm the sauce before assembling.

Estimated Cooking Time: 2 hours and 30 minutes
Estimated Total Preparation Time: 5 hours

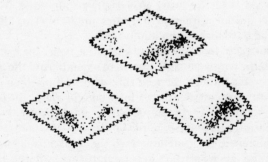

∾ TIMBALLO DI TORTELLINI ∾
Tortellini Baked in a Crust

For 4

CRUST
2 cups sifted all-purpose flour
¼ tsp. salt
5 oz. (10 tbs.) chilled butter, cut
  into small pieces
2 egg yolks
2 tbs. chilled water

TORTELLINI
  FILLING
½ lb. fresh spinach
    or
½ 10-oz. package frozen spinach,
  partially thawed
salt
½ cup fresh ricotta
½ 8-oz. package cream cheese,
  softened

⅓ cup freshly grated Parmesan
  cheese
1 egg yolk
¼ tsp. freshly grated nutmeg

PASTA
2 strips of very thin fresh pasta
  (½ Basic Fresh Egg Pasta,
  p. 200)
salt

SAUCE
2 cups Basic Tomato Sauce I,
  p. 14
6 tbs. butter
½ cup heavy cream

¾ cup freshly grated Parmesan
  cheese

1 egg yolk, lightly beaten

1. To prepare the crust, place the flour, the salt, the butter, the 2 egg yolks, and the water in a large mixing bowl. Mix the ingredients quickly with your fingertips until they are blended. Do not knead the dough. Form it into a ball.

If you use a food processor, place the flour, the salt, and the butter in the container, and process 10 seconds. Add the 2 egg yolks and the water through the feed tube while the machine is running, and continue processing for 30 to 50 second longer, until a ball of dough is formed. Wrap the dough in waxed paper, and chill in the refrigerator for about 2 hours.

2. To prepare the tortellini, wash the spinach well, and without shaking the leaves, place it in a saucepan with ¼ tsp. salt. Cook, covered, over medium heat for about 15 minutes, or until just tender. If you use frozen spinach, cook it with ¼ tsp. salt, covered, over low heat for 4 to 6 minutes. Drain, and let cool. Squeeze it with your hands to remove as much liquid as possible, and chop until fine.

3. In a medium bowl cream the ricotta, the cream cheese, the

Parmesan cheese, and the egg yolk with a wooden spoon. Add
the spinach, the salt, and the nutmeg, and mix thoroughly. Taste
for salt.

4. Make the pasta strips. Pass the first strip of pasta through
the machine, and place it on a flat, lightly floured surface. Keep
the remaining dough wrapped in plastic. Take a round pastry cutter
or a glass 2¼" in diameter, and cut out circles of dough. Using a
teaspoon and a rubber spatula, take a little of the filling at a time,
form it into small balls, and place them in the center of each circle.
With a finger dipped in cold water, moisten the edge of the upper
half of the circle. Fold the circle in half, and press the edges together to seal them. Holding the half moon in the left hand with
the straight edge toward you, press this edge in the center with the

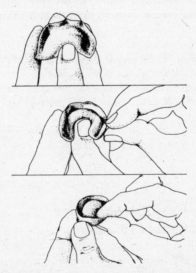

thumb. Then place the right forefinger downward with the nail
against this indentation and wrap the ends around it, pressing them
together with the thumb, sealing them well. Pass the second strip
of dough through the machine, and repeat the procedure.

5. Heat the tomato sauce over medium heat. Add 2 tbs. butter
and the cream, and cook 1 to 2 minutes longer, until warm.

6. Preheat the oven to 375° F.

7. Drop the tortellini into 4 to 5 quarts boiling salted water.
If the tortellini are fresh, cook for 2 minutes; if they are frozen,
cook for about 4 minutes. Drain.

8. In a bowl toss the tortellini with the remaining 4 tbs. butter and half the Parmesan cheese.

9. Divide the dough for the crust into two parts, one twice as large as the other. On a flat floured surface roll out the larger piece into a circle ⅛" thick. With this sheet line an 8" springform. Press the dough well against the bottom and sides, making sure that it reaches over the top of the form. Roll out the smaller piece of dough for the top.

10. Place ⅓ of the tortellini on the bottom of the crust. Spread ⅓ of the sauce on top, and sprinkle with ⅓ of the Parmesan cheese. Repeat the process twice. Cover the top with the second circle of dough, and pinch the border all around to seal the timballo. Brush the top with the egg yolk.

11. Bake the timballo for about 40 minutes. Allow to settle for about 10 minutes before unmolding it onto a round platter. Serve immediately.

Note: The tortellini can be prepared two days ahead. Refrigerate them, dusted with flour, in a closed tin box in layers separated by a plastic wrap. The sauce can be prepared the day before and refrigerated. Warm the sauce before assembling.

Estimated Cooking Time: 2 hours and 30 minutes
Estimated Total Preparation Time: 5 hours

∽ TIMBALLO DI FETTUCCINE VERDI ∽
Timbale of Green Fettuccine   For 4

1 lb. fresh mushrooms	3 eggs
4 tbs. plain dry bread crumbs	1½ cups heavy cream
7 tbs. butter	1½ cups cooked ham, chopped
salt	½ cup freshly grated Parmesan
1 lb. green fettuccine (see Basic	cheese
Spinach Egg Pasta, p. 204)	freshly ground black pepper

1. Preheat the oven to 400° F.
2. Trim off the ends of the mushroom stems. If the mushrooms are relatively clean, wipe them thoroughly with a damp paper towel. If there is a lot of soil and dirt clinging to the caps, rinse

thoroughly but quickly in cold water, rubbing them against each other to dislodge the dirt. Dry with paper towels, and cut into thin slices.

3. Generously butter an 8-cup souffle dish. Sprinkle the bottom and sides with the bread crumbs, covering all the surfaces evenly. Shake off any excess crumbs.

4. Heat 3 tbs. butter in a medium skillet. Add the mushrooms and 1¼ tsp. salt, and sauté over high heat for about 10 minutes, until soft and almost dry.

5. Drop the fettuccine into 4 to 5 quarts boiling salted water. If the fettuccine are fresh, cook 1 minute; if they are frozen, cook for about 2 minutes.

6. Drain the fettuccine.

7. Put the fettuccine back into the cooking pot, and toss with 4 tbs. butter.

8. In a large bowl beat the eggs slightly. Add 1 cup cream, the ham, the cheese, and the pepper, and mix thoroughly. Add the fettuccine, toss well, and taste for salt.

9. Place ⅓ of the fettuccine mixture in the buttered dish, and top it with ⅓ of the mushrooms. Repeat the process, ending with the fettuccine. Reserve the final ⅓ of the mushrooms for the sauce.

10. Bake the timballo for about 20 minutes. Remove from the oven, and allow to settle in the dish for about 8 to 10 minutes.

11. Add the remaining cream to the reserved mushrooms, and cook over low heat for about 5 minutes, to thicken. Taste for salt.

12. Unmold the timballo on a heated round dish. Serve the sauce separately.

Estimated Cooking Time: 45 minutes
Estimated Total Preparation Time: 1 hour and 15 minutes, not including the pasta

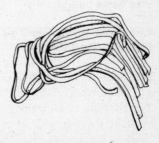

∽ SOUFFLE DI TAGLIOLINI VERDI ∽
Green Tagliolini Souffle For 4 to 6

This spectacular dish with the surprise inside (the tagliolini) will delight everyone. Light in texture and delicate tasting, it would be perfect for a luncheon.

2 scant cups very thick bechamel sauce with 3 tbs. butter, 4 tbs. flour, 1½ cups milk, and ¼ tsp. salt (see Bechamel Sauce, p. 16)
1 cup heavy cream
8 oz. green tagliolini, cut into 2" lengths (½ Basic Spinach Egg Pasta, p. 204)

salt
1 cup freshly grated Parmesan cheese
4 tbs. butter
6 egg yolks, slightly beaten
freshly ground black pepper
7 to 8 egg whites

1. Preheat the oven to 375° F.
2. Make the bechamel sauce in a medium saucepan.
3. Add the cream, and cook over low heat for 1 to 2 minutes. Remove from the heat.
4. Drop the tagliolini into 2 to 3 quarts boiling salted water. If the tagliolini are fresh, cook 1 minute; if they are frozen, cook for about 2 minutes.
5. Drain the tagliolini. You should have about 1½ to 1¾ cups.
6. Add the tagliolini, the Parmesan cheese, and the butter to the bechamel sauce, and stir well. Stir in the egg yolks and the pepper, and taste for salt.
7. Butter an 8-cup souffle dish.
8. Whip the egg whites until stiff but not dry. Fold them into the tagliolini mixture.
9. Pour the mixture into the souffle dish, and bake for 40 minutes. Serve immediately.

Estimated Cooking Time: 1 hour and 10 minutes
Estimated Total Preparation Time: 2 hours

∽ FRITTATA DI PAGLIA E FIENO ∽
Omelette with Yellow and Green Tagliolini   For 4 to 5

This colorful omelette is an elegant finger food, buffet dish, or main course.

7 *eggs*
salt
freshly ground black pepper
4 *oz. yellow tagliolini (a little less than ⅓ Basic Fresh Egg Pasta, p. 200)*
4 *oz. green tagliolini (about ¼ Basic Spinach Egg Pasta, p. 204)*

6 *tbs. butter at room temperature*
½ *cup freshly grated Parmesan cheese*
3 *1-oz. imported soft cheese wedges (such as La Vache Qui Rit) cut into small pieces*

1. In a large bowl beat the eggs with ¼ tsp. salt and the pepper.
2. Drop the yellow and green tagliolini into 4 to 5 quarts boiling salted water. If the pasta is fresh, it will be done in 1 to 2 minutes; if it is frozen, it will take 3 to 4 minutes.
3. Drain the tagliolini.
4. In another bowl toss the tagliolini with 2 tbs. butter, the Parmesan cheese, and the pieces of soft cheese. Add to the egg mixture, and stir gently.
5. Heat 3 tbs. butter in a medium skillet over medium heat. Pour in the egg mixture, turn the heat to low, and cook for about 7 minutes.
6. Loosen the frittata from the pan (the cheese will make it stick a little), and turn it onto a dish, cooked side down.
7. Add the remaining 1 tbs. butter to the pan. When it has melted, slide the frittata, soft side down, into the pan, and cook for about 5 minutes, or until well set. Press down with a spatula to make sure there is no liquid egg in the center.
8. Turn the frittata onto a platter, and let sit for at least 10 minutes before serving.
9. Cut the frittata into wedges or smaller pieces if it is to be eaten with the fingers.

Estimated Cooking Time: 30 minutes
Estimated Total Preparation Time: 45 minutes, not including the pasta

∾ NIDI DI PAGLIA E FIENO ∾
Nests of Yellow and Green Tagliolini For 4

3 eggs
salt
freshly ground black pepper
¼ cup freshly grated Parmesan
  cheese
4 oz. (⅔ cup) cooked ham,
  chopped
5 oz. yellow tagliolini (slightly
  more than ⅓ Basic Fresh Egg
  Pasta, p. 200)

5 oz. green tagliolini (slightly
  less than ⅓ Basic Spinach Egg
  Pasta, p. 204)
1 cup flour
10 tbs. butter
1 cup Basic Tomato Sauce III,
  p. 16

1. In a large bowl, beat the eggs together with ¼ tsp. salt and the pepper. Add the Parmesan cheese and the ham, and stir.
2. Drop the yellow and green tagliolini into 4 to 5 quarts boiling water. If the pasta is fresh, it will cook in 1 to 2 minutes; if the pasta is frozen, it will take 3 to 4 minutes.
3. Drain the tagliolini.
4. Add the tagliolini to the egg mixture, and stir gently.
5. Put the flour into a shallow bowl.
6. Divide the pasta mixture into 12 portions. Twist each of the 12 portions of pasta around a fork to form little "nests." Gently dip each nest into the flour, press down slightly, and set aside.
7. Heat the butter in a skillet over medium-low heat. Fry the nests on both sides in the hot butter, and place on a heated platter.
8. Heat the tomato sauce, and serve separately.

Estimated Cooking Time: 30 minutes
Estimated Total Preparation Time: 45 minutes, not including the pasta

7 Dumplings
Gnocchi

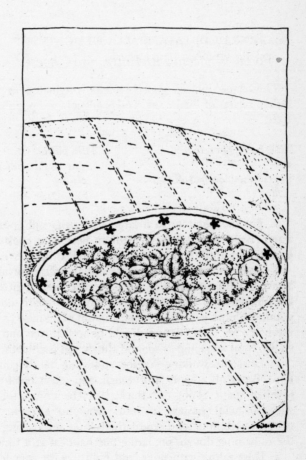

*G*nocchi—dumplings in English—appear in many different forms. Although they don't fit strictly into the rice/pasta category, they play a similar role in Italian cuisine. Here are several appealing varieties, most based on the classic potato version, and a few made with other ingredients.

∽ GNOCCHI DI PATATE ALLA PIEMONTESE ∽
● *Potato Gnocchi with Butter and Cheese*　　　For 4

This classic potato gnocchi recipe originated in the northern Italian region of Piedmont. Today gnocchi are popular throughout Italy.

2 lbs. boiling potatoes	8 tbs. butter
salt	¾ cup freshly grated Parmesan
1¼ cups unbleached all-purpose	cheese
flour	

1. Put the potatoes in a large saucepan, and cover them with water. Bring to a boil over medium heat, and cook for about 45 minutes, or until tender. Drain, and peel while they are still warm.

2. Pass the potatoes through a food mill onto a flat surface. Sprinkle with ¼ tsp. salt, and add the flour a little at a time, kneading it into the potatoes to form a smooth dough. Not all potatoes absorb exactly the same amount of flour, so the amount you use will vary. The mixture should be well mixed and soft but not sticky. Stop kneading as soon as the dough is smooth.

3. Dust the working surface and your hands generously with flour. Break off a handful of dough, and roll it out to form a long ropelike shape about ¾″ thick. Cut the dough into ½″ pieces with diagonal slashes to form diamond shapes. Sprinkle the gnocchi with flour, and repeat the rolling and cutting process with the remaining dough, preparing one handful at a time.

4. Dust a fork with flour, and hold it with your left hand at a vertical angle, pressing the prongs against the table. Using your right thumb, roll each of the gnocchi against the back or front of the fork, pushing down quickly. Each "gnocco" will have a hollow curved shape with the ridges on the convex outer side. Shaped

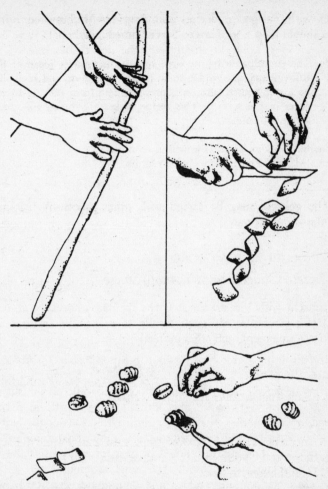

gnocchi are preferable because the sauce gets caught between the ridges. However, the simple cut gnocchi are quite acceptable if you don't want to go through the shaping process.

5. Drop the gnocchi, a few at a time, into 5 to 6 quarts boiling salted water. After they come to the surface, in 3 to 4 minutes, let them cook for another 20 to 30 seconds.

6. While the gnocchi are cooking, heat the butter over low heat until it is slightly browned.

7. When the gnocchi are done, remove them, with a skimmer or slotted spoon, to a heated dish one layer at a time. Sprinkle each

layer with Parmesan cheese, and drizzle with browned butter. You should have 2 to 3 layers. Serve immediately.

Note: The gnocchi can be prepared two to three hours ahead of time through step 4. Sprinkle them lightly with flour, and keep them on a well-floured surface to prevent them from sticking to each other or the surface. This recipe makes about 140 gnocchi, or about two pounds.

Estimated Cooking Time: 1 hour and 10 minutes
Estimated Total Preparation Time: 2 hours

The gnocchi may be served with other sauces. A few good combinations follow.

⌁ GNOCCHI AL POMODORO ⌁

Potato Gnocchi with Tomato Sauce   For 4

Gnocchi with tomato sauce is the Thursday specialty at most Roman restaurants. Although simple to make, the textures and flavors complement each other perfectly.

2 lbs. potato gnocchi (about 140)
salt
2 cups Basic Tomato Sauce III,
*   p. 16*

2 tbs. butter
½ cup freshly grated Parmesan
*   cheese*

1. To prepare gnocchi, follow steps 1 to 4 of Potato Gnocchi with Butter and Cheese (p. 244), and see note.
2. Heat the tomato sauce.
3. Drop the gnocchi, a few at a time, into 5 to 6 quarts boiling salted water. After they come to the surface (3 to 4 minutes), let them cook for another 20 to 30 seconds.
4. When the gnocchi are done, remove them, with a skimmer or a slotted spoon, to a heated serving dish one layer at a time. Top each layer with tomato sauce, dot with butter, and sprinkle with cheese. You should have 2 to 3 layers. Serve immediately.

Estimated Cooking Time: 1 hour and 10 minutes
Estimated Total Preparation Time: 2 hours

ᔎ GNOCCHI AL GORGONZOLA ᔎ
Potato Gnocchi with Gorgonzola Sauce   For 4

2 lbs. potato gnocchi (about 140)
salt
4 tbs. butter
4 oz. mild Gorgonzola cheese,
softened

¾ cup light cream
½ cup freshly grated Parmesan
cheese

1. To prepare gnocchi, follow steps 1 to 4 of Potato Gnocchi with Butter and Cheese (p. 244), and see note.
2. In a small saucepan combine the butter, the Gorgonzola, and the cream, and cook over low heat, stirring and mashing with a wooden spoon to form a smooth, creamy sauce. Keep warm.
3. Drop the gnocchi, a few at a time, into 5 to 6 quarts boiling salted water. After they come to the surface (3 to 4 minutes), let them cook for another 20 to 30 seconds.
4. When the gnocchi are done, remove them, with a skimmer or slotted spoon, to a heated serving dish one layer at a time. Top each layer with sauce and Parmesan cheese, reserving at least half to sprinkle on top. You should have 2 to 3 layers. Serve immediately.

Estimated Cooking Time: 1 hour and 10 minutes
Estimated Total Preparation Time: 2 hours

ᔎ GNOCCHI ALLA BAVA ᔎ
Potato Gnocchi with Fontina Cheese   For 4

2 lbs. potato gnocchi (about 140)
salt
6 tbs. butter

6 oz. Italian Fontina cheese,
shredded

1. To prepare gnocchi, follow steps 1 to 4 of Potato Gnocchi with Butter and Cheese (p. 244), and see note.
2. Preheat the oven to 425° F.
3. Butter a round oven-to-table baking dish.
4. Drop the gnocchi, a few at a time, into 5 to 6 quarts boiling

salted water. As they come to the surface, remove them, with a skimmer or a slotted spoon, to the baking dish one layer at a time. Cover each layer with cheese and a few dots of butter, reserving at least half the butter for the top. You should have 2 to 3 layers.

5. Bake the gnocchi for 6 to 8 minutes. Serve immediately.

Estimated Cooking Time: 1 hour and 20 minutes
Estimated Total Preparation Time: 2 hours

～ GNOCCHI DI ZUCCA ～
Squash Gnocchi　　　　　　　　　　　　　　For 4

This is our version of a wonderful dish savored at Mama Gina in Florence, recreated from the artistic description of its preparation given to us by a friendly waiter.

2 lbs. butternut squash
½ lb. boiling potatoes
salt
1 egg
2½ cups unbleached all-purpose
　flour

1 cup Basic Tomato Sauce I,
　p. 14
½ cup heavy cream
½ cup freshly grated Parmesan
　cheese

1. The evening before preparing the gnocchi bake the squash— halved or quartered and wrapped in aluminum foil—in a 350° F. oven for about 1½ hours, or until soft. Scoop out the pulp, put it into a piece of cheesecloth or a thin dish towel, and hang it overnight above the sink to drain.

2. Put the potatoes in a large saucepan, and cover with water. Bring to a boil over medium heat, and cook for about 45 minutes, or until tender. Drain, and peel while they are still warm.

3. Pass the potatoes through a food mill onto a flat surface. Add the squash, ¼ tsp. salt, and the egg, and mix with a fork. Add the flour by kneading it into the mixture to make a smooth dough. This mixture will not always absorb exactly the same amount of flour, so the amount you use will vary. The dough should be well mixed and soft but not sticky. Stop kneading as soon as the dough is smooth.

4. Dust the working surface and your hands generously with flour. Break off a handful of dough, and roll it out to form a long

ropelike shape about ¾" thick. Cut the dough into ½" pieces with diagonal slashes to form diamond shapes. Sprinkle the gnocchi with flour, and repeat the rolling and cutting process with the remaining dough, preparing one handful at a time.

5. Heat the tomato sauce over low heat. Add the cream, and cook for a few minutes more, making certain not to let the sauce boil.

6. Drop the gnocchi, a few at a time, into 5 to 6 quarts boiling salted water. After they come to the surface, in 3 to 4 minutes, let them cook for another 20 to 30 seconds.

7. When the gnocchi are done, remove them, with a skimmer or a slotted spoon, to a heated serving dish one layer at a time. Cover each layer with sauce and Parmesan cheese. You should have 2 to 3 layers. Serve immediately.

Estimated Cooking Time: 2 hours and 50 minutes
Estimated Total Preparation Time: 3 hours and 40 minutes

∽ GNOCCHI DI RICOTTA ∽

Ricotta Gnocchi For 4

These gnocchi made with ricotta are a bit lighter than those made with potatoes. They are also convenient to make since they can be prepared in advance and reheated.

1 lb. fresh ricotta	1¼ cups freshly grated Parmesan
1 egg	cheese
2 egg yolks	1 to 1¼ cups unbleached
salt	all-purpose flour
⅛ tsp. freshly grated nutmeg	8 tbs. butter

1. If the ricotta seems to be too moist, put it in a dish towel, and gently squeeze out any excess liquid.

2. In a bowl beat the egg and egg yolks together slightly. Add the ricotta, ½ tsp. salt, the nutmeg, and 1 cup Parmesan cheese, and blend thoroughly. Add 1 cup flour. After it has been completely worked into the mixture, flour your hands, and check to see whether the dough is firm enough to be formed into teaspoon-sized balls. If not, continue adding flour a little at a time until the dough has reached the right consistency.

3. Flour your hands generously, and shape the ricotta mixture into little balls about the size of a rounded teaspoon. Place them on a lightly floured surface.

4. Drop the gnocchi into 4 to 5 quarts boiling salted water. After they come to the surface, in 3 to 4 minutes, let them cook for another 30 seconds. Remove the gnocchi with a skimmer or a slotted spoon to a heated serving dish.

5. Heat the butter over low heat until it is slightly browned. Sprinkle the gnocchi with the remaining Parmesan cheese, and drizzle with the browned butter. Serve immediately.

Note: These gnocchi can be prepared in advance and reheated in a 400° F. oven for about 15 minutes. Don't add the cheese and butter until just before heating in the oven.

Estimated Cooking Time: 20 minutes
Estimated Total Preparation Time: 1 hour and 10 minutes

⮫ GNOCCHI VERDI ⮪
Spinach and Ricotta Dumplings   For 4

1 lb. fresh spinach
    or
1 10-oz. package frozen leaf
  spinach, partially thawed
salt
2 cups fresh ricotta

⅓ to ⅔ cup unbleached all-
  purpose flour (depending on
  the consistency of the ricotta)
2 eggs, slightly beaten
1¼ cups freshly grated Parmesan
  cheese
¼ tsp. freshly grated nutmeg
8 tbs. butter

1. Wash the spinach well, and without shaking the leaves, place it in a saucepan with ¼ tsp. salt. Cook, covered, over medium heat for 15 to 20 minutes, or until tender.

If frozen spinach is used, cook it with ¼ tsp. salt, covered, over low heat for 5 to 8 minutes. Drain the spinach, and let cool. Squeeze it with your hands to remove as much liquid as possible.

2. Put the spinach through the medium disc of a food mill. The spinach should have a coarse texture, as if it were finely chopped.

3. In a large bowl mix the spinach, the ricotta, ⅓ cup flour, the eggs, 1 cup Parmesan cheese, the nutmeg, and ½ tsp. salt with a

wooden spoon until thoroughly blended. The mixture will be soft and somewhat sticky. If it is too difficult to handle, add more flour a little at a time.

4. Flour your hands generously, and shape the mixture into little balls about the size of a rounded teaspoon. Place them on a lightly floured board.

5. Drop the gnocchi into 4 to 5 quarts boiling salted water. After they come to the surface, in 3 to 4 minutes, remove them, with a skimmer or a slotted spoon, to a heated serving dish.

6. Heat the butter in a small saucepan over low heat until it is slightly browned. Sprinkle the gnocchi with the remaining Parmesan cheese, and drizzle with the browned butter. Serve immediately.

Note: This dish can be prepared several hours in advance. In that case, place the gnocchi in a buttered ovenproof serving dish in one layer. Drizzle first with the butter and then the grated cheese. Bake in a 400° F. oven for about 15 minutes.

Estimated Cooking Time: 25 minutes
Estimated Total Preparation Time: 1 hour

～ GNOCCHI ALLA ROMANA ～
Semolina Gnocchi Roman Style For 4

Although an unpretentious dish, these gnocchi are very popular with adults as well as children because of their soft, creamy texture.

3½ cups milk	*2 egg yolks*
1¼ cups (½ lb.) semolina flour	*½ cup freshly grated Parmesan*
(see note)	*cheese*
salt	*5 tbs. butter, melted*

1. Bring the milk to a boil in a medium saucepan over medium-high heat. Add the semolina by sprinkling it gently over the milk, stirring constantly with a wooden spoon. Lower the heat to medium-low, continue to stir, and cook for about 15 minutes.

2. Remove the semolina from the heat. Add ¼ tsp. salt and the

egg yolks, stirring well after each addition; add ¼ cup Parmesan cheese. Stir well, and pour out onto a cold, flat surface (marble or formica). With a spatula dipped in cold water smooth the surface of the semolina until it is about ⅓″ thick. Let cool for about 1 hour.

3. Cut the semolina into small circles with a cookie cutter or glass about 1¾″ in diameter.

4. Preheat the oven to 400° F.

5. Butter a round oven-to-table baking dish.

6. Place the scraps from the cut out circles on the bottom of the dish. Sprinkle with some of the Parmesan cheese and melted butter. Make additional layers with the circles. Pour the remaining butter over the top, and sprinkle with the remaining Parmesan cheese.

7. Bake the gnocchi for about 15 minutes, or until golden. Serve immediately.

Note: Semolina is available in most large supermarkets and at Italian specialty stores. These gnocchi can be prepared several hours in advance through step 6.

Estimated Cooking Time: 35 minutes
Estimated Total Preparation Time: 1 hour and 50 minutes

8 Salads
Insalate

*I*n Italy salads of both cooked and raw vegetables are usually seasoned simply with oil and vinegar or oil and lemon juice. More elaborate dressings that include mayonnaise, anchovies, or egg yolks are reserved for appetizers. Italians eat their salads with or after the main course rather than before.

∽ INSALATA MISTA ∽
Mixed Salad
For 4

1 small head Boston lettuce
½ small head curly chicory
½ small head escarole
½ small bunch arugola
    or
½ small bunch watercress
1 small celery heart
2 scallions
1 carrot

4 radishes
1 small cucumber, preferably the
    pickling type
6 cherry tomatoes
salt
⅓ cup olive oil
2 tbs. red wine vinegar
freshly ground black pepper

1. Remove and discard any dark green or bruised leaves from the lettuces. Remove the thick stems from the arugola or watercress.
2. Wash all the greens in 2 or 3 changes of cold water. Drain, and dry thoroughly in a salad spinner or basket.
3. Remove any leaves from the celery heart and the green part from the scallions.
4. Peel and shred the carrot into a large salad bowl, preferably glass or china.
5. Cut the celery and the scallions into ¼″ pieces, and add them to the bowl. Thinly slice the radishes and the cucumber, and add them, with the tomatoes.
6. Tear the lettuce leaves into 3 or 4 pieces, and add them and the arugola.
7. Sprinkle the salad with 1 tsp. salt. Pour the oil over it in a thin stream, and sprinkle the vinegar on top. Add the pepper, and toss the salad gently but thoroughly. Taste for salt and/or vinegar. Serve the salad immediately.

Estimated Total Preparation Time: 20 minutes

∾ INSALATA VERDE MISTA ∾

Mixed Green Salad   For 4

1 *small head Boston lettuce*	½ *small bunch arugola*
1 *small head bibb lettuce*	or
or	½ *bunch watercress*
½ *small head romaine lettuce*	*salt*
¼ *head escarole*	⅓ *cup olive oil*
¼ *head curly chicory*	2 *tbs. red wine vinegar*
	freshly ground black pepper

1. Remove and discard any dark green or bruised outer leaves from the lettuces. Remove the thicker stems from the arugola or watercress.

2. Wash all the greens in 2 or 3 changes of cold water. Drain, and dry thoroughly in a salad spinner or basket. It is very important that the lettuce leaves be free of water so that the oil will coat them evenly.

3. Tear the lettuce leaves into 3 or 4 pieces, and place them in a salad bowl, preferably glass. Add the arugola or watercress.

4. Sprinkle the greens with ½ tsp. salt. Pour the oil over the salad in a thin stream. Sprinkle with the vinegar. Toss the leaves gently but thoroughly, and taste for salt and/or vinegar. Serve the salad immediately with a pepper mill on the side.

Note: The greens can be washed even a day in advance and kept in the refrigerator in a plastic bag.

Estimated Total Preparation Time: 20 minutes

∾ POMODORI SPACCATI ∾

Seasoned Tomato Halves   For 4

4 *firm round tomatoes*	*freshly ground black pepper*
salt	4 *tbs. olive oil*

1. Cut the tomatoes in half, and arrange on a glass or china platter cut side up.

2. Sprinkle the tomatoes with ½ tsp. salt and the pepper, and drizzle with the oil.

Estimated Total Preparation Time: 10 minutes

∽ INSALATA DI POMODORI ∽
Tomato Salad   For 4

2 scallions, minced
1 tbs. fresh parsley, minced
½ tsp. dried oregano
4 tbs. olive oil

salt
freshly ground black pepper
3 large tomatoes, thinly sliced

1. In a small bowl combine the scallions, the parsley, the oregano, the oil, ¼ tsp. salt, and the pepper. Stir thoroughly with a fork, and let stand for 20 to 30 minutes.

2. Arrange the tomato slices in a shallow serving dish, and spoon the seasoning over them. Let rest for 10 minutes before serving.

Estimated Total Preparation Time: 45 minutes

∽ INSALATA DI CAROTE ∽
Carrot Salad   For 4

Colorful and low in calories, this is the perfect salad to accompany a creamy pasta or rice dish.

1 lb. carrots, washed and peeled
3 tbs. lemon juice

4 tbs. olive oil
salt

1. Using the largest holes on a standing grater or the shredding disc of a food processor, grate the carrots.

2. Place the grated carrots in a salad bowl. Add the lemon juice, the olive oil, and ¼ tsp. salt. Toss, and serve.

Note: Although it is best to make this salad shortly before serving, any leftovers kept in the refrigerator will remain moist and tasty for a couple of days.

Estimated Total Preparation Time: 25 minutes

∾ INSALATA DI CRESCIONE ∾
Watercress Salad For 4

2 bunches watercress
salt
⅓ cup olive oil

2 tbs. red wine vinegar
freshly ground black pepper

1. Remove most of the stems from the watercress, and wash in several changes of cold water. Dry the watercress in a salad spinner or basket.

2. Put the watercress in a salad bowl, preferably glass, and sprinkle with ½ tsp. salt. Drizzle with the oil and the vinegar, and toss well. Serve immediately with a pepper mill on the side.

Estimated Total Preparation Time: 15 minutes

∾ INSALATA DI FINOCCHIO ∾
Fennel Salad For 4

1 large round fennel bulb
4 tbs. olive oil
1 tbs. white wine vinegar

salt
freshly ground black pepper

1. Cut off the tops of the fennel, and discard any tough or bruised outer layers. Cut the fennel bulb in half lengthwise, and then cut each half crosswise into very thin slices.

2. Wash the fennel in cold water. Drain, and pat dry.

3. Place the fennel in a glass or china salad bowl. Pour the oil and vinegar over it, sprinkle with ¼ tsp. salt and the pepper, and toss well.

Note: When buying fennel, always choose the round, bulbous ones— called the female in Italy. They are more tender than the flatter, oblong "males."

Estimated Total Preparation Time: 15 minutes

∿ INSALATA DI SCAROLA ∿
Escarole Salad   For 4

⅓ cup blanched walnuts,
    chopped
⅓ cup vegetable oil
1 large head escarole (about
    1 lb.)

salt
freshly ground black pepper
3 tbs. Parmesan cheese, crumbled
    or shaved

1. Soak the walnuts in the oil for at least 2 hours.
2. Remove and discard any dark green or bruised outer leaves from the escarole, and wash in 2 or 3 changes of cold water. Drain, and dry thoroughly in a salad spinner or basket. Cut the leaves into ½" pieces. Sprinkle with ¼ tsp. salt and the pepper; add the oil and walnuts, and toss well. Sprinkle the Parmesan cheese on top, and serve.

Estimated Total Preparation Time: 20 minutes, not including soaking
the walnuts

∿ VERDURE IN PINZIMONIO ∿
Bowl of Raw Salad Vegetables   For 4 to 6

This is a great salad for a buffet—it makes a lovely centerpiece —or for any occasion when you want a colorful, decorative display of vegetables. Once you get the idea, the variations are infinite.

3 celery stalks with leaves
1 bunch radishes
2 to 3 long carrots
1 large green or red sweet pepper

1 small cauliflower
salt
freshly ground black pepper
1 cup olive oil

1. Wash and dry all the vegetables.
2. Peel the tough outer layer from the celery stalks, and cut each crosswise into two pieces. One piece will have the celery leaves and a short stem, and the other will be all stem. Cut the stem pieces in half lengthwise.
3. Trim the roots and the leaves from the radishes, leaving part of the green stems for decoration and dipping.

4. Peel the carrots, and cut into strips.

5. Halve the pepper, remove the seeds and the filaments, and cut into wide strips.

6. Remove the hard core from the cauliflower without separating the florets (they will be separated at the table).

7. Mix 1½ tsp. salt, the pepper, and the oil and divide the oil mixture between two small bowls.

8. In a good-sized shallow bowl, preferably glass, arrange the cut vegetables in a decorative pattern. Put the cauliflower in the center. Surround it with little bundles of celery stalks, carrot sticks, and pepper strips. Scatter the radishes over the whole arrangement. Place near bowls of oil for dipping.

Note: Other suitable vegetables for this salad are fennel, broccoli, asparagus, artichokes, and cherry tomatoes. All the vegetables except the pepper can be prepared the day before and refrigerated in plastic bags.

Estimated Total Preparation Time: 30 minutes

∽ INSALATA DI ARANCE ∽
Orange Salad

For 4

In spite of the curious match of these ingredients, the sugar and the oil complement the orange surprisingly well. The result is very flavorful—neither tangy nor sweet.

4 navel oranges   3 tbs. olive oil
½ tsp. sugar

1. Peel the oranges, taking care to remove all the skin, to expose the flesh.

2. Cut the oranges crosswise into thin slices.

3. Arrange the slices on a serving dish in a spiral.

4. Sprinkle the slices with the sugar, and drizzle them with the oil. Let sit for about 30 minutes. Serve the salad at room temperature.

Estimated Total Preparation Time: 45 minutes

∾ INSALATA DI BARBABIETOLE ∾
Beet Salad

For 4

salt
1 lb. beets
freshly ground black pepper

2 tbs. red wine vinegar
2 tbs. olive oil

1. Bring 1½ to 2 quarts water with 2 tsp. salt to a boil. Add the beets, and cook, covered, over medium heat for about 30 minutes, or until tender but firm.
2. Drain the beets, cool slightly, and peel. While still warm, cut the beets into thin slices, and place in a shallow dish. Sprinkle with ¼ tsp. salt, the pepper, and the vinegar, and toss to make sure that the slices are well coated. Add the olive oil, and toss again. Allow the beets to marinate for at least 30 minutes before serving.

Note: This salad can be prepared several hours in advance. It does not need to be refrigerated.

Estimated Cooking Time: 35 minutes
Estimated Total Preparation Time: 1 hour and 15 minutes

∾ INSALATA DI CAVOLFIORE ∾
Cauliflower Salad

For 4

1 head cauliflower (about
1½ lbs.)
salt

4 tbs. olive oil
2 tbs. white wine vinegar
freshly ground black pepper

1. Remove and discard the leaves from the cauliflower, and carefully separate the florets. Rinse under cold water.
2. Bring 1½ to 2 quarts water with 2 tsp. salt to a boil. Add the florets, and cook, covered, over medium heat for 10 to 12 minutes, or until just tender.
3. Drain the florets, and place in a glass or china salad bowl. Drizzle with the oil and the vinegar, sprinkle with the pepper, and toss gently. Taste for salt. Serve the salad at room temperature.

Estimated Cooking Time: 25 minutes
Estimated Total Preparation Time: 35 minutes

∽ INSALATA DI FAGIOLINI ∽
Green Bean Salad   For 4

1 lb. green beans	*3 tbs. olive oil*
salt	*1 tbs. red wine vinegar*
2 tbs. fresh parsley, minced	*freshly ground black pepper*
2 tsp. scallions, minced	

1. Snap off the ends of the beans, and remove any strings along the edges. Rinse in cold water.
2. Bring 1½ to 2 quarts water with 2 tsp. salt to a boil. Add the green beans, and cook, uncovered, over medium-high heat for 10 to 12 minutes, or until barely tender.
3. Drain the beans in a colander. Refresh quickly under cold water, and remove to a bowl. Toss the beans with the parsley, the scallions, the oil, the vinegar, ¼ tsp. salt, and pepper to taste.

Note: This salad can be eaten immediately or prepared several hours beforehand.

Estimated Cooking Time: 25 minutes
Estimated Total Preparation Time: 35 minutes

∽ INDIVIA O SCAROLA ALLA GRIGLIA ∽
Grilled Chicory or Escarole   For 4

This is perhaps the quickest and most elegant way to prepare these vegetables. Venetians use radicchio rosso, but if you can't get it, chicory or escarole gives a comparably delicious result. Chicory is sharper than escarole. Try both to see which you prefer.

2 medium heads curly chicory	*½ cup olive oil*
or	*or*
2 medium heads escarole	*6 tbs. butter*
	salt
	freshly ground black pepper

1. Remove and discard the hard outer leaves of the lettuce. Cut each head vertically into 4 pieces, and wash well in cold water. Shake the lettuce vigorously, and pat it with paper towels to remove as much moisture as possible.

2. If you use olive oil, place the lettuce on a dish, drizzle the pieces with the oil, and sprinkle with ¼ tsp. salt and the pepper. Heat a heavy iron skillet over high heat. Add the lettuce, and sear it briskly for 2 minutes on each side. Or you may place the lettuce on a rack and broil it under a broiler for 3 to 4 minutes on each side.

If you use butter, heat the butter in the heavy skillet over high heat being careful not to let it burn. Immediately add the lettuce, sprinkle with ¼ tsp. salt, and the pepper, and turn the heat to medium high. Fry the lettuce for about 4 minutes on each side. Serve immediately.

Note: This salad is also good at room temperature.

Estimated Cooking Time: 8 to 10 minutes
Estimated Total Preparation Time: 20 minutes

⌁ RAPINI ALL'AGLIO E OLIO ⌁
Rapini with Oil and Garlic   For 4

1 lb. rapini (broccoli rape)   3 tbs. olive oil
salt   1 large garlic clove

1. Separate the florets from the leaves and stems of the rapini. Peel the tough dark green skin off the stems, and cut the stems into 1½" pieces.
2. Steam the rapini in a medium saucepan for 5 to 7 minutes. While they are cooking sprinkle with ¼ tsp. salt. Drain well.
3. Heat the oil in a medium saucepan, preferably enamel or stainless steel, add the garlic, and sauté for a few seconds. Add the rapini, and sauté over medium-low heat for another 5 minutes. Serve warm.

Estimated Cooking Time: 20 minutes
Estimated Total Preparation Time: 30 minutes

∽ SPINACI ALL'AGRO ∽
Cooked Spinach Salad For 4

3 lbs. fresh spinach   4 tbs. olive oil
salt   2 tbs. lemon juice
freshly ground black pepper

1. Remove the stems from the spinach, and wash well in several changes of water.
2. Without shaking the leaves, place the spinach with ½ tsp. salt in a medium saucepan, and bring to a boil over medium heat. Push the leaves down with a spoon. Cover the saucepan, and cook for 10 to 12 minutes, or until tender.
3. Drain the spinach in a colander, and let cool. Squeeze gently to remove most of the liquid.
4. Put the spinach in a glass salad bowl. Sprinkle with ¼ tsp. salt and the pepper. Pour on the olive oil and the lemon juice. Toss gently, and serve at room temperature.

Note: The spinach can be cooked several hours ahead of time or even the day before and seasoned up to one hour before serving. If the spinach is cooked the day before, refrigerate it overnight and remove from the refrigerator several hours before serving.

Estimated Cooking Time: 15 minutes
Estimated Total Preparation Time: 35 minutes

∽ INSALATA D'INVERNO ∽
Winter Salad For 4

3 medium potatoes   1 cup canned chickpeas
salt   2 ripe tomatoes
½ lb. green beans   3 to 4 scallions, thinly sliced
3 tbs. red wine vinegar   8 to 10 fresh basil leaves, torn
freshly ground black pepper   into small pieces (optional)
½ cup olive oil   or
1 cup canned red kidney beans   1 tbs. fresh parsley, chopped

1. Put the potatoes in a small saucepan, and cover them with water. Add ½ tsp. salt, and bring to a boil over medium heat. Cook for about 35 minutes, or until tender.

2. While the potatoes are cooking, snap off the ends of the green beans, removing any strings.

3. Bring 1 quart water with 1 tsp. salt to a boil. Add the green beans and cook, uncovered, over medium-high heat for 10 to 12 minutes, or until barely tender.

4. Combine the vinegar, ½ tsp. salt, and the pepper in a small bowl, and stir until the salt is dissolved. Add the oil, and mix well.

5. In a bowl combine the kidney beans, the chickpeas, and 2 tbs. of the vinegar and oil mixture. Toss gently together.

6. Cut the tomatoes into thin wedges.

7. Drain potatoes, and let cool. Peel, and cube. Drain green beans.

8. Arrange a mound of the kidney beans and chickpeas in the center of a shallow round serving dish. Surround with smaller mounds of potatoes, green beans, and tomatoes. Spoon the remaining vinegar and oil dressing over the vegetables, and sprinkle with the scallions and the basil or parsley.

Estimated Cooking Time: 40 minutes
Estimated Total Preparation Time: 50 minutes

9 Fruit
for Dessert

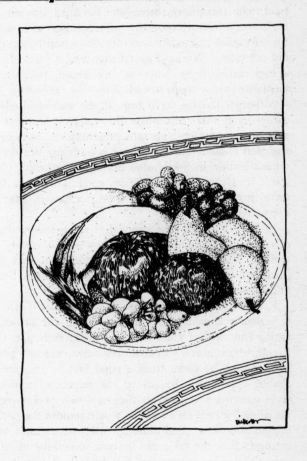

*F*ruit is almost always the preferred finale to a meal in Italy. When you gaze through the windows of Italian restaurants, the sumptuous display of fruit is often as prominent as the fresh pasta, the antipasti, and the rest. To an Italian, fresh seasonal fruit is not incidental to the meal; it is always something to savor, a special treat to be anticipated throughout the meal. I've almost never seen an Italian refuse after-dinner fruit, regardless of how he had eaten. Fruit freshens the palate and provides a healthy close that is sweet but not filling. We have found that fruit is particularly pleasing in a high-carbohydrate pasta or rice menu; the meal itself is so satisfying that it tends to cancel out the craving for a rich dessert.

Although Italians serve fruit at the end of almost every meal, even very formal ones where there may be a sweet as well, they have no interest in elaborate presentations. When fruit is fresh and well chosen, the eye appeal is built in. We do not have the same selection in the United States; nevertheless, you can always select fruit that looks and tastes good. To add to the aesthetics, serve fruit in a basket, a glass bowl, a stemmed fruit dish, or on a decorative platter.

In Italy, fruit is usually served at room temperature. The taste of certain fruit such as melons, however, is clearly enhanced by chilling. You can chill the fruit beforehand or serve it on a platter garnished with pieces of ice, as is often done in Italy, especially in the summer.

Except for melons, peaches, and fruit salad (macedonia), fruit is generally served whole. Italians learn the art of peeling and eating fruit with a knife and fork at an early age. One Milanese friend, who is now a successful physician, was very poor as a young man though he came from a good family. In spite of his often shabby appearance, he gained the respect of waiters and fellow train passengers as soon as they saw him peel a piece of fruit— impaling the fruit on a fork, he would remove the peel with a knife in one unbroken spiral. Though most of us can't aspire to that, eating fruit at the table can become something of an art.

Fruit salad has a long tradition in Italy. Naturally, the composition depends upon the season. Italians like their fruit salad with lots of liquid—usually fruit juice or white wine or a combination of both—and sugar. In summer peaches are also sliced and marinated in white wine and sugar.

Fruit with cheese is a delicious variation. It may come as a surprise, but the most common after-dinner cheese is a good Parmesan (Parmigiano Reggiano). Its rich, nutty flavor goes particularly well with fall and winter fruit such as apples, grapes, and pears.

Regardless of how you decide to serve your fruit-as-dessert, always choose what's in season. The cost will be lower, and the fruit itself will probably be fresher and of higher quality than out-of-season delicacies. To help you get started in planning your fruit desserts, the menu suggestions that follow the recipes offer some ideas.

No Italian meal concludes without coffee, sometimes *corretto*, or laced, with a liqueur or a brandy such as Sambuca or grappa. Although Italians often enjoy coffee by itself at various times of the day, they never drink it during a meal. Italian coffee—that is, espresso—is served black, in demitasse cups, usually with sugar. It is never served with lemon peel, a touch, unknown in Italy, that diminishes rather than enhances the wonderful aroma of the espresso.

To prepare a good cup of dark, rich, smooth, and aromatic espresso is a simple process, but there are some rules that must be followed to avoid the disaster of a watery and bitter black potion. Most important, of course, are the beans, which should not only be a good blend for espresso (more on this later) but should also be freshly roasted, freshly ground, and the correct grind for the machine being used.

The water is equally important. It should be fresh, cold, and, ideally, soft and free of chemicals. In Rome the two coffee bars that compete for primacy in coffee-making—Tazza d'Oro and Bar Sant'Eustachio—are both located near the Pantheon, an area that receives its water from a fresh spring called *acqua vergine* (virgin water) which was brought to this site at the time of Augustus. The best espresso we ever had was in Turin, many years ago, a rich and fragrant concoction so smooth and thick that it richly deserved its appellation *crema di caffe* (cream of coffee). It was the combination of a top-rate blend of coffee and fresh mountain water. You can achieve satisfactory results with fresh tap water, but if you're a real purist, you may make your espresso with bottled spring water.

Fine espresso coffee is the result of a good blend of high-grade beans and the right roasting. In Italy we had the pleasure of interviewing Arrigo Comar, the owner of the *torrefazione* Mattioni—a coffee-roasting business—in Gorizia. His best and most expensive blend is half Brazilian coffee—the Santos type—and half Guatemalan or Costa Rican. Other good blends consist of beans from Brazil, Costa Rica, Jamaica, the Ivory Coast, and Zaire. After the blend has been prepared, the beans are roasted at 480 to 500° F for about 13 minutes to bring out their flavor. The result is a dark, luscious, slightly oily product with a wonderful aroma. When ground, the coffee is the color of dark cocoa.

We find that what is sold in the United States as French roast, which is lighter that the U.S. Italian roast, is close to, if slightly darker than, the coffee served in Italy. The so-called Italian roast or espresso bears little resemblance to Italian coffee.

Ideally coffee should be ground just before it is prepared. For this reason we find a coffee grinder very useful. Store your beans in an airtight container in the refrigerator, for they tend to get stale; they can also be frozen for one to two months. If you buy your coffee already ground, refrigerate or freeze it until you use it.

Grinding your own coffee enables you to control its texture. If the coffee is ground too fine, the water will not seep through, and if it is too coarse, your coffee will be weak and watery. Your coffee machine will determine how fine to grind the coffee.

The American market is flooded with a confusing multitude of espresso makers. The main distinction is between stove-top machines and electric ones. The stove-top machines do not exactly produce that creamy and foamy delicacy called espresso, but they make an excellent brew, very close to the real thing. There are two kinds of stove-top machines: the old-fashioned *napoletana* (the Neapolitan) and the more recent and increasingly popular *moka*. The *napoletana* functions by the drip method. For it you need coffee ground to the consistency of fine sand. Fill the bottom part of the machine with water, pack the filter section with coffee, screw on the top of the filter section, and insert it in the water container. Cover with the empty reservoir (the one with the spout), and place the *napoletana* over medium heat. When the water begins to boil, it will start to drip out of a tiny hole just below the rim of the water container. This is the signal to remove the machine from the stove and quickly turn it upside down on a warmer. The water will then seep through the coffee to fill the bottom pot. In seven to ten minutes the coffee will be ready.

The *moka* Express comes in a variety of sizes and materials— cast aluminum, stainless steel, and flameproof porcelain; if possible avoid aluminum, which gives off a slight aftertaste. For the *moka* use a slightly coarser grind of coffee than for the *napoletana*. To prepare the coffee, fill the bottom with cold water. Pack the coffee into the filter in the middle, and screw the top on tightly. Place the *moka* over a low flame. Within four to ten minutes, depending on the size, the steam and water forced through the coffee will fill the top vessel.

Always drink espresso fresh, never warmed up. Prepare just the amount you need, and serve it right away.

Among the almost infinite variety of electric coffee makers, the best kinds make one or two cups at a time. These are miniature versions of Italian coffee-bar machines, which produce wonderful, authentic espresso. We like the Krups Gaggia, imported from Italy, and Olympia Cremina, imported from Switzerland. To prepare the coffee, turn the machine on to heat for about five minutes. Fill the filter cup with coffee, press it down with the tool that comes with the machine, and insert the filter holder back into the machine. Turn on the switch that regulates the flow, or if it is a lever-operated machine, move the lever up and down. The coffee will flow in a very thin, droplike, and bubbly rivulet into the cup. Be sure to read the operating instructions that come with the machine carefully.

To make a good, aromatic drink, it is important that the machine, whether stove-top or electric, be absolutely clean. Wash it with hot water and a brush to remove any sediment. Do not use soap.

Espresso's most popular relative is cappuccino, a lovely espresso and milk concoction that is the perfect accompaniment to breakfast or simply delightful by itself for a coffee break. In Italy cappuccino is never drunk at the end of lunch or dinner. Most electric espresso machines have a steamer attachment for cappuccino. To make cappuccino, immerse the nozzle of the steamer into a small pitcher of milk. Turn the valve on, and when the milk is bubbly and foamy, pour it over the espresso. The proportions for cappuccino range from two thirds espresso and one third milk to half espresso and half milk, depending on whether you prefer your cappucino dark or light. Top with a light sprinkling of cocoa, not cinnamon.

If you use a stove-top coffee maker, you may end up with some leftover coffee. This is excellent chilled, slightly sweetened, or served over crushed ice (known as granita de caffe) or with a scoop of vanilla ice cream.

One final word about espresso. You may have heard that since Italian coffee is strong, you cannot drink it as often as American coffee. In fact, Italian espresso, because of its longer roasting time, contains less caffeine than American coffee. So don't hesitate to enjoy it.

11 Guide to Italian Wine

*A*fter a long period of undeserved neglect and underappreciation, Italian wines have finally achieved respectable status in the estimation of American wine enthusiasts. Only a few years ago most Americans' familiarity with Italian wines barely extended to the Bolla wines—Valpolicella, Soave, Bardolino—and the most pedestrian varieties of Chianti. Today experts sing the praises of such classic Italian wines as Amarone and Barolo and some of the more modest and formerly little-known Italian wines that share the same fine winemaking traditions.

Wine experts have long recognized that Italian wines have certain advantages over comparable wines from other countries. They are often of high quality even at a young age, and they are lower in acidity than French wines. Among both reds and whites, good Italian wines are not hard to find, in many cases, at very moderate prices, lower even than California wines of similar quality. This combination of moderate prices and high quality often makes Italian wines the best value around. This stems from the fact that Italy produces wine in enormous quantities—more than any other country in the world. Although only a small percentage of Italian wines are exported, every region—almost every locality—in Italy produces wine. Naturally not all of it is worthy of consideration, but, amazingly, much of it is satisfactory and a significant portion is truly outstanding. As Italian wines increase in popularity, their extraordinary value/price ratio may not hold. In the 1960s, when serving Italian wines had little status, Efrem, as a diplomat's wife, made a point of ordering directly from reliable producers she knew in northern Italy. At that time the firm of Antinori was just beginning to export its wines, and through a Florentine friend whose main interests were discovering and collecting contemporary Italian paintings and outstanding wines, she received several cases of particularly superior vintages. She also went with her father, who knew the best-kept secrets about wine producers, to some of the smaller establishments in the Veneto region to order wine. Among these wines she considers Pinot Grigio di Angoris and Verduzzo her discoveries. Her guests were always very surprised to discover that she dared to serve Italian wines and that the wines were, in fact, so good. It gave her great satisfaction when a close friend and great wine snob who considered any wine beyond Margaux not worth even a sip offered to buy whatever Antinori Classico she had left on her departure from Ceylon. In this small way Efrem hoped to carry on her own personal crusade to develop an appreciation for the wines of Italy.

Today knowledgeable wine lovers cannot possibly ignore the high quality and enormous range of Italian wines. However, the long-standing status enjoyed by French wines and the increasing sophistication of wine production in California continue to dominate the American market, so that Italian wines remain a great bargain. As wine dealers have become more enthusiastic about Italian wines, they have broadened the selection available, so any reasonably well-stocked store has an extensive variety.

Listed below are the selections we both made among the many Italian wines marketed in the United States. While not a complete guide in any sense, it should be helpful in your quest for Italian wines that will enhance your meals. Recommendations for wines with specific dishes are included with the menus in Chapter 12.

All vintage red wines should be uncorked ahead of time to allow them to breathe. Exposure to air enhances their natural bouquet and flavor. The older the wines, the more time they need. Some Amarones, Barolos, Brunello di Montalcinos, and Gattinaras may require two to three hours to reach their optimum state; others will benefit from half an hour to an hour's breathing.

Great Reds

Amarone, whose full name is Recioto Amarone della Valpolicella, is a dry Recioto, a wine made from half-dried grapes and a specialty of the Verona area in Veneto. It has a velvety, full body comparable to a superior Bordeaux. The slightly bitter yet pleasant flavor gives this wine its name, from *amaro*, which means "bitter." Amarone ages well and ideally should be drunk when it is about ten years old. The best vintage year is 1964; very good vintages are 1966, 1967, 1969, 1974, 1977, 1979, and 1980. This wine hasn't had a bad vintage in recent years, so the years in between also offer above-average wine.

Barolo is considered one of the finest wines of the Piedmont region and, indeed, one of the best wines produced in Italy. Coming from the Nebbiolo grape, Barolo is a deep, intense, full-bodied wine with a powerful scent. Its rich flavor is characterized by an unusual velvety texture, and the Turinese find it so superb and satisfying that they call it *re dei vini,* or "king of wines." Like most full-bodied reds, Barolo should not be drunk too young. It is usually best when at least ten years old. The best vintages are 1961, 1964, 1971, and 1978 (the last is considered a fine investment for aging). Very good vintages are 1962, 1965, 1967, 1970, 1974, 1979, and 1980.

Brunello di Montalcino has been produced for the past 100 years in the medieval Tuscan town of Montalcino, south of Siena, from San Giovese grapes. Rich without being heavy and characterized by a distinctive vitality, this big and fragrant wine is another contender for the title "king of Italian wines." It is certainly among the most expensive. Although after five years it is called *riserva* ("aged"), it takes many years to mature and is at its best when more than a decade old. Probably the best vintage available in the United States is 1964. Selling for as much as $100 a bottle, it is a collector's item. The other best vintages are 1970, 1975, and 1981. Very good vintages are 1966, 1967, 1971, 1977, 1978, 1979, and 1980.

Chianti Classico Riserva, usually identified by the black rooster on the collar, is perhaps the most widely available and popular of the best Italian wines sold in the United States. Produced from a mixture of red and white grapes grown in the Tuscan hills between Florence and Siena, it is aged in oak casks for at least three years. Sometimes compared to Bordeaux, Chianti Classico Riserva is a fragrant wine with good tonality and great versatility. You can always feel secure with a wine in this category. Although there are great variations among brands, the wine is eminently reliable. The best vintages are 1971 and 1978. Very good vintages are 1970, 1975, 1977, 1979, and 1980.

Gattinara, like Barolo, is a Piedmontese wine produced from the Nebbiolo grape. And like Barolo, it is regarded as one of Italy's greatest reds. Compared with a wine like Chianti, these two wines—Barolo and Gattinara—are produced in very small quantities, which contributes to their status and prestige. Gattinara is a smooth, robust wine with elegance and the balance that ideally requires at least ten years of aging. The best vintages are 1964 and 1974. Very good vintages are 1968, 1969, 1970, 1976, 1979, 1980, and 1981.

Grumello is another wine made from the Nebbiolo grape, but those for Grumello are grown in Valtellina, the Alpine area of Lombardy north of Milan. Grumello is a well-developed, medium-bodied red wine characterized by a certain delicacy that increases with age. It is noticeably lighter than the Piedmontese Nebbiolo wines such as Barolo and Gattinara. Although some vintages reach their peak at nine or ten years, other vintages are excellent at six or seven years old. Very good vintages are 1971 and 1978. Other good vintages are 1973, 1975, 1979, 1980, and 1981.

Sassella, like Grumello, is produced in Lombardy from the Nebbiolo grape and is equally highly regarded. Although it bears many of the same characteristics as Grumello, Sassella has a longer history, going back to Roman times. Celebrated during the Renaissance, it was one of Leonardo da Vinci's favorite wines. There are no recent exceptional vintages; the very good and good vintages are the same as for Grumello.

Sfursat is still another Lombardian wine from the Valtellina area produced from the Nebbiolo grape. However, it is the dried Nebbiolo grapes that are responsible for Sfursat's distinctive taste and strong, velvety texture. Because of the dried grapes, it bears some resemblance to Amarone, at the same time displaying some of the qualities of Grumello and Sassella. It ages very successfully and reaches its optimum state between eight and ten years old. Some very good vintages are 1971 and 1978. Good vintages are 1973, 1975, 1979, 1980, and 1981.

Torgiano Riserva, also known as Rubesco di Torgiano, is produced in limited quantities in Umbria near Assisi. A pleasant, rounded, medium-bodied red with a unique accent whose fine flavor improves with age, it bears a resemblance to Chianti Classico Riserva. At seven to ten years, Torgiano Riserva approaches its full potential. The best recent vintages are 1975 and 1980. The very good vintages are 1973, 1974, 1977, 1978, 1979, and 1981.

Venegazzu', a red from the area around Treviso, near Venice, is among the great Italian wines, but it remains an unknown treasure in the United States. Venegazzu' is a warm, mellow wine characterized by a rich bouquet and delicate fragrance. Venegazzu' Della Casa, the category of this wine that is aged longer in wooden casks, is a richer wine with fuller body and a slight bitter aftertaste. Very good vintages are 1971, 1977, and 1979. Good vintages are 1972, 1975, 1976, 1978, 1980, and 1981.

Other Recommended Reds

ROBUST

Barbera, from Piedmont, is a dark, tannic, grapey wine with a powerful, intense fragrance. It should be reserved for rich pasta dishes and heavy soups. The best variety of this wine is Barbera d'Asti; the most common is Barbera d'Alba. Barbera is already good at two years and is excellent at three or four. The best vintage is 1978. Very good vintages are 1979 and 1980.

Ciro' Rosso, a Calabrian wine, exhibits a flavorful, strong character and pleasant bouquet. Its magnificent ruby color has been revered since the time of the ancient Greek colonies in Italy. Fruity when young, it improves when aged for four or five years. Very good vintages are 1977, 1978, 1980, and 1981. Good vintages are 1975 and 1979.

Etna Rosso, made from grapes grown on the slopes of Mt. Etna, is a rich, hearty, well-balanced, garnet-colored wine with a fruity bouquet. It ages well. Good vintages are 1975, 1977, 1978, and 1979.

Refosco is from Friuli-Venezia Giulia. Named after a local grape, Refosco is a smooth, well-rounded red with great versatility. The best type is Refosco Colli Orientali del Friuli; Refosco Grave del Friuli is highly satisfactory but lighter. Very good vintages are 1977, 1978, and 1979. A good recent vintage is 1980.

Vino Nobile di Montepulciano, well known since the fourteenth century, is an even, mellow dry red Tuscan wine. It is produced from the same combination of grapes as Chianti, with which it shares certain characteristics. Excellent vintages are 1970 and 1975. Very good vintages are 1973, 1977, 1979, and 1981. Good vintages are 1974, 1978, and 1980.

MEDIUM BODIED

The Italian *Cabernet* wines produced in Veneto, Trentino, and Friuli-Venezia Giulia are made from a grape originally imported from France. Unlike the California Cabernets, which are aged in wooden casks, the Italian Cabernets are bottled young. The result is a very different wine. Slightly tannic with an herby fragrance, these wines are very good after two or three years. Some of the best Cabernet wines available in the United States are Cabernet Franc, Cabernet Sauvignon del Piave, Cabernet Grave del Friuli, and Cabernet Trentino. Very good recent vintages are 1979 and 1980.

Although the Chianti Classicos are considered the best of the *Chianti* wines, a non-classico, such as Chianti Colli Fiorentini, Chianti Rufina, Chianti Montalbano, and Chianti Colli Senesi can be very satisfactory. These Tuscan wines are excellent drunk young. Always a pleasant and versatile wine, the young Chianti is fruity, fresh, easily drinkable, and a good accompaniment for light pasta and vegetable dishes. Very good vintages are 1978 and 1979. Good vintages are 1977 and 1980.

Corvo Rosso, a very popular Sicilian wine from the area around Palermo, is charming and slightly aromatic, with a clean flavor. Very good vintages are 1974, 1975, 1977, and 1979. Good vintages are 1976 and 1978.

Freisa, from Piedmont, comes in two varieties—a slightly sweet and a dry. When you buy it to accompany a meal, be sure to specify the dry version. The most common dry Freisa is Freisa di Chieri from an area near Turin. Dry Freisa is a flowery, aromatic wine that is best drunk young. An excellent vintage is 1978. Very good vintages are 1979 and 1981.

Grignolino comes from an area near that which produces Freisa. A crisp, agreeable red of no great distinctiveness, it has a high alcoholic content. Like Freisa, it is best when drunk young. An excellent vintage is 1978. Very good vintages are 1979, 1980, and 1981.

Like the Cabernet wines, the *Merlot* wines, produced in Veneto, Trentino, and Friuli-Venezia Giulia, come from a grape originally imported from France. Among the best available in the United States are Merlot del Piave, Merlot del Friuli, and Merlot Collio Goriziano. In general, they are excellent table wines somewhat softer and more balanced than the Cabernets. At times they are distinguished by an herby aroma. They should not be drunk before they are two or three years old. Very good vintages are 1977, 1978, and 1979. A good vintage is 1980.

Nebbiolo d'Alba, produced from the same grape as Barolo and Gattinara, is often described as a light Barolo. This Piedmontese wine is refined in taste and smooth in character. A genuinely fine wine which is best when young, it is often underrated. Very good vintages are 1978, 1979, 1980, and 1981.

Rosso Conero, a crisp, lively red similar to Chianti, comes from the Adriatic coast near Ancona. Its pleasing taste goes well with most spaghetti dishes. An excellent vintage is 1979. Very good vintages are 1975, 1977, and 1980.

Torgiano Rosso, from Umbria, is also known as Rubesco. Similar to the Riserva, the younger Torgiano is lighter, fresher, and less impressive.

LIGHT BODIED

Bardolino is produced in the area of Lake Garda near Verona in Veneto. A pale and refreshing wine with a slight tartness, it is the ideal wine for a summer picnic. Bardolino is best drunk young. The Bardolino most widely available in the United States is Bolla. Bertani, a very fine producer, is also available in most good wine stores. The 1981 vintage is very good.

Lambrusco, from Emilia Romagna, is a semidry, fizzy, crisp wine with a slightly acid taste and fruity scent. It seems to go well with rich dishes characteristic of the area around Modena, where this wine is produced. This wine should be drunk as young as possible.

Valpolicella, a relative of Bardolino, is grown in the same area near Lake Garda in Veneto. Valpolicella is characterized by a clear, bright red color and a slightly heavier body than Bardolino. A very pleasant versatile wine with a touch of bitterness, it is also at its best when young.

Great Whites

Fiano di Avellino, from Campania, is a rich, balanced, medium-bodied white reminiscent of hazelnuts. An elegant wine with the potential for aging, it is usually best when four to five years old. An excellent vintage is 1977. Very good vintages are 1978, 1979, 1980, and 1981.

Greco di Tufo, another wine from Campania, is harmonious, flavorful, and slightly fruity, distinguished by a flowery fragrance reminiscent of orange blossoms. It is made from a grape that was brought to Italy by the ancient Greeks. Unlike most Italian white wines, Greco di Tufo, like Fiano di Avellino, improves with age. An excellent vintage is 1977. Very good vintages are 1978 and 1979. Good vintages are 1980 and 1981.

Picolit is a very rare semisweet wine sometimes difficult to find even in its own region of Friuli. Expensive and almost mythic in its renown, it has an elegant and sophisticated scent. Picolit's intense, round flavor is enhanced by the high alcoholic content. Some very good vintages are 1977, 1978, and 1979. Save this wine for a special occasion.

Verduzzo is another distinguished white from the Friuli-Venezia Giulia region that comes from the grape of the same name. Known for its full body and balanced character, its slightly tannic flavor adds another dimension to this luscious wine.

Other Recommended Whites

Cortese di Gavi, produced from the Cortese grape, is the foremost white wine from the Piedmont area. It is a smooth white of a certain character and texture.

Corvo Bianco is a pleasant, well-rounded Sicilian white with a refreshing acidity.

Luminous and golden in color, *Orvieto* has a firm, smooth, classic taste. It is made in Umbria. There is also a slightly sweet version known as Orvieto Abboccato that is pleasant and very delicate.

Pinot Grigio, produced in Friuli-Venezia Giulia, has a clean, agreeable flavor and refined taste. This is a versatile, benign white that would satisfy almost any white wine lover. Among the best ones available in the United States is Pinot Grigio Collio Goriziano.

Regaleali is a smooth, gracious Sicilian white with a mellow flavor. Slightly aromatic and unquestionably appealing, it's so good it may disappear at a faster rate than expected.

Soave, from Veneto, is probably the most popular Italian white wine in North America. A pleasant, flowery, pale white with no overwhelming character, it is a particularly good wine for summer.

Traminer, from Trento, is a distinctive white wine with a spicy scent. Although one of our favorites, its unusual flavor and strong aroma will not please everyone.

The best-known *Verdicchio* is the Castelli di Jesi in the amphora-shaped bottle. A rather crisp and austere white from Marches, it is characterized by a greenish straw color.

Vernaccia di San Gimignano, a clean, firm white with a distinct presence, is a strong Tuscan wine that flows with surprising ease. It has been popular since Renaissance times and was said to be one of Michelangelo's favorites.

Sparkling Wines

Asti Spumante, from Piedmont, is the most famous, but not necessarily the best, of the Italian sparkling wines. Its reputation derives from its pleasantly sweet, fruity taste.

Cinzano Riserva Principe di Piemonte is a more harmonious, dry sparkling wine than Asti Spumante that exhibits a crisp, yet aromatic character.

Ferrari sparkling wines produced according to the champagne method are considered Italy's best in this category. Made in the Alto Adige, Ferrari can be dry (Ferrari Secco), slightly sweet (Gran Spumante Ferrari), extra dry (Riserva), or Brut.

Produced in Piedmont from Pinot grapes, Pinot di Pinot Gancia is a pleasant dry sparkling wine with a slight acidity.

The best version available of Prosecco di Conegliano in the United States is Superiore di Cartizze, produced by Carpene-Malvolti. There are both dry and sweet varieties of this white wine from Veneto. Generally they are characterized by a pleasant, flowery bouquet. The sweet version is fruity in flavor.

Venegazzu' Brut Loredan Gasparini, from Veneto, is a superb sparkling wine whose virtues have been discovered only recently. In fact, it can match most fine champagnes. Like Ferrari, this clean, very dry and fully satisfying wine is produced according to the champagne method.

Wines as Aperitifs

Any of the sparkling wines above would make an elegant before-dinner drink. Among the other whites described, we would recommend Picolit, Verduzzo, Orvieto Abboccato, Regaleali, Traminer, and Vernaccia di San Gimignano.

Dessert Wines

Although there are many types of *Malvasia*, dry and sweet, red and white, the best is Malvasia di Lipari. This Malvasia, which comes from an island north of Sicily, is a rich, sweet, golden wine with a powerful aroma and high alcoholic content; nevertheless, it is clean and easy to drink. Other good versions of Malvasia are Malvasia di Cagliari from Sardinia and Malvasia di Casorzo d'Asti from Piedmont.

Moscato is usually a flowery, sweet, amber-colored wine that can be either plain or sparkling. Perhaps the most delightful type is the Moscato di Pantelleria from a small island south of Sicily. Other good choices are Moscato di Trani from Apulia and Moscato Naturale (non-sparkling) d'Asti from Piedmont, which is lighter and slightly fruitier than the others.

Passito di Caluso is a Piedmontese dessert wine made from partially dried grapes. This wine has a velvety texture and a delicate fragrance. There is a stronger version—Passito di Caluso Liquoroso. Another distinguished Passito is Passito del Santo from Tuscany. The Tuscan version is perhaps more opulent and intense than Passito di Caluso.

Picolit di Oleis is a sweeter version of the Picolit described earlier. A delicious and impressive dessert wine, it has an unusual perfume that adds to its appeal.

Recioto refers to the whole category of wines from the Verona area made from dried grapes. The best selection for dessert wine is Recioto della Valpolicella (the sweet counterpart of the great Recioto Amarone della Valpolicella previously discussed). This sweet Recioto is an exceptionally rich, deep red wine that is produced in limited quantities. Two good versions of this wine available in the United States are Masi Mezzonella and Masi Classico degli Angeli. The former is intense and powerful; Classico degli Angeli is somewhat lighter.

Vin Santo means "wine for the saints," which is an indication of the wine's veneration in the Tuscan region near Siena where it is produced from dried grapes. It is a lovely, smooth, amber-colored sweet wine that Italians enjoy drinking with a special kind of dry almond cookie called Biscottini di Prato. Among dessert wines, Vin Santo is unique because it has more alcohol than sugar.

Liqueurs

Italians generally take their liqueurs with their coffee. There are several types. The digestive liqueurs (*digestivi*), which range from very sweet to extremely bitter, are low in alcoholic content. Most are very aromatic and somewhat medicinal in taste because they are distilled from herbs. Other types are sweet liqueurs and brandies. Some of the Italian after-dinner drinks that have recently become popular in the United States, like Galliano and Strega, are not usually served in Italy.

Amaro is the most common digestive liqueur distilled from aromatic herbs. There are numerous varieties, ranging from such mass-produced brand names as Averna or China Martini to those made in relatively small quantities for a limited market. Many of the latter come from monasteries or family estates. In any case, Italians insist they have a noticeably positive effect on the digestive process.

There are several liqueurs and brandies we recommend. *Grappa*, a kind of aquavite distilled from the remains of grapes after wine-making, was originally from the Venice area. It is now produced by many of the best-known winemakers. Grappa is very dry and aromatic and very high in alcoholic content. Bocchino Nero from Asti and Grappa Nardini are particularly fine ones. *Sambuca* is a sweet, anise-flavored liqueur. The classic way to drink Sambuca is with coffee beans, which Italians call "mosche"—meaning flies—in the glass. *Centerbe* means "100 herbs," which indicates how aromatic this drink is. Dry and very alcoholic, it boasts a magnificent transparent green color. Herb brandies have a long tradition in Italy. Various formulas have been handed down since the Middle Ages by monks who used them for medicinal purposes. *Amaretto di Saronno* is a light, sweet liqueur with a strong almondy flavor.

12 Menu Suggestions

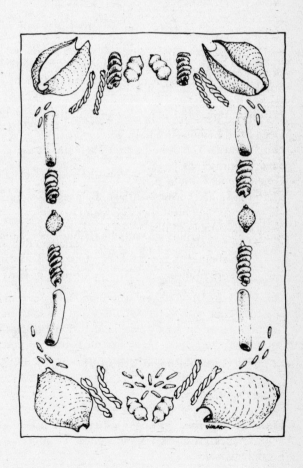

*T*here are many ways of organizing a lovely and exciting meal around rice and pasta dishes. Our seasonal menus for a variety of occasions represent just a sample of the possibilities. With these suggestions in mind, you can create limitless combinations of your own that will both delight and impress your guests.

⌣ *Informal Wine Party for all Seasons* ⌣

Black and Green Italian Olives
Bread Pizzas, p. 50
Smoked Salmon Toasts, p. 51
Stuffed Eggs, p. 53
Deep-Fried Red Rice Balls with Mozzarella, p. 141
Deep-Fried Lemon Rice Balls, p. 139
Omelette with Yellow and Green Tagliolini, p. 241
Savory Mushrooms, p. 42
Green Pepper Frittata, p. 57
Platter of Italian cheeses—Asiago, Belpaese, Gorgonzola, Provolone
Italian bread and breadsticks (Grissini)
Wines: Nebbiolo d'Alba   Traminer
       Grumello   Vernaccia di San Gimignano
       Cabernet   Orvieto Abbocato
       Corvo Rosso   Cortese di Gavi or Verdicchio

⌣ *Children's Lunch* ⌣

Semolina Gnocchi Roman Style, p. 251
                and
Bread Pizzas, p. 50
Carrot Salad, p. 256
Fruit—strawberries (spring); watermelon balls (summer); seedless grapes (autumn); apple wedges (winter)
Fresh lemonade

∽ *Spring Brunch* ∾

Savory Grilled Tomatoes, p. 46
Asparagus Frittata, p. 54
Zucchini Frittata, p. 58
Italian bread
Platter of orange and grapefruit sections
Caffelatte o cappuccino (Italian coffee with milk)

∽ *Elegant Spring Luncheon* ∾

Asparagus Mimosa, p. 27
Tagliolini with Smoked Salmon, p. 212
Escarole Salad, p. 258
Strawberries with lemon juice and sugar
Espresso
Wine: chilled Venegazzu' Brut Loredan Gasparini or chilled Pinot di Pinot Gancia

∽ *Spring Dinner Alla Veneta* ∾

Seafood Salad, p. 60
Risotto with Spring Vegetables, p. 91
Fennel Salad, p. 257
Small honeydew halves filled with strawberries or large honeydew wedges served with strawberries
Espresso
Wine: chilled Soave

∽ Quick Spring Menu ∽
(about 60 minutes)

Stuffed Eggs, p. 53 (30 minutes)
Fusilli with Tuna and Butter, p. 176 (30 minutes)
Seasoned Tomato Halves, p. 255 (10 minutes)
Green apples with dried ricotta
Espresso
Wine: Valpolicella Bolla

∽ Summer Buffet ∽

Marinated Eggplant, p. 34
Marinated Zucchini, p. 48
Risotto with Seafood, p. 116
Cold Tomatoes Stuffed with Rice, p. 123
Spaghetti Hooker Style I, p. 166
Penne with Basil and Cream, p. 187
Mixed Green Salad, p. 255
Watermelon basket filled with mixed summer fruit
Espresso
Wines: chilled Orvieto Secco Melini
       Torgiano Rosso

∽ Summer Picnic ∽

Frittata with Fresh Herbs, p. 57
Marinated Eggplants, Peppers, and Tomatoes, p. 39
Spaghetti Frittata, p. 167
Watercress Salad, p. 257
Italian bread
Bing cherries
Espresso freddo (chilled and sweetened)
Wine: Bardolino Bertani

∿ *Elegant Supper at the Beach* ∿

Raw Artichoke Salad, p. 25
Ring of Risotto with Seafood Sauce, p. 133
Mixed Salad, p. 254
Canteloupe halves filled with raspberries and drizzled with Port
Espresso
Wine: chilled Greco di Tufo

∿ *Quick Summer Menu from the South* ∿
(about 60 minutes)

Roasted Peppers, p. 44 (25 minutes)
Spaghetti in Anchovy Sauce, p. 153 (30 minutes)
Tomato and Mozzarella Salad with Fresh Basil, p. 51 (15 minutes)
Sliced peaches in white wine (10 minutes)
Espresso
Wine: chilled Corvo Bianco

∿ *Autumn Sunday Lunch* ∿

Raw Mushrooms in Piquant Sauce, p. 40
Jumbo Shells Filled with Ricotta, p. 172
Bowl of Raw Salad Vegetables, p. 258
Black grapes with mixed nuts in the shell
Espresso
Wine: Sassella Rainoldi 1971

～ *Piedmontese Country Menu for Autumn* ～

Bagna Cauda, p. 20
Risotto with Barolo, p. 89
Cooked Spinach Salad, p. 263
Red and green apples
Espresso
Wine: Barolo dei Marchesi di Barolo 1974

～ *After-Football Get-Together* ～

Potato and Cheese Pancake, p. 52
Minestrone Milanese Style with Rice, p. 64
Beet Salad, p. 260
Fresh Anjou pears
Espresso
Wine: Cabernet Grave del Friuli

～ *Piedmontese Country Menu for Autumn* ～
(*about 60 minutes*)

Rice with Four Cheeses, p. 117 (40 minutes)
White Beans with Tuna, p. 28 (15 minutes)
Orange Salad, p. 259 (15 minutes)
Dried figs and walnuts
Espresso
Wine: Chianti Colli Senesi

～ *Hearty After-Ski Lunch* ～

Onion Frittata, p. 56
Bean Soup with Pasta, p. 72

Fennel Salad, p. 257
Peeled and sliced navel oranges
Espresso
Wine: Refosco

⁓ *Winter Buffet* ⁓

Squid Salad, p. 58
Mushrooms in Olive Oil, p. 41
Pasta Roll with Spinach and Ricotta Filling, p. 213
Baked Lasagna with Cream Cheese and Prosciutto, p. 231
Rice Ring with Zucchini, p. 130
Risotto with Seafood, p. 114
Mixed Green Salad, p. 255
Italian bread and breadsticks (Grissini)
Fruit salad and tray of Italian cheeses—Asiago, Fontina, Gorgon-
    zola, ricotta salata
Espresso
Wines: chilled Pinot Grigio Colli Orientali del Friuli
           Merlot Collio Goriziano

⁓ *After-Theater Supper* ⁓

Risotto with Champagne, p. 87
Grilled Chicory or Escarole, p. 261
Sliced fresh oranges sprinkled with sugar and chopped walnuts and
    served with Amaretti (Italian almond cookies)
Espresso
Wine: chilled Prosecco di Conegliano or chilled Ferrari Brut

⁓ *Quick Winter Menu* ⁓
(*about 60 minutes*)

Smoked Salmon Toasts, p. 51 (25 minutes)
Linguine with Walnuts, p. 178 (20 minutes)

Watercress Salad, p. 257 (20 minutes)
Basket of assorted fruit
Espresso
Wine: chilled Corvo Bianco

13 Mail Order Suppliers

Italian ingredients

Italian Heritage
53 Westfield Drive
Cranston, R.I. 02920
(401) 942-4958

Manganaro Foods
488 Ninth Avenue
New York, N.Y. 10018
(212) 563-5331

Todaro Brothers
555 Second Avenue
New York, N.Y. 10016
(212) 532-0633

Il Conte di Savoia
555 West Roosevelt Road
Chicago, Ill. 68607
(312) 666-3471

Pasta machines

Williams-Sonoma/Dept. CFC
P.O. Box 3792
San Francisco, Calif. 94119
(415) 652-1515

Williams-Sonoma
5300 Wisconsin Avenue, N.W.
Washington, D.C. 20015
(202) 244-4800

Kitchen Bazaar
Mailorder
4455 Connecticut Avenue
Washington, D.C. 20008
(202) 363-4625

Index

in butter and cheese, 148
with clam sauce, 154–56
with eggplant, 160–61
in egg sauce, 151
with eggs and bacon, 149–51
frittata, 167–68
with garlic, oil, and chili pepper,
    153
hooker style, 166–67
with mushrooms, 162
    and cheese, 164
    and peas, 163
with mussels, 156
peasant style, 164–65
pushcart style, 151–52
with seafood, 158–59
with squid, 157
summer, 165–67
with tomato sauce, 157
    and mozzarella, 152
with tuna and tomato sauce, 157
Spaghetti
all'aglio, olio, e peperoncino, 153
alla burina, 164–65
al burro, 148–49
con i calamari, 157–58
alla carbonara, 146, 149–51
con carciofi, 159–60
con le cozze, 156
estivi, 165–66
con funghi, 162–64
alla malafemmina, 167
alla marinara, 158
con le melanzane, 160–61
con mozzarella, 152
alla puttanesca, 166–67
con le vongole, 154
    macchiati, 155
Spinach
rice mold with, 127
and ricotta with rigatoni, 190–91
and ricotta filling, 213–14,
    219–20, 226
salad, cooked, 263
Spinach pasta, egg, 204
Spinaci all'agro, 263

Squash
gnocchi, 248–49
and pasta soup, 76
tortelli filling, 227
Squid
risotto, 109–10
salad, 58–60
with spaghetti, 157
Strawberry risotto, 106–7
Supplí
al limone, 139–40
al riso rosso, 141
Suppliers, mail-order, 293

Tagliolini
with caviar, 211–12
with Greek tarama, 210–11
in lemon and cream sauce, 212
with smoked salmon, 212–13
soufflé, green, 241
yellow and green, 242
Tagliolini
al caviale, 210–12
al limone, 212
al salmone, 212–13
Tarama, tagliolini with, 210–11
Tiella pugliese, 70–71
Timballo
di fettuccine verdi, 238–39
di raviolini verdi, 233–35
di rigatini e melanzane, 195
di rigatoni con zucchine, 196
di riso al formaggio, 126
di riso e melanzane, 128
di riso con spinaci, 127
di tortellini, 236–38
Tomatoes
with artichokes, 22–23
baked, stuffed with rice, 122–23
canned, 10
with endive, 30–31
with macaroni, 182
marinated with eggplant, 39
with mozzarella and rigatini, 190
and mozzarella salad with fresh
    basil, 51
paste, 10